COMPANION

TO

OLD ENGLISH POETRY

For Chris, my friend
— remembering the good old days

HeL

COMPANION

TO

OLD ENGLISH POETRY

edited by

HENK AERTSEN

and

ROLF H. BREMMER, JR.

VU UNIVERSITY PRESS

Amsterdam 1994

The illustration on the cover shows The Sacrifice of Isaac, Fol. 38r, MS. Cotton Claudius B.iv, British Library, London.

VU University Press is an imprint of:
VU Boekhandel/Uitgeverij bv
De Boelelaan 1105
1081 HV Amsterdam
The Netherlands

printed by Wilco, Amersfoort

ISBN 90-5383-116-9
Nugi 953

PREFACE

The study of Old English poetry has undergone some marked changes in the past two decades. For one thing, this has resulted in a greater appreciation for the Christian backgrounds of many of the poems. Also, the value of the poetic canon, as it was mainly established by nineteenth-century scholarship, has sometimes effectively been challenged. Finally, manuscript studies have given us a new insight into the context in which the poems have come down to us.

The present collection of original essays is especially intended to enable undergraduate students to become acquainted with some of these new developments, but will also be of use to the more advanced student. At the same time, it will appear that not all accepted views should be dismissed as old-fashioned. We hope that the variegated approaches to genres and individual poems alike presented here will be found informative and interesting. Clearly, the present book is not meant to be used as a manual on the subject of Old English poetry, but it will offer the student new ways to critically approach the popular and lesser known poetic monuments of Anglo-Saxon England.

We take this opportunity of thanking all colleagues, in the New World and the Old, for their contributions to this volume.

Vrije Universiteit, Amsterdam
University of Leiden
June, 1994

Henk Aertsen
Rolf H. Bremmer, Jr.

CONTENTS

THE DIVERSE NATURE OF OLD ENGLISH POETRY

ALLEN J. FRANTZEN

In his 1967 introduction to Old English literature, C.L. Wrenn sought to demonstrate the centrality of poetry to Anglo-Saxon culture. Attempting to widen the definition of "culture" beyond the limits of a single scholarly discipline and its technical language, he divided the term into four parts— material, intellectual, moral, and spiritual—and began with material culture as exemplified by the artifacts of the Sutton Hoo ship burial (Wrenn, 1967:2-5; Chambers, 1959:417-18). Material culture so splendid was known from descriptions in *Beowulf* but, before the burial was uncovered, had been regarded as having merely literary rather than historical significance. The find, which confirmed that the glories hinted at in *Beowulf* actually existed, greatly enhanced the value of the poem as a record of its age.

If Wrenn saw Old English poetry as a witness to aristocratic taste, he also saw verse as something quite different—as a "natural expression" of the Anglo-Saxon folk and their ethos:

> Poetry arises in early times as a natural expression of men's feelings, and uses natural rhythms which grow and become traditional because they spring from a selection of the patterns of actual speech, from the rhythms of songs and dances, and from employing designs of formulaic phrases to suit the ethos of the people.　　　　　　(Wrenn, 1967:195)

Anglo-Saxon poetry, as Wrenn saw it, both corroborated the achievement of the culture's elite and simultaneously expressed the lived experience of the masses. Since Wrenn wrote, the critical climate has changed a great deal, but students still form first—and lasting—impressions of Anglo-Saxon literary culture through its poetry. *Beowulf* was and is chief among the texts that introduce the Anglo-Saxon world to them.

Impressive though Wrenn's vision is, we cannot easily deduce the complexities of Anglo-Saxon (or any other) culture from its written tradition, much less from poetry alone. An introductory volume should emphasize the poetry's diversity and its connections to writing of other kinds, for the poetry is, as new readers immediately recognize, powerful and appealing; its influence is intensified by criticism that admires the verse's uniformity and regards it as indicative of the culture's coherence. Because Old English poetry continues to be seen as Wrenn saw it—as an

epitome of Anglo-Saxon culture and a central reference point from which
to view the Anglo-Saxon age—it is essential to understand not only that
Old English poetry engages Anglo-Saxon culture at many levels, but that it
does so selectively. Observations about the unity of Anglo-Saxon culture
are especially beneficial to students new to the subject. But introductions
are also the point at which generalizations about the "nature" of the verse
need to be qualified by the particulars of its history.

1. Fixed Features and Conventional Contexts

The editorial and critical traditions of Old English poetry emphasize features of style, syntax, and vocabulary that characterize virtually all the
poems, no matter what their genre or purpose and no matter when during
the Old English period they were composed. According to Donald G.
Scragg, "All Old English poetry is of such uniformity in form and language that it is impossible to establish even relative dating with any certainty" (1991:57). The alliterative half-lines of Old English poetry, although divided by a caesura and printed in modern editions in two columns, are written continuously in the manuscripts and are recognizable as
verse by sound rather than by sight; they fall into five categories of stress
(Type A through Type E) that began to break down only at the end of the
period. These fixed metrical patterns, supported by a repertory of stock
phrases (or "formulas") and traditional motifs, constitute both compositional and structural confines. But within them poets achieved great expressive variety. Scragg demonstrates, for example, how the *Beowulf*-
poet's mastery of metre, wordplay, vocabulary, and syntax alternately
compresses and expands narrative space, artfully imitating the suspense
that builds as Beowulf and the Danes pursue Grendel's mother to her mere
(Scragg, 1991).

Like metre, the vocabulary of Old English poetry was highly spe-
cialized. It incorporated "a large stock of distinctly poetic words, words
that never or very rarely occur in prose," Helmut Gneuss notes, and employed such words "side by side with others that belong to the common
vocabulary of Old English" (Gneuss, 1991:47). Many of these poetic
words look back to Germanic roots shared by Old English with Old Frisian, Old Norse, Old Saxon, and Old High German, and so point to a verse
tradition apparently very old by the time it acquired written form in
Christian Anglo-Saxon England. This uniformity in poetic conventions
suggests a very conservative tradition. But poets proved adept at applying
these techniques both to specifically religious poetry and to verse that
deals only incidentally with spiritual matters. Students need to read but a
small sampling of the verse to detect these similarities; a much deeper

acquaintance with the texts is necessary before one can appreciate the subtle powers with which poets manipulated the rules that bound their craft.

The fixed features of Anglo-Saxon poetry are most apparent at the linguistic level, but even there diversity is important. The lexicon, for example, demonstrates some regional variation, with the corpus containing a mixture of West Saxon and Anglian words that can be used to specify the provenance and (sometimes, and less reliably) the date of a text. Although few poems have been localized or dated precisely, it is amply clear that the poetry emerged from different literary centres and different ages and that it employed a "general poetic dialect" that varied as the verse was transmitted from age to age and region to region (Campbell, 1959:10).

Indeed, the paradox of seeing Anglo-Saxon poetry as a unified expression of Anglo-Saxon culture is that poetry, for all its linguistic uniformity, constitutes a diverse record of a developing culture. As we see in Bede, Anglo-Saxon England was, for centuries, a patchwork of kingdoms that moved towards unity only in the second half of the ninth century. The poetry written during this period would seem to have the power to reveal the transformation of culture as Bede's England became Alfred's and then passed into Danish rule in the eleventh century. But did poetry participate in this process or merely report or reflect it? What uses for poetic texts have been identified? What kinds of use have yet to be analysed and appreciated?

Attempting to answer these questions, we find, first, that the uniformity of the verse effectively impedes systematic dating and thus prohibits the construction of a historical sequence for the poems that would reveal successive stages of a developing culture. Views of the culture derived from the poetry will therefore, in the main, be synchronic rather than diachronic. But they need not be synthetic: that is, they can emphasize differences rather than similarities in the corpus. So we also find that the texts speak more variously than the critical tradition allows. For critics have focused on a small number of texts that are, despite their differences, strikingly similar. Too easily, and too frequently, the culture seen through these texts appears to be composed of undifferentiated and unifying stereotypes. The most important of these is surely "the Anglo-Saxon hero", who has acquired both male and female as well as pagan and Christian manifestations (Chance, 1986). This "hero", a simplified literary construct both in the Old English period and in modern criticism, is placed at the centre of "the Anglo-Saxon world-view". This world-view is itself another oversimplification for the complex and contradictory social phenomena we see in the Anglo-Saxon period. If we believe that traditional categories, such as those employed for the poems in this volume and others like it, are indispensable, we must also see that they ultimately obscure the social differences that mark literary culture.

The critical tradition has constructed a hierarchy of genres around these cultural stereotypes and has fit Anglo-Saxon poems into it. The foremost genre is the heroic, which is seen as having early and late phases, with *Beowulf* representing the former and *The Battle of Maldon* and *The Battle of Brunanburh* seen as late, weakened examples of the tradition. Christian narratives follow, with *The Dream of the Rood* and *Genesis B* recognized as the finest examples. Next are the elegies, the famous narrative of exile, spiritual and otherwise, a category in which *The Wife's Lament* has recently become especially recognized. Last come the riddles and a handful of allegorical poems noteworthy for their elaborate and somewhat enigmatic figures of speech (e.g. *The Phoenix*).

Nearly all criticism of Old English poetry concerns this corpus. A glance at the categories used by major annual bibliographies shows that the place of *Beowulf* is unique. *Anglo-Saxon England*, for example, divides "Poetry" into "General", "*Beowulf*", and "Other poems". The annual review of scholarship in *The Old English Newsletter* treats "Individual Poems" in one category and *Beowulf* (not an "individual poem"?) in another. The new *Cambridge Companion to Old English Literature* makes this hierarchy especially plain: *Beowulf*, "other heroic poetry", *The Battle of Maldon*, elegies, Biblical poetry, *The Dream of the Rood*, Cædmon [!], Cynewulf, and "wisdom poetry" (Godden and Lapidge, 1991:287-9).

The criticism indexed in these categories shows that this hierarchy rests on a firm foundation of accumulated taste and informed opinion. In *Old English Verse*, one of the most lively and persuasively argued introductions to the subject we have, T.A. Shippey uses *Beowulf*, its verse forms, and its heroic code as markers against which the vitality of the Old English poetic tradition can be measured. He also stresses elegiac texts, which he reads effectively as "wisdom" poetry. The remainder of his analysis is devoted to hagiographical and scriptural narratives. Didactic and "homiletic" poems are barely mentioned; they remain ancillary to the great strains of the tradition Shippey traces. Shippey takes pains to "look at the whole range of surviving material", and to acknowledge the individual and "marked peculiarities" of the major poetic codices (Shippey, 1972:80). But it is nonetheless clear from his introduction that certain genres are thought to be more typical and revealing of Anglo-Saxon culture than others, and that heroic narratives, Christian or Germanic, come first.

2. Words in the World

Conventions of genre—modes of classification established only in the nineteenth century—dictate the shape of the bibliographies but do little to suggest the variety of the poems classified there. As an alternative to these categories, I suggest that we consider the social use of poetry as measured by its *eventfulness*. "Eventfulness" is a term derived from political criticism that maintains, in the words of Edward W. Said, that "texts are worldly" and that they are, "to some degree, events", "part of the social world, human life, and of course the historical moments in which they are located and interpreted" (Said, 1983:4).[1] Eventfulness makes us aware of the function of texts in social contexts, whether celebratory, memorial, educational, devotional, commercial, or erotic. Eventfulness reminds us that the word lives in the world and that the texts we read were once alive to meanings we cannot imagine. Some texts are about events, such as battles, coronations, or burials. But an event is not only an occurrence; it can also be a result or a consequence—an effect—and even a cause. Texts that valorize heroic conduct or mournfully recollect better times are the effects of loss; they are also causes, since they seek to keep the past alive and to console listeners in the present. Allegorical poems that reconfigure spiritual conflict as mortal combat—a frequent device in hagiographical poetry—can be seen both as a result (of conversion) and as a cause (of militant Christian behaviour). But many Old English poems respond to social concerns less typical of the Germanic warrior's code and more characteristic of the Christian at prayer or reflection. Poetry taught and admonished; but it also asserted, complained, criticized, puzzled, reinforced, subverted, and seduced. All these activities are events: they are acts in speech and writing that seek to provoke or respond to actions in the world.

The eventfulness of poetry is apparent in many ways. New work by James W. Earl, John P. Hermann, Martin Irvine, Clare A. Lees, Gillian R. Overing, and others, while not using eventfulness as a critical model, employs psychoanalysis, deconstruction, feminism, and intertextuality to discover new modes of connection between poetry and its social and intellectual worlds (Earl, 1982, 1989, 1991; Hermann, 1989; Irvine, 1986, 1991; Lees, 1991; Overing, 1990, 1991). Those wary of contemporary critical modes can find eventfulness in a traditional source: the manuscripts that hold the verse. The manuscripts attest to the eventfulness and diversity of Old English poetry in numerous ways; they hold a history of reading and writing that began before the codices were written, continued when the texts were performed and heard, and grew as the texts were written about—and the manuscripts often written on—in the post-Anglo-Saxon

---

[1] The concept of "eventfulness" has been most fully developed by J.G.A. Pocock (1987). I discuss a number of interpretations of "eventfulness" and give specific applications in Frantzen, 1991:126-7. And see Lees (1991) for the link between eventfulness and reception theory.

world. Old English poetic codices are in fact a highly diverse index to the texts, and one of the striking facts about them is that a number of the manuscripts are not Anglo-Saxon (that is, written between 700 and 1100) at all. Some Old English poetry is connected to the period of its creation only through the work of Renaissance and eighteenth-century scholars, without whose transcriptions certain texts—including *The Battle of Maldon*—would have been lost. Understanding the diversity of Old English poetry requires us to see the texts in both their Anglo-Saxon contexts and in later contexts in which they were read, a series of historical periods connected by the manuscripts themselves.

No one has done more than Fred C. Robinson to establish the importance of manuscript contexts for the interpretation of Old English poetic texts (1980, 1981, 1989). Having reexamined numerous manuscripts, he has forced us to review the dependence of the critical tradition on editorial conventions. Other scholars whose close work with manuscripts has led us to important physical evidence are Patrick W. Conner (1986) and Kevin S. Kiernan (1981, 1986, 1990). The brief survey of the manuscripts of Old English poetry that follows, although much indebted to Robinson's work, focuses not on their codicological or paleographical details but rather on their nature as collections of verse—and prose—that suggest diverse social applications and, therefore, textual eventfulness.

Nearly ninety manuscripts contain some Old English verse. All the manuscripts supply rich and varied contexts for the short poems they include. But this large number of codices is itself no guide to the variety of poetic tradition, although it reminds us of the dominance of Latin texts as contexts for Old English poetry. Approximately half of these ninety manuscripts contain only one or two very short texts—either *Cædmon's Hymn* (nine lines, in 17 MSS) or *Bede's Death Song* (five lines, in 29 MSS).[2] *The Anglo-Saxon Poetic Records* (*ASPR*) print the corpus in six volumes. Four manuscripts dominate: the *Beowulf* manuscript, which also includes *Judith*; the Exeter Book (116 or 117 poems); the Junius manuscript (*Genesis* [A and B], *Daniel, Exodus, Christ and Satan*); and the Vercelli Book (six poems, including *The Dream of the Rood* and *Elene*). What kinds of collections are these?

Two of the four manuscripts contain only poetry. The Junius manuscript was once known as the "Cædmon Manuscript" because its texts are predominantly biblical and loosely conform to the list of subjects that, according to Bede, this prolific but elusive early master created for his astonished audiences (*Historia Ecclesiastica* 4.24). This manuscript is particularly important because of its illustrations, some of the finest drawings

---

[2] See *ASPR* 5:xxxvii and xliv for this information.

from the period. The Exeter Book is another kind of collection altogether; it contains some of the most famous poetry in the corpus, including both *The Wanderer* and *The Seafarer*. Persuasive arguments about its formation by Conner suggest that the codex is composed of three booklets, each with its own coherence. Hence some overall logic to the organization of the manuscript is possible, although the groupings—riddles, the most famous elegies, and other kinds of texts—are not likely to fit into a clear pattern (Conner, 1986, 1993).

The other two codices, the Vercelli Book and the *Beowulf* manuscript, mix poetry and prose, and the mixture, in both cases, has been seen as having interpretive consequences for the poetry. Yet it is difficult to appreciate the significance of these combinations of poetry and prose because the *Anglo-Saxon Poetic Records* exclude the prose. Few Anglo-Saxonists have read *The Wonders of the East*, the *Letter of Alexander the Great to Aristotle*, or the *Life of St. Christopher*, the three prose texts that precede *Beowulf* and are written in the same hand as the first scribe of the poem (Rypins, 1924). The mixture of prose and verse is even more significant in the case of the Vercelli Book, since it is both a major collection of homilies and the repository of some of the best known poems, including *The Dream of the Rood* (after *Beowulf* possibly the most-admired poem in Old English), *Elene*, and *Andreas*.

These codices, the first four volumes in the *ASPR*, are unique, and most of the poetry in them—they contain nearly two-thirds of the Old English verse that survives—exists in only one copy. Both the Vercelli and Exeter collections contain *Soul and Body*, and other codices include texts of which we have more than one copy. But this material, however important, has been paid little heed. The fifth volume of the *ASPR* includes the *Meters of Boethius*, a series of poems extracted from two manuscripts of King Alfred's translation of the *Consolation of Philosophy*. Only one of these poems or "meters", a description of the Goths attacking Rome often included in anthologies, has become well-known. As Earl has argued, this text, "the one battle poem Alfred wrote", owes its status in the canon, however modest, to critical preference for heroic poetry. One manuscript of the meters is a copy of an Anglo-Saxon manuscript that was badly damaged in the 1731 fire in Sir Robert Cotton's library, and this is the manuscript that contains the poem about the attack on Rome. The copy, made by the Dutch scholar Francis Junius (Oxford, Bodleian Library, Junius MS 12), is the sole source for four of the meters and for the proem to the work (Shippey, 1972:80-81; O'Keeffe, 1990:24). Another important poetic text linked to Alfred, less studied even than the Boethius poems, is a verse translation of the Psalms (Psalms 51:7, to Psalm 150:3). This manuscript is the fifth *ASPR* volume, the *Paris Psalter*; in it the poetry follows a prose translation of the first fifty Psalms. Now that the prose translations of the Psalms has been accepted as Alfred's, it is more likely that new work with the poetic translation of the Psalms will be undertaken (Bately, 1982; Griffith, 1991).

Other poems attributed to Alfred, whose fondness for poetry supposedly dates to his childhood,[3] are found in manuscripts of translations either carried out under the king's direction or written during his reign (872-899). These poems belong to the fringes of the *Anglo-Saxon Poetic Records* (volume 6), which designates the verse, most unhappily, as the "minor poems". These "minor"—that is, short rather than insignificant— poems include two more possibly by Alfred, among them a metrical preface to the *Cura Pastoralis* (found in four manuscripts) and an epilogue to the same (found in two copies). They also include a metrical preface to Bishop Wærferth's translation of the *Dialogues* of Gregory the Great (found in one copy only). That poems were attached to prose texts on which a great many of the king's much-heralded educational reforms rested tells us that more than heroism and elegiac lament occupied the minds of literate Anglo-Saxons when they wrote, read, and heard poetry.

The separation of verse from prose throughout the *ASPR* has had significant consequences for our understanding of Old English poetry, particularly in those few cases in which a poem occurs in more than one manuscript, including *Soul and Body* and *Riddle 30* (which is found in two forms in the Exeter Book). Douglas Moffat, a recent editor of *Soul and Body*, notes that some critics (myself included) have seen the two forms as two different poems, and, responding to an editorial history of "bifurcation based on manuscript", have referred to the *"Soul and Body* poems" (Moffat, 1990:10). Given that two of the four principal manuscripts of Old English poetry contain only poetry, and that nearly all poetry occurs in only one manuscript, we can see the appeal of editing the verse without the prose. The *ASPR* has conditioned scholars to think of the Old English corpus not only as a collection of manuscripts rather than a collection of texts, but as a collection of purely poetic manuscripts—as poetry without any context except that of the edited manuscript purged of prose. The distortion is most significant in the cases of the poetic translations of the Psalms, Alfred's *Meters*, and the "minor" poems, which, edited as a collection that stands in the same series as *Beowulf* and the Junius poems, inevitably seem inconsequential. The *"ASPR* effect" has been far from beneficial, and the isolation of poetry from prose is particularly detrimental. The reasons for this isolation are not clear; the editors apparently never considered the distortions such a practice might produce. That the

---

[3] See Asser's *Life of King Alfred*, trans. S. Keynes and M. Lapidge, in *Alfred the Great*, ed. Keynes and Lapidge (Harmondsworth: Penguin Books, 1983), p.75 (chapter 23).

ASPR appeared during the period when the New Criticism was taking over English Departments in the United States is significant but hardly decisive in explaining the editors' procedure (Frantzen, 1990: 78-9, 82-3). As we have seen, poetry was already an ascendent category in Wrenn's view, a view that was highly characteristic of the traditional, historical criticism; he regarded prose as "very largely non-literary", and like him many Anglo-Saxonists continue to think of prose as a "stepping-stone" to poetry, seeing poetry as "literature" and prose as a "background" to (or more recently a source for) it (Wrenn, 1967:195; Lees, 1991:157-8).

Yet the authority of the manuscripts is, some scholars believe, too great, and prevents editors from emending texts adequately. Describing the nineteenth-century editorial tradition of Old English, Michael Lapidge has argued that manuscript collections were overly influential. "Because they are so few in number," Lapidge writes, "the surviving manuscripts of Old English verse were accorded an immense reverence, and this reverence is palpable in Anglo-Saxon studies today." He adds, "The manuscript, rather than the author, has come to dominate the consciousness of editors of Old English verse," who strive to reproduce "every last detail of the manuscript" in their editions (Lapidge, 1991:39). But in the case of the *ASPR*, which are otherwise conservative editions, the manuscripts are hardly treated with reverence, "palpable" or not, since four out of the six volumes present poems without reference to the prose that contextualizes them. It seems that Lapidge's implied call for an editorial "consciousness" dominated by authors instead of manuscripts is really a consciousness dominated instead by editors, who should be free to idealize the text by reconstructing its original language and then substituting that standardized language for the language of the manuscript. Such editions tend to homogenize texts by regularizing divergent linguistic and scribal practices.

The diversity and eventfulness of Old English poetry, therefore, are obscured by editorial traditions in several ways. The kinds of eventfulness I catalogue here involve the relations of some poems—chiefly "minor" poems—to prose in the codices. The undistinguished critical reputation of the "minor" poems has, as Robinson has demonstrated several times, allowed early editorial judgments to go unchallenged. One example is Cambridge, Corpus Christi College 201, a corpus of laws, homilies, and a penitential that also contains a sequence of four (or five) poems on themes of penance and judgement (Caie, 1976). Robinson has argued that two poems, *Exhortation to Christian Living* and *A Summons to Prayer*, make one better text if they are joined as *The Rewards of Piety*. They have been divided because only the second is macaronic (incorporating both Latin and Old English), and this shift in itself suggested to editors the start of a new text rather than a continuation of a poem already in progress (Robinson, 1989:195-6). If this linguistic difference has caused a division of one text into two, there is another case in which thematic looseness—a vague category of "penitential poetry"—helped to fuse two parts of different texts, as Alan Bliss and I argue about the poems we designated as *Resignation A* and *Resignation B* (Bliss and Frantzen, 1976; see Klinck, 1992).

Another important prose collection that includes poetry is Oxford, Bodleian Library, Junius 121, which contains the Gloria (the same text as Corpus 201), the Creed, the Pater Noster, and fragments of the Psalms. At this point, Junius 121 holds a devotional prose office, "De Officiis diurnalium nocturnalium horarum" (Ker, 1957:414). In the Corpus manuscript, the poetic prayers are written on the first leaves of a quire that also includes (in a different hand) Latin prayers for confessional devotion. To find the versified Old English prayers and Latin prose on the same pages is not particularly startling, and no organic relationship between these materials need be postulated. What the juxtaposition calls our attention to is not only the diversity of texts but of scripts; this part of the manuscript contains three different hands and suggests a compilation drawn from varied sources but not random in its aims (Ker, 1957:90). The mixture of poetry and prose in what Robinson calls the "envoi" to Bede's *Ecclesiastical History* is also a multi-authored text that again shows how the Anglo-Saxons comfortably combined genres and poetic applications that modern traditions try to keep separate (Robinson, 1981).

Other texts whose genres are signalled by their manuscript contexts are the poems in the *Anglo-Saxon Chronicle*, which are found in four manuscripts. These poems include *The Battle of Brunanburh*, *The Capture of the Five Boroughs*, *The Coronation of Edgar*, *The Death of Edgar*, *The Death of Alfred*, and *The Death of Edward*. The first of these poems imparts a broad, historically distanced view of a battle and differs sharply from another famous battle poem, *The Battle of Maldon*, which speaks to local and immediate concerns. Both *The Battle of Brunanburh* and *The Capture of the Five Boroughs* are regarded as competent Old English verse, but critics have had few compliments for the others. Shippey calls the third and fourth "painfully laboured" and "totally lifeless", the poem of Edgar's death "rhymed jog-trot", and that on Alfred "the nadir of Old English verse" (Shippey, 1972:186-7). Arguments about the artistic merits of these poems have overshadowed their social functions. Their defects in style may witness the decline of a verse tradition, but dwelling on their demerits has kept readers from asking why poetry became an acceptable medium for the *Chronicle* in the late years of its composition, and what ideological aims were made overt in the departures from tradition signalled by poetry. Especially interesting implications about the function of *The Battle of Brunanburh* as part of the *Chronicle* have recently been discussed by Irvine, who notes that the poem refers to "what the books tell us, the old scholars", about the history of England ("*us secgað bec / ealde uðwitan"*, lines 65-73). There is, Irvine notes, a history behind this poem that is specifically written and that links this event to the oldest recorded victories in the West Saxon history (Irvine, 1991:204-8).

The textual dimensions of the *Chronicle* poems must be considered in the light of other uses for Old English poetry that modern readers do not recognize for poetry in their own cultures. One of these uses is demonstrated by what Earl describes as "talking poems", metrical prologues and epilogues that share the prosopopoetic function of *The Dream of the Rood*, the riddles, and other texts that speak (Earl, 1989; Whobrey, 1991). These poems include those that accompany some of King Alfred's translations; others in this interesting genre are *Thureth* and *Aldhelm*. The latter follows the table of contents in a manuscript of Aldhelm's *De virginitate* in Cambridge, Corpus Christi College 326; it contains both Latin and Greek words, taking the infrequent combination of Old English and Latin (as in *The Rewards of Piety* and the *Phoenix*) one step further. "The speaker of the poem is Aldhelm's treatise," Robinson (1989:196) observes, as the opening words, *"þus me gesette"*, indicate. *Thureth* is an even more interesting text. It is found in a manuscript that contains a benedictional and a coronation liturgy and that is designated, in the poem, as a *"halgung-boc"*, a benedictional (line 1). The poem names the authority an eorl, Thored (*"Þure ð"*, line 3) named in a charter in this manuscript who apparently commissioned the collection that the poem prefaces.[4]

These texts draw attention to the production of texts in the period—their sponsorship, their physical characteristics—and to the communicative processes that reading and writing were engaged in. These books speak in the first person, not about wisdom or good conduct, but about being books—about their textuality, which, Earl writes, is "an independent intelligence, mediating between the author and the reader—stressing, in fact, the distance between author and reader", and emphasizing the distance between the author and the text, now forever out of his or her hands, and also the gap between the text and the reader who now stands before it (Earl, 1989:54). Such gestures, Earl writes, are "inconceivable in oral poetry", since they incorporate the idea of a fixed, written text; these colophons also draw our attention to one of the most frequently expressed concerns of Old English, by Ælfric and others, that there was a gap between the word and the sacred truths it communicated, a gap that could be closed only by securing the reader's most devout intentions.

Another example is the poem known as *Durham*, a version of the *encomium urbis* genre written between 1104 and 1109. This poem once existed in two manuscripts, both from the twelfth century, one an an-

---

4 See *ASPR* 6:lxxxviii-xc for comments, p. 97 for the text.

thology of historical texts about Durham (Cambridge, University Library
Ff.i.27), another a manuscript destroyed in the Cottonian fire (London,
British Library, Cotton Vitellius D.xx). This poem was probably written
in connection with the translation of St. Cuthbert to the new cathedral at
Durham in 1104. Shippey regards this text as a sad example of late Old
English poetry, and once again there is no disputing the metrical evidence
(Shippey, 1972:176-7). But *Durham* is an occasional poem of exceptional
importance.[5] The only example of the *encomium urbis* in Old English, as
Margaret Schlauch noted long ago, it looks back to Alcuin's famous poem
on the saints of York (written 780-82). This comparison should prompt us
to wonder why this conventional and popular form of Latin poetry left no
earlier traces in English vernacular records. It is significant that, so many
years after the Conquest, a poet should have evoked this ancient form in a
language not traditional to it but a language that evoked fading traditions
of a different sort.

The phenomenon of late Old English poetry is usually discussed in
the context that Shippey supplies in his astute critique of the "decline" of
the techniques of great Old English verse, more recently described as
"decay" by Griffith (Shippey, 1972:175-90; Griffith, 1991). These terms,
while logical from the Anglo-Saxon perspective, begin to look very
strange when we think instead in terms of early Middle English literary
culture. For what causes the decline or decay of one culture except the
emergence and growth of another? It is not axiomatic that the same features that make Old English poetry valuable are also those that testify to
its linguistic integrity or its fidelity to tradition. The later Old English
texts also complicate conventional distinctions between poetry and prose.
Near the end of the Anglo-Saxon period, authors seem to have lost touch
with the tradition their verse continued. Some poems depart so far from
the conventions of earlier verse as to become "rhythmical prose instead",
and two Old English authors, Wulfstan of York and London (d. 1023),
and the abbot Ælfric (d. *c.*1010), wrote prose that is rhythmical in nature
and evocative of the verse (Shippey, 1972:183-9).

Finally, considering the manuscripts of Old English poetry reminds
us that some poems come to us in manuscripts from a much later period.
One is *The Battle of Maldon*, the single manuscript of which was lost in
the Cottonian fire. The poem was printed by Thomas Hearne from a transcript made by John Elphinston (Scragg, 1981:4). The poem has always
been overshadowed by its reputation as a weakened representation of the
heroic code seen in more vigorous form in *Beowulf* especially. Another
poem known only through a Renaissance copy is *Seasons for Fasting*,

---

[5] See *ASPR* 6:xliii-xlv for comments, p. 27 for the text.

which was transcribed by Laurence Nowell in 1562; its original manuscript too was destroyed in the Cottonian fire. This poem belongs to a broad category of texts that give specific advice for religious observances, including the Ember fast days. The poem also criticizes the corruption of the clergy; addressing *"folces mann"*, 'men [and women] of the people', it was apparently written for the laity (Hilton, 1986).[6] Such a text is more than straightforward instruction in matters of religious observance, although that is its first aim, evidently an important function for poetry in the period. The poem's attack on the clergy would have come from an authority such as Archbishop Wulfstan, who was in a position not only to complain about laxity but to legislate against it. It is significant that other occurrences of the phrase *"folces mann"* are found in such prose texts as the *Old English Penitential* and *Scriftboc* (two penitentials from the tenth century or after), the *Regularis Concordia*, and the laws of Wihtred (Hilton, 1986). We see, through this textual affiliation between *Seasons* and Old English regulatory prose, that poetry was used to reiterate ideas propounded in other genres. *The Seasons* is interesting for several reasons, including its apparently unique eight-line stanzas. What no doubt accounts for this poem being recopied in the sixteenth century is precisely its emphasis on clerical corruption, this being one of the major concerns with the Roman Church that English Protestant scholars and antiquaries, including John Bale and John Foxe, emphasized. Nowell belonged to a group of scholars who found precedent for the English Reformation in Anglo-Saxon texts (Frantzen, 1990); *Seasons for Fasting* is a rare poetic member in their group of texts.

Old English historical poetry that departs from the immediately recognizable features of the heroic code, or participates in that code in somewhat ambiguous terms, offers another kind of diversity in its link to later English writing. Any reader of Layamon's *Brut* recognizes the Anglo-Saxon "survivals" implicit in its language and ethos. In this matter of the scholarly recovery of Old English literature culture, however, the prose far outstripped the poetry. The important texts printed by early Anglo-Saxon scholars included law codes and homilies and pastoral letters by Ælfric, not *Beowulf*, *The Wanderer*, or *The Seafarer*. Indeed, the first edition of Bede's *Historia Ecclesiastica Gentis Anglorum* did not even recognize the poetic shape of *Cædmon's Hymn*, arguably the most famous of all Old English poems (Frantzen, 1990:157-9).

6 See *ASPR* 6:xcii-xciv for comments, pp. 98-104 for the text (which is incomplete).

3. Conclusion

Old English poetry is usually introduced within the framework of a hierarchy of genres that allow readers to imagine only a few social uses,
chiefly literary musing (the elegies) and heroic reflection. Such uses
favour aristocratic entertainment but, curiously, ignore the preoccupations
of Alfred, one of the few aristocrats who, we can be fairly sure, set his
hand—at least figuratively—to writing poetry. Such poetry is selective
and predominantly aristocratic; even pious poetry is not likely to have
reached beyond the relatively small learned circles, although presumably
poems that expressed and expounded on prayers might have been more
widely known. Charms, gnomes, and riddles almost certainly knew life
both inside and outside learned circles.

If the poetry is socially selective in ways we cannot circumvent, we
can nevertheless view it less selectively than we have been wont to do.
Ways of viewing the poetry outside the framework of nineteenth-century
generic categories have long been at hand. Michel Foucault's "author function", for example, is a useful way to focus on the impact of reputation on
the reception of a writer's work (Foucault, 1977). King Alfred's name
carries a powerful "author function" in prose, but in verse it is barely
recognized. Is this because we do not envision a king writing poetry, even
though King David, also a poet, remains a likely and logical model for the
West Saxon king? Or is it because we cannot imagine the place of poetry
in a ninth-century educational reform because verse occupies so small a
place in modern education? Just as Alfred's poetry is found in several
manuscripts connected chiefly by his name as their author, so too are the
celebrated poems of Cynewulf dispersed in two manuscripts (*Juliana* and
Christ II in the Exeter Book; *Elene* and *Fates of the Apostles* in the Vercelli Book). We are so wary of falling into the traps of romantic criticism
that held earlier scholars of Cynewulf—and A.S. Cook in particular—that
we seem to shun the manuscript implications of common authorship, including the possibility that a codex in which all of Cynewulf's work was
once collected stands behind the surviving copies. Conner observes that the
shorter texts in the Exeter Book that occur elsewhere (including *Soul and
Body*, *Judgment Day I*, and *The Lord's Prayer I*) are all found in the third
of the three booklets that compose the Exeter codex. He believes that this
booklet is a "self-sufficient unit" with a textual history different from that
of the rest of the Exeter collection. Here too textual histories help break
up the tyranny of manuscript contexts and open scholarly eyes to textual
forms whose outlines are still present, if obscured, in the poetic records
(Conner, 1986:241). Another useful reading model, also derived from
Foucault, is the archaeological metaphor in which we isolate and identify
layers of scribal activity, beginning with the manuscript and its glosses,

corrections, and notes, and extending to the appearance of the text in print (Frantzen, 1990:114-19; Irvine, 1991:182-7).

Such ways of reading break the hold of the editorial and critical tradition on texts and refocus our reading energies on the possibilities of difference among them. We are familiar with arguments that some elegies are layers of Christian and pagan thinking, or even dialogues between two speakers or one consciousness divided into two parts, as has been suggested for *The Seafarer* (Pope, 1974). But here I am thinking instead of reading that is concerned not with dramatic voices but with the textual voices of the manuscripts and their post-Anglo-Saxon and post-medieval histories.

Old English poetry survives in many more registers, and in far more ambiguous registers, than the critical and scholarly traditions seem to allow for. Admittedly such divisions are introduced as part of the "introductory" mode; without some categories (whether they be types of verse, types of metrical patterns, or classes of verbs), the learner new to the subject would be lost. But these categories are the modes in which new students discover the Anglo-Saxon world—in the *ASPR*, in the bibliographies that follow generic conventions, and introductory texts such as this one.

By understanding the contexts and the histories of the manuscripts that contain the poems, we can begin to appreciate how many purposes poetry answered to in the culture. The power of the poetry of prayer, epilogues, or didactic texts is too obvious to modern readers, who prefer the literary mysteries of *The Dream of the Rood* (also prayerful, also didactic) instead. But this understanding of poetry as literary and hence in need of interpretation and mediation is a consequence of modern taste; it is no judgment on medieval mentalities. We are conditioned to see Old English poetry applied only to a few of the expressive purposes it seems to have served: we think of heroic—and hagiographic—boasts and of celebrations of the bonds that link lords (and the Lord) and thanes; we hear elegiac laments in female and male voices; we enjoy witty riddles; and we defer to the solemnity of the apocalyptic and the eschatological. Much of the rest is written off as "homiletic" or "pious" poetry, and it is in this category that I urge new readers to look for new insights into the literary culture of the Anglo-Saxons.

The poetry in these lusterless categories is by no means as routine as the categories themselves would seem to suggest. Even the titles given by editors to moral and didactic texts—*An Exhortation to Christian Living, Homiletic Fragment I, Maxims, A Father's Advice to his Son*—invite boredom and suggest that such poems are, as one commentator put it, "lifeless moralizing in conventional phrases" (Gordon, 1954:ix). But there is much life to be found in this moralizing; what we need is a critical tradition less focused on the fixed features of Old English poems—and the equally fixed canon of preferred texts—and more open to ways of reading that accommodate the diversity of the culture and its poetry.

REFERENCES

Bately, J. (1982). Lexical Evidence for the Authorship of the Prose Psalms in the Paris Psalter. *Anglo-Saxon England* 10. 69-95.

Bliss, A., and A.J. Frantzen (1976). The Integrity of *Resignation*. *Review of English Studies* 27. 385-402.

Caie, G. D. (1976) *The Judgment Day Theme in Old English Poetry*. Copenhagen: Nova.

Campbell, A. (1959) *Old English Grammar*. Oxford: Oxford University Press.

Chambers, R.W. (1959). *"Beowulf": An Introduction to the Study of the Poem with a Discussion of the Stories of Offa and Finn*. 3rd ed., with a Supplement by C. L. Wrenn. Cambridge: Cambridge University Press.

Chance, J. (1986). *Woman as Hero in Old English Literature*. Syracuse, NY: Syracuse University Press.

Conner, P.W. (1986). The Structure of the Exeter Book Codex. *Scriptorium* 40. 233-42.

Conner, Patrick (1993). *Anglo-Saxon Exeter: A Tenth-Century Cultural History*. Woodbridge, Suff.: D.S. Brewer.

Earl, J.W. (1982). Apocalypticism and Mourning in *Beowulf. Thought* 57. 363-70.

Earl, J.W. (1989). King Alfred's Talking Poems. *Pacific Coast Philology* 24. 49-61.

Earl, J.W. (1991). *Beowulf* and the Origins of Civilization. In: Frantzen, 1991:65-89.

Foucault, M. (1977). "What is an Author." In: *Language, Counter-Memory, Practice: Selected Essays and Interviews by Michel Foucault*. Ed. D.F. Bouchard, trans. D.F. Bouchard and S. Simon Ithaca, NY: Cornell University Press. 113-38.

Frantzen, A.J. (1990). *Desire for Origins: New Language, Old English, and Teaching the Tradition*. New Brunswick, NJ: Rutgers University Press.

Frantzen, A.J. (ed.) (1991). *Speaking Two Languages: Traditional Disciplines and Contemporary Theory in Medieval Studies*. Albany, NY: State University of New York Press.

Gneuss, H. (1991). The Old English Language. In: Godden and Lapidge, 1991. 23-54.

Godden, M., and M. Lapidge (ed) (1991). *The Cambridge Companion to Old English Literature*. Cambridge: Cambridge University Press.

Gordon, R.K. (1954). *Anglo-Saxon Poetry*. Everyman's Library. London: Dent, and New York: Dutton.

Griffith, M.S. (1991). Poetic Language and the Paris Psalter: The Decay of the Old English Tradition. *Anglo-Saxon England* 20. 167-86.

Hermann, J.P. (1989). *Allegories of War: Language and Violence in Old English Poetry*. Ann Arbor, MI: University of Michigan Press.

Hilton, C.B. (1986). The Old English *Seasons for Fasting*: Its Place in the Vernacular Complaint Tradition. *Neophilologus* 70. 155-59.

Irvine, M. (1986). Anglo-Saxon Literary Theory Exemplified in Old English Poems: Interpreting the Cross in *The Dream of the Rood* and *Elene. Style* 20. 157-81.

Irvine, M. (1991). Medieval Textuality and the Archaeology of Textual Culture. In: Frantzen, 1991:181-210.

Ker, N.R. (1957). *Catalogue of Manuscripts Containing Anglo-Saxon*. Oxford: Clarendon Press.

Kiernan, K.S. (1981). *Beowulf and the Beowulf Manuscript*. New Brunswick, NJ: Rut-

gers University Press.
Kiernan, K.S. (1986). *The Thorkelin Transcripts of Beowulf.* Anglistica 25. Copenhagen: Rosenkilde and Bagger.
Kiernan, K.S. (1990). Reading Cædmon's "Hymn" with Someone Else's Glosses. *Representations* 32. 157-74.
Klinck, Anne (1993). *Old English Elegies: A Critical Edition and Genre Study.* Montreal: McGill-Queens University Press.
Krapp, G.P., and E. van K. Dobbie (eds.) (1931-54). *The Anglo-Saxon Poetic Records,* 6 vols. New York: Columbia University Press.
Lapidge, M. (1991). Textual Criticism and the Literature of Anglo-Saxon England. *Bulletin of the John Rylands University Library Manchester* 73. 17-45.
Lees, Clare A. (1991). Working with Patristic Sources: Language and Context in Old English Homilies. In: Frantzen, 1991:157-180.
Moffat, Douglas (ed. and trans.) (1990). *The Old English* Soul and Body. Woodbridge, Suff.: Boydell and Brewer.
O'Keeffe, K.O. (1990) *Visible Song: Transitional Literacy in Old English Verse.* Cambridge: Cambridge University Press.
Overing, G.R. (1990). *Language, Sign, and Gender in Beowulf.* Carbondale, IL: Southern Illinois University Press.
Overing, G.R. (1991). On Reading Eve: *Genesis B* and the Readers' Desire. In: Frantzen, 1991:35-63.
Pocock, J.G.A. (1987). Texts as Events: Reflections on the History of Political Thought. In: *The Politics of Discourse: The Literature and History of Seventeenth-Century England.* Ed. Kevin Sharpe and Steven N. Zwicker. Berkeley: University of California Press.
Pope, John C. (1974). Second Thoughts on the Interpretation of *The Seafarer. Anglo-Saxon England* 3. 75-86.
Robinson, F.C. (1980). Old English Literature in its Most Immediate Context. In: *Old English Literature in Context.* Ed. J.D. Niles. Totowa, NJ: Rowman and Littlefield. 11-29.
Robinson, F.C. (1981). 'Bede's' Envoi to the Old English History. *Studies in Philology* 78. 4-19.
Robinson, F.C. (1989). "The Rewards of Piety": Two Old English Poems in their Manuscript Contexts. In: *Hermeneutics and Medieval Culture.* Ed. P.J. Gallacher and H. Damico. Albany, NY: State University of New York Press. 193-200.
Rypins, S. (1924). *Three Old English Prose Texts in MS. Cotton Vitellius A.xv.* Early English Text Society, O.S. 161. London: Oxford University Press.
Said, E. W. (1983). *The World, the Text, and the Critic.* Cambridge, MA: Harvard University Press.
Schlauch, Margaret. (1941). An Old English *Encomium Urbis. Journal of English and Germanic Philology* 40. 14-28.
Scragg, D. (ed.) (1981). *The Battle of Maldon.* Manchester: Manchester University Press.
Scragg, D. (1991). The Nature of Old English Verse. In: Godden and Lapidge, 1991:55-70.
Shippey, T.A. (1972). *Old English Verse.* London: Hutchinson.
Whobrey, W.T. (1991). King Alfred's Metrical Epilogue to the *Pastoral Care. Journal of English and Germanic Philology* 90. 175-86.
Wrenn, C.L. (1967). *A Study of Old English Literature.* London: Harrap, and New York: Norton.

OLD ENGLISH POETRY IN ITS MATERIAL CONTEXT

MILDRED BUDNY

The Anglo-Saxons practised the art of book-production through a period of some five centuries, which extended from their conversion to Christianity in the seventh and eighth centuries to their conquest by the Normans in the eleventh. They produced books of many kinds and styles, including some major contributions to the history of book-design.[1] Among them are some of the principal witnesses to Old English poetry. Other witnesses survive in later copies, while a few Anglo-Saxon witnesses survive in other media: stone sculpture, bone carving and decorated metalwork. Understanding the character of the witnesses as material objects can greatly aid comprehension and appreciation of their texts.

1. The Art of Writing and Book-Production

Whereas the pagan Anglo-Saxons practised writing in runes already from an early date, before they migrated to England in the fifth and sixth centuries, Christian missionaries from Ireland and the Mediterranean brought the Latin alphabet and books to them in England in the seventh and eighth centuries. Imported books and scribes introduced many styles of script and techniques of book-production. These in turn were transmitted to the Continent through intensive missionary activity from much of the British Isles, under Sts Gall (died c.630), Willibrord (658-739), Boniface (c.675-754) and others. Few witnesses to Old English poetry survive from this early period (Plates 1-2). During the eighth and ninth centuries Viking raids on England dispersed many libraries, disrupted manuscript production and redirected the course of literacy.

After securing his kingdom against such incursions, King Alfred (871-99) turned much attention to educational reform and vernacular book-production. The translations of Latin texts which he deemed important include some poetic texts, either derived from the Latin originals or appended to the translations (Plate 3). The former include the Psalms of

---

[1] Accounts of the surviving books and their achievement appear in Ker (1957), Temple (1976), Alexander (1978), Brown (1991), Ohlgren (1992) and Budny (forthcoming). Their historical and cultural setting is surveyed in J. Campbell (1982), Backhouse *et al.* (1984), Webster and Backhouse (1991) and Ford (1992).

the Old Testament and the *Metres* of Boethius (*c.*480-524) which alternate with prose portions within *The Consolation of Philosophy*; the latter include the *Metrical Preface* and *Epilogue* to Alfred's translation of the *Pastoral Care* of Pope Gregory the Great (590-604). Alfred's programme declined after his death, but the Benedictine monastic reform movement which gained momentum through Continental inspiration under his successors in the tenth century created a revival of education and literacy through the rest of the Anglo-Saxon period. This led to a flowering of both vernacular and Latin book-production. To this period belong most of the surviving witnesses to Old English poetry (Plates 4-10 and 12) as well as the development of rhythmical prose.

Old English texts continued to be composed and copied after the Norman Conquest. They include versions or extensions of the *Anglo-Saxon Chronicle* and the poem *De situ Dunelmi* (Plate 13). Annotations in some Anglo-Saxon manuscripts show occasional consultation later in the Middle Ages. This occurred notably at Worcester in the thirteenth century, where an anonymous, assiduous and autodidactic—but not always accurate—reader of Old English texts entered glosses and other notes in many manuscripts, including two copies of the *Pastoral Care*. The annotator is now known as the 'Tremulous Worcester Hand', from his distinctive quivery script, which became increasingly unsteady in later stages of his activity, while his command of Old English improved. As might be expected, Old English poetry caused him greater difficulty than prose, to judge by his glosses to the *Metrical Preface* and *Epilogue* of the *Pastoral Care* (Plate 3). After all, for many prose texts he could consult the Latin original to check the meaning of individual words or phrases and passages as a whole, but with the appended poetry he was on his own. Its densely compacted and interlaced word-order offered special challenges (or obstacles) to comprehension.

After the dispersal of English monastic collections under King Henry VIII (1509-47), a concerted recovery of medieval texts in the second half of the sixteenth century led to the revival of Old English studies. Major early proponents include Lawrence Nowell (*c.*1520-*c.*1569), who owned and annotated the *Beowulf* Manuscript (Plate 7); Matthew Parker (1504-75), who assembled the largest surviving private collection of Anglo-Saxon manuscripts and sponsored the earliest printed editions of Anglo-Saxon texts; and John Joscelyn (1529-1603), Parker's Latin secretary, who aided those editions and prepared Old English word-lists and a dictionary, in collaboration with Parker's son John (1548-1618). Such collectors, scholars and antiquaries left their marks in many manuscripts, as with Joscelyn's distinctive spidery script alongside the glosses by the Tremulous Worcester Hand in the *Metrical Preface* to the *Pastoral Care* (Plate 3). During this period Anglo-Saxon manuscripts were carefully collected; they were examined and compared, to collate the different witnesses to the same texts; transcripts were made; editions of specific texts were published; and word-lists and an Old English dictionary were compiled, but not published. Such means set the stage for the modern study of Old English.[2]

Editions of poetic texts first appeared in the seventeenth century, albeit in the midst of prose texts. In 1643 the scholar Abraham Wheloc (1593-1653) published both the Latin and Old English versions of Bede's *Ecclesiastical History of the English People*, which incorporates *Cædmon's Hymn*; and the *Anglo-Saxon Chronicle*, which contains seven poems among its annals, including *The Battle of Brunanburh*. This edition prints the verse in long lines like prose, much as it appears in the Anglo-Saxon originals (Plate 6). Editions of poetic texts as such, together with a recognition of the structure of poetic half-lines, emerged by the early eighteenth century, with the pioneering work of Franciscus Junius (1591-1677), George Hickes (1642-1715) and Humfrey Wanley (1672-1726). The first to print a sizeable number of Old English poems was Junius, who published all four poems from MS Junius 11 (Plate 10) in 1655. Hickes's *Thesaurus* of 1705 contains editions of several texts, including *The Battle of Finnsburh*, *The Battle of Brunanburh*, and *The Rune Poem*, as well as an account of Anglo-Saxon metrics; it prints the verse half-lines as individual lines. Editions and studies have appeared increasingly from the nineteenth century onwards, with the work of the Icelandic scholar Grímur Jónsson Thorkelin (1752-1829), the English scholar John Mitchell Kemble (1807-57) and many others. Work continues apace in many parts of the world on the texts; their character, structure and layout; the nature of Old English prosody; and the material context in which the poetic corpus appears.[3]

2. Patterns of Survival and Distribution

Old English poetry survives in divers contexts: mostly in manuscripts and rarely in other media (Plates 1-10 and 12-14). Many texts survive in copies made during the Anglo-Saxon or Anglo-Norman period, but some are known only through later copies. The witnesses mostly comprise some one hundred manuscripts and a handful of inscriptions in stone, bone or

[2] This work is surveyed in Adams (1917), Douglas (1951:52-76), Ker (1957:l-lvi) and Berkhout and Gatch (1982).
[3] Accounts of this work appear in Douglas (1951:77-118), Sisam (1953), Shippey (1972), Kiernan (1986), O'Brien O'Keeffe (1990), Godden and Lapidge (1991), Mitchell and Robinson (1992), and Moffat (1992). See also Wheloc (1643), Hickes (1705) and Junius (1994).

metalwork. Some poetry survives only in extracts quoted in prose texts, which range from homilies to correspondence. Some lost witnesses are known through transcripts, printed editions, sketches or photographs made before their disappearance or destruction.[4]

Usually the poetry, like the prose, is written or inscribed with Latin letters (*a*, *b*, *c* and so on) mixed with the special Old English letters *eth* (*ð* and *Đ* in minuscule and capital forms), *thorn* (*þ* and *Þ*) and *wynn* (*ƿ* and *Ƿ*), along with some signs for abbreviations, as with the symbol 7 representing the word or element *and* or *ond* (as in Plates 6 and 7). Scribes who had not received Anglo-Saxon training frequently had difficulty with the special Old English letters. These include Continental scribes of the early medieval period as well as copyists of later periods. Their common mistakes or substitutions involve rendering *ð* as *d*; *þ* as *th*; and *ƿ* as *p*, *pu*, *u*, *uu* or *w*, variously reflecting the shape or phonetic value of the letter (Plate 13).[5]

Occasionally the poetry is written with or partly with runes, the angular script which the Anglo-Saxons brought to England and used mostly for inscriptions upon stone, bone, wood, metalwork and pottery. Partly from this script derive the Old English letters *ð* and *ƿ* which augment the Latin alphabet. Poetic texts with runes include *The Rune Poem*, *The Ruin*, the *Dialogues of Solomon and Saturn I*, four poems by Cynewulf (active perhaps in the first half of the ninth century), several *Riddles*, two inscriptions on the Franks Casket and the version of the *Dream of the Rood* on the Ruthwell Cross (Plates 1 and 5). The runes stand for their phonetic values or for their rune-names and the corresponding words, so that they might form the text itself or parts within it, including cryptic or acrostic elements.[6]

Runes represent the poetic texts in full on both the Ruthwell Cross and the Franks Casket (Plate 1). On the casket the inscriptions run clockwise around its panels in alternately horizontal and vertical lines; on the cross the poetry stands upright in vertical series of horizontal lines around its east and west faces. The metrical inscriptions carved in runes on the Great Urswick cross shaft and the Thornhill and Chester memorial stones occupy their own panels in block-like series or columns of horizontal lines. The inscription on the Falstone memorial stone places side by side one panel in Latin letters and one in runes. In other poems the runes stand

---

[4] The corpus and its locations are described in Ker (1957), Bradley (1982:553-9) and Robinson and Stanley (1991). Its texts are printed in Krapp and Dobbie (1931-54).

[5] Some are listed in Ker (1957:475-84).

[6] Accounts of runes and their uses on objects and in poetic texts appear in Menner (1941), Nicholson and Frese (1975:301-34), Williamson (1977), Backhouse *et al.* (1984: 101-3), Page (1987) and Bammesberger (1991).

interspersed either singly or in groups among lines of Latin letters, where the scribes usually distinguished the runes by placing a medial point to either side, in the same way that roman numerals were treated in early medieval manuscripts (Plates 6 and 7). In *The Rune Poem* the runes begin each stanza and occur in their standard alphabetic sequence, the *futhark*; the poem gives an account of their meanings. In Cynewulf's poems *Christ II*, *Juliana*, *Elene* and *The Fates of the Apostles* the runes spell out the author's name *Cynwulf* or *Cynewulf*. In *Solomon and Saturn I* (Plate 5) the runes represent or duplicate the Latin letters of the *Pater Noster* as they do battle with the devil. In this poem the runes are extra-metrical, demonstrating that they comprise an interpolation into the original composition.

Such features emphasise the importance of the visual layout of the written text. The presentation of some poetic texts with elegant script, decorated initials and/or illustrations (Plates 1-4, 7, 9 and 10) similarly indicates close attention to their material embodiment.

The poetry occupies many different settings. It either stands on its own or along with other texts, which comprise Old English prose, Latin prose or verse or a combination of these. For example, *The Dream of the Rood* survives in portions (along with Latin inscriptions) on the eighth-century Ruthwell Cross carved in stone; in two lines (along with an Old English donorship inscription in prose) on the eleventh-century Brussels Cross engraved in partly gilt silver over a wooden core; and in full (among numerous Old English texts in prose and verse) transcribed in the tenth-century Vercelli Book (Vercelli, Biblioteca Capitolare, MS CXVII).

Four manuscripts contain most of the poetic corpus (Plates 7-10). The Vercelli Book also contains *Andreas*, *The Fates of the Apostles*, *Elene*, other verses and twenty-three homilies. The epic poem *Beowulf* solely survives among miscellaneous texts in prose and verse, including *Judith*, in the late tenth- or early eleventh-century Nowell Codex (London, British Library, MS Cotton Vitellius A.xv, fols. 94-209). Collections of secular or religious poetry occupy both the tenth-century Exeter Book (Exeter, Cathedral Library, MS 3501, fols. 8-130) and the late tenth- or early eleventh-century Caedmon or Junius Manuscript (Oxford, Bodleian Library, MS Junius 11). The Junius Manuscript contains *Genesis*, *Exodus*, *Daniel* and *Christ and Satan*. The many poems in the Exeter Book include *Christ I-III*, *Guthlac A-B*, *The Phoenix*, *Juliana*, *The Wanderer*, *The Seafarer*, *The Panther*, *Deor*, *Wulf and Eadwacer*, *The Wife's Lament*, *The Husband's Message*, *The Ruin* and nearly one hundred *Riddles* grouped in three sections alternating with other genres.

Other representatives of the corpus appear in many contexts. For example, poems devoted to religious observance—*Judgment Day II*, *An Exhortation to Christian Living*, *A Summons to Prayer*, *Lord's Prayer II* and *Gloria I*—occur in a cluster in an eleventh-century ecclesiastical and secular handbook (Cambridge, Corpus Christi College, MS 201, pages 161-70). Poems appear in some versions of the *Anglo-Saxon Chronicle*, starting with MS 'A', the Parker Chronicle (Cambridge, Corpus Christi College, MS 173, Part I), a copy begun in the late ninth or early tenth century and continued in stages to the late eleventh. These poems comprise *The Battle of Brunanburh*, *The Capture of the Five Boroughs*, *The Coronation of Edgar*, *The Death of Edgar*, *The Death of Alfred*, *The Death of Edward* and *William the Conqueror*. They occur in the annals for the years 937, 942, 973, 975, 1036, 1065 and 1087, although each surviving version of the *Chronicle* contains only some of the poems. Some copies of Old English translations made by or for King Alfred (871-99) contain the *Metrical Preface* or *Epilogue*, or both, as with the ninth-century Hatton *Pastoral Care*, which Alfred arranged to send to Worcester (Oxford, Bodleian Library, MS Hatton 20: Plate 3), and the tenth-century Corpus *Pastoral Care*, which belonged to Worcester (Cambridge, Corpus Christi College, MS 12).

Metrical versions of the Psalms probably by Alfred occur in the mid eleventh-century bilingual Paris Psalter (Paris, Bibliothèque Nationale, MS lat. 8824), which sets the Latin text and the Old English version in double columns upon each page. Its Old English rendering of Psalms 1-50 is in prose, while that of Psalms 51-150 is metrical. A variant version of the *Metrical Psalms* occurs in parts of the interlinear Old English gloss in the mid twelfth-century Eadwine Psalter made at Christ Church, Canterbury (Cambridge, Trinity College, MS R.17.1 [987]). In groups of columns on each page this book juxtaposes the Hebrew, Roman and Gallican versions of the Latin Psalter. The Old English gloss accompanies the Roman version. The metrical sections of the gloss span Psalms 90:16-91:15, 92:3-95:2 and perhaps other portions.[7] Here it seems that the Old English poetry interlaces not only with prose in the gloss but also with the several Latin versions and their accompanying commentary.

Old English poetry combines with Latin and transliterated Greek in the anonymous macaronic poem *Ealdhelm*. It survives in one elegant tenth-century copy of the Latin *Praise of Virginity* by Aldhelm (*c.*639-709 x 710) in the prose version (Cambridge, Corpus Christi College, MS 326), where *Ealdhelm* stands between the chapter-list and the author's preface to his work (Plate 4). The poem alternates the different languages in alliterative half-lines, which accord with Old English poetic structure. The copy breaks off abruptly, seemingly abandoned partway by the scribe, so the full version of the poem remains unknown. Yet its emulation of Aldhelm's intricate style of Latin composition using unusual vocabulary and inter-

---

[7] They are assessed by Baker (1984) and O'Neill (1988).

laced word-order perhaps affords a glimpse of his approach to Old English verse which has been otherwise lost.

Some prose texts include elements of rhythmical prose. These mainly comprise works in the mature style of Ælfric of Eynsham (*c.*950-*c.*1010) and some compositions by Wulfstan, archbishop of York (1002-23).[8] Two late versions of the *Anglo-Saxon Chronicle*—MS 'D' (London, British Library, Cotton MS Tiberius B.iv) and MS 'E', the Peterborough Chronicle (Oxford, Bodleian Library, MS Laud Misc. 636)—employ rhythmical prose in the annals for 959 and 975; they contain few of the other poems of the other versions, although the Peterborough Chronicle alone contains *William the Conqueror*.

The distribution pattern of Old English poetry and poetic elements within the extant manuscripts and other media provides a challenge to assessing their intended audiences and functions, which appear to have been varied and complex.

The survival pattern of the poetic corpus is equally complex. Some Anglo-Saxon and later sources refer to literature which no longer survives, as with Aldhelm's vernacular poetry, which King Alfred is reported to have admired. Some poetic texts survive only in unique copies, as with most poems in the four major codices. Others appear in multiple copies, dialects and versions. *Cædmon's Hymn* exists in Northumbrian and West-Saxon versions in seventeen manuscripts of varying dates, starting with the eighth-century St Petersburg Bede (St Petersburg, Publichnaya Biblioteka imeni M.E. Saltykova-Shchedrina, Cod. Q. v. 1. 18). In this manuscript the poem stands in the lower margin of one page as an entry by the original scribe, providing the Old English original alongside the Latin translation by Bede (673-735) in his monumental *Ecclesiastical History of the English People* (Plate 2).

All the copies of *Cædmon's Hymn* appear in manuscripts of the *Ecclesiastical History* in either Bede's Latin original or the Old English version completed by the early tenth century. The Old English poem occurs as part of the main text (if Old English) or as an addition in the margin or at the end; in either case it comprises an appropriate element in the manuscript. Similarly the poetic inscriptions on the Ruthwell Cross, the Brussels Cross and the Franks Casket (Plate 1) ably address and express the character of the objects, even to the extent of making the object appear to speak in the first person. Using the first person is common among inscriptions on objects, in either prose or verse, as well as in verse *Riddles*, which challenge the reader or beholder to guess the speaker's

---

[8] These are described by McIntosh (1949), Funke (1962), Pope (1967-8), Godden (1979) and Stanley (1984).

identity (Plate 9).

By contrast, some other poetic texts appear to be extraneous or in-congruous within their settings. The two copies of the poetic *Dialogues of Solomon and Saturn* exemplify these extremes (Plates 5 and 12). Damaged texts of the two verse *Dialogues* (*Solomon and Saturn I-II*), in which the second *Dialogue* lacks some leaves, sandwich the prose *Dialogue*—itself a fragment—in a small-format tenth-century copy now part of the Red Book of Darley (Cambridge, Corpus Christi College, MS 422), which otherwise contains a portable collection of liturgical texts. An incomplete version of *Solomon and Saturn I* occurs as an eleventh-century addition to the large-format eleventh-century Corpus Old English Bede (Cambridge, Corpus Christi College, MS 41). The survival of both copies means that their two damaged and fragmentary texts of *Solomon and Saturn I* can be conflated to reconstruct an almost complete version. In the Corpus Old English Bede the poem stands among the many miscellaneous texts in Latin and Old English added in the margins or other originally blank areas. They include some Old English *Metrical Charms*, aimed variously to control a swarm of bees, to protect against theft of cattle, to remedy the loss of cattle and to safeguard a journey. In the Red Book of Darley the fragmentary dialogues in both prose and verse comprise a coherent main text, but in the Corpus Old English Bede the poetic texts belong to a hap-hazard collection, as the margins of the manuscript served as an unusual type of 'commonplace book' to contain divers texts.

Some other locations for various *Metrical Charms* seem more appropriate, as with two tenth-century manuscripts devoted to recipes, charms and related texts. One comprises collections of Old English charms and medical recipes (London, British Library, MS Royal 12 D. xvii). The other contains a herbal and a collection of recipes, charms and other texts mainly in Old English (London, British Library, MS Harley 585).

Many texts survive only in copies made long after their composi-tion. This is clearly the case with most copies of *Cædmon's Hymn*, the sole survivor of the work of a poet who lived in the second half of the seventh century; and it might be the case with *Beowulf*, whose date of composition remains controversial. Besides its copies dating between the eighth and eleventh centuries, *Cædmon's Hymn* occurs in four twelfth-century copies (Hereford, Cathedral Library, MS P. v. 1 + Oxford, Bod-leian Library, MS e Mus. 93 [3632]; Oxford, Lincoln College, MS Lat. 31, fols. 14-113; Oxford, Magdalen College, MS Lat. 105; and Dijon, Bibliothèque Municipale, MS 574). Copies of the fourteenth and fifteenth centuries also survive (for example in Cambridge, Trinity College, MS R.5.22 [717]; and Brussels, Bibliothèque Royale, MS 8245-57). A twelfth-century copy destroyed in 1940 (formerly Tournai, Bibliothèque Munici-pale, MS 134, fol.78v) can be glimpsed through a photographic record

PLATES

Plate 1

Plate 2

Plate 3

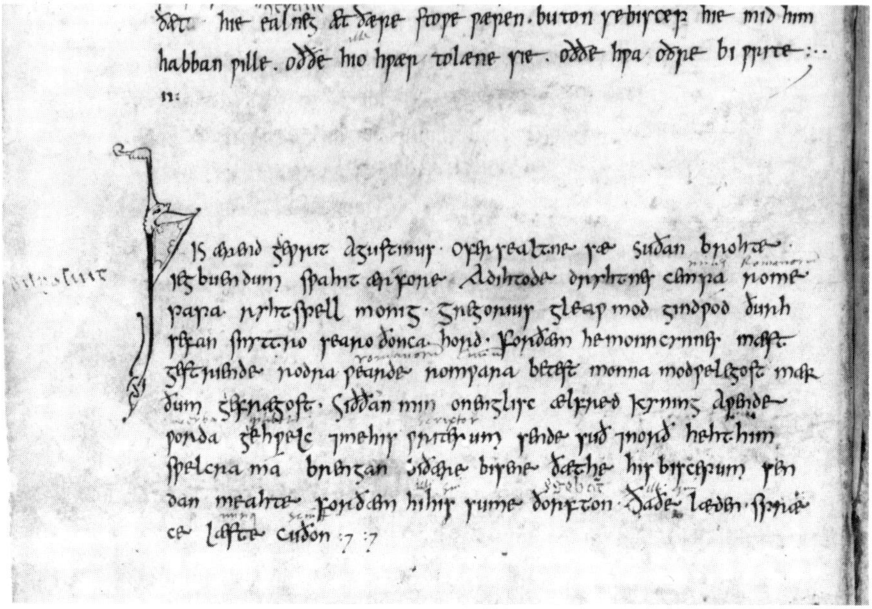

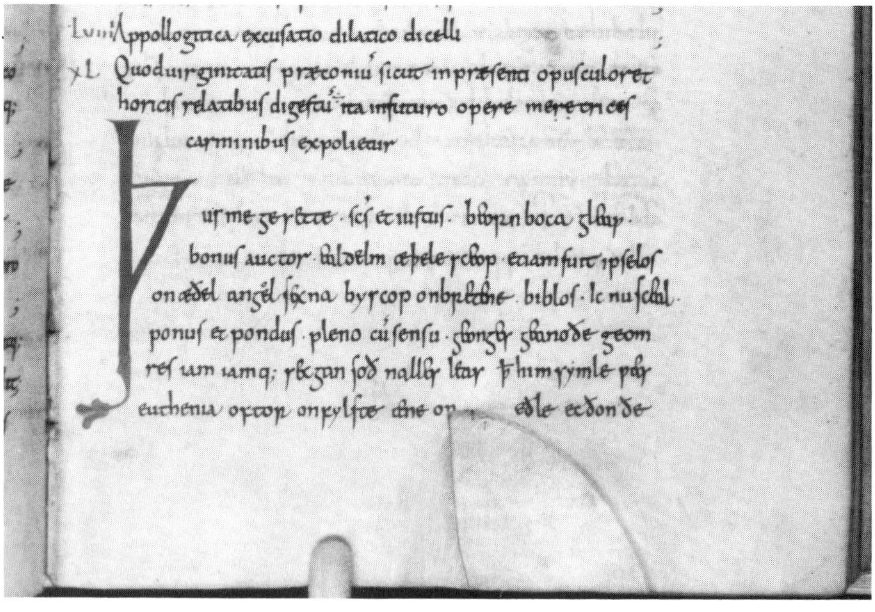

Plate 4

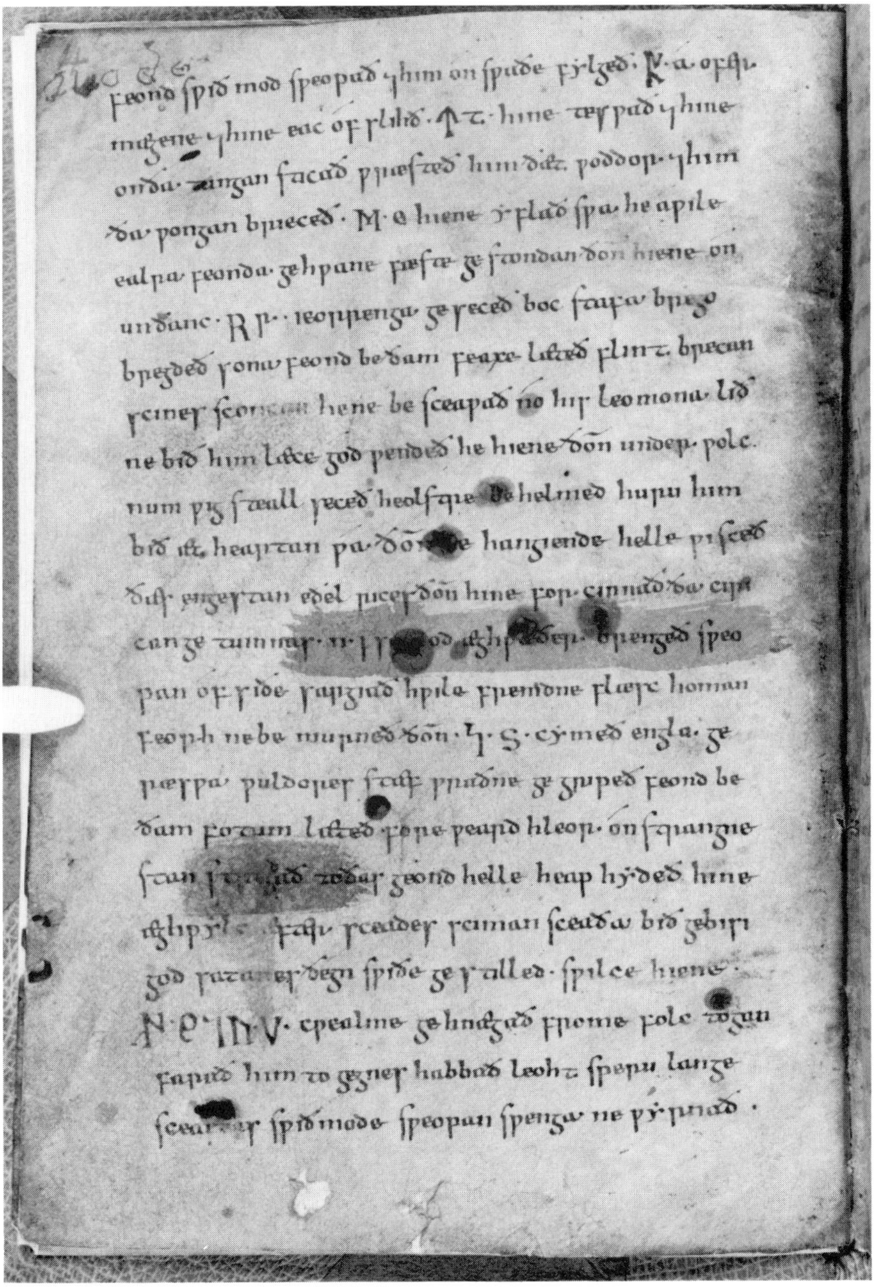

Plate 5

Plate 6

breotene þæmne cyning ⁊ æþeling eᷓ ȝeᷓ þᷓ rohton þᷓ reaxina land
riᷤþᷤ hᷓᵘmiȝe. læᷓtan him behindan hrᵃ byrt tianȝalu riᷤ
þadan. þone ᷤpaᵓtan hᷓaȝen. hᷓynneð nebban. ⁊þanehaᵘeþan
þadan eaᵘm aȝᵉtan hᷓyᷓ aȝᷓ. bᷓucan ᷤpᵉⱺyȝne ȝuð haᷓpoᷤ.
⁊þᷓt ᷤpaᵉⱥeⱺiᷤᷓy ᷓulᷓ onþalⱺe ne þeaᷓⱺ þᵉl maᷓie on þiᷤ
eiȝlanⱺe eᷓ þᷓy ȝiᷤᷓa ᷓoleᷓᷤ ȝe þylleⱺ be þoᷓᵃn hᷓᷓu ᷤþᷓⱺ ⱺiᷤ
eȝum þᷓy þeuᷓ þᷓe ȝaⱺ bᷓe ealⱺeᵘⱺ þᷓan. ᷤiþþan eaᷤᷓan hᷓⱺᷓᵘ
tiȝle ⁊þᷓaxe upbᷓeoman. oþᷓ bᷓaⱺbᷓimu bᷓyᷓ ᷓine þoᷓᷓan.
þlanᷓe þiᷤ ᷤini þaᷓ. þealliᷤe oþᷓn ᷓoman. ᷤoᷓþaᷓ aᵘ hᷓaᷓe eaᵓⱺ
beȝeaᷓaᷓ⁊

Aᷠ. ⱺ̇ᷓᷓᷓ XXXVIII.
Aᷠ. ⱺᷓᷓᷓ XXXVIIII

Aᷠ. ⱺᷓᷓᷓ xl. Hᷓn æþelᷤᷓan cyning ᷓo ᷤᷓ þᷓnⱺe on vi. kᷓl
noᵛ ymbe xl þinᷓþa buᷓan anþeniht þᷓyᷤᷓe æᷓenⱥo cyning
ᷓonᷓ þᷓnⱺe ⁊eaⱺmunⱺ æþeling þᷓnȝ ᷓoþiᷓe. ⁊heþᷓᷓ þa. xviii.
þinᷓþe. ȝeþelᷤᷓan cyning þixaⱺe. xiiii. ȝeaᷓ ⁊ᷓ þuᷓan h...

ᷓ ulþelm aᷓᷓceᷓiᷤᷓeap on eanᷓ.

Aᷠ. ⱺᷓᷓᷓ xli. Hᷓn eaⱺ munⱺ cyning ᷤnȝla þᷓoⱺᷠ maȝa
uᷠ ⱺᷓᷓᷓᷓxlᷓ.
munⱺ boᷓa myᷓþe ȝeᷤoⱺe ⱺyᷓeⱺeⱺ þᷓuᷓa
ᷓaⱺoᷓ ᷤeaⱺeᷤ hᷓᷓanᷓylliᷤ ȝaᷓe. ⁊humbᷓa ea bᷓaⱺa bᷓim
ᷤᷓᷓa bᷓnȝa þiᷓe liȝoᷓa ᷓaᷓᷤᷓn ⁊lin ᷓᷓlene. ⁊ᷤno ᷓinȝahᷓᷠ
iᷓᷓl eᷤᷓan þoᷓⱺeaᷓ ⱺᷤoᷓa byᷓ ⱺᷓne þᷓᷓnanⱺᷓ unⱺᷓ
noᷓⱺmannum myᷓⱺe ȝeᷓeȝ ⱺe onhᷓᷤᷓᷓᷓ þᷓa hᷓᷓᷓeⱺᷓ mu
lanȝe þᷓaȝa oᷓ hᷤᷓ alyᷓⱺeᷤᷓ þoᷓhᷤᷓþᷓþ þ ᷓeiᷤe þiᷤ
ȝᷓoᷓa hliþ aᷓᷓna eaⱺþeaᷓoᷤᷤ eaⱺmunⱺ cyning onᷓᷓnȝanlæᷓᷓ

Plate 7

geweald, ond þæt word acwæð: Næfre ic ænegu[m]
men ær alyfde, siþðan ic hond ond rond hea-
ban mihte, ðryþærn Dena buton þe nu ða.
Hafa nu ond geheald husa selest, gemyne
mærþo, mægenellen cyð, waca wið wraþum.
Ne bið þe wilna gad, gif þu þæt ellenweorc aldre

·X·   gedigest

ÐA him Hroþgar gewat mid his hæleþa gedryht, eodur Scyldinga, ut
of healle; wolde wigfruma Wealhþeo se-
can, cwen togebeddan. Hæfde kyning-
wuldor Grendle togeanes, swa guman
gefrungon, seleweard aseted; sundornyt-
te beheold ymb aldor Dena, eotonweard
abead. Huru Geata leod georne truwode
modgan mægnes, metodes hyldo. Ða he
ofdyde isernbyrnan, helm of hafelan,
sealde his hyrsted sweord, irena cyst, om-
biht þegne, ond gehealdan het hildegeatwe.
Gespræc þa se goda gylpworda sum, Beowulf

Plate 8

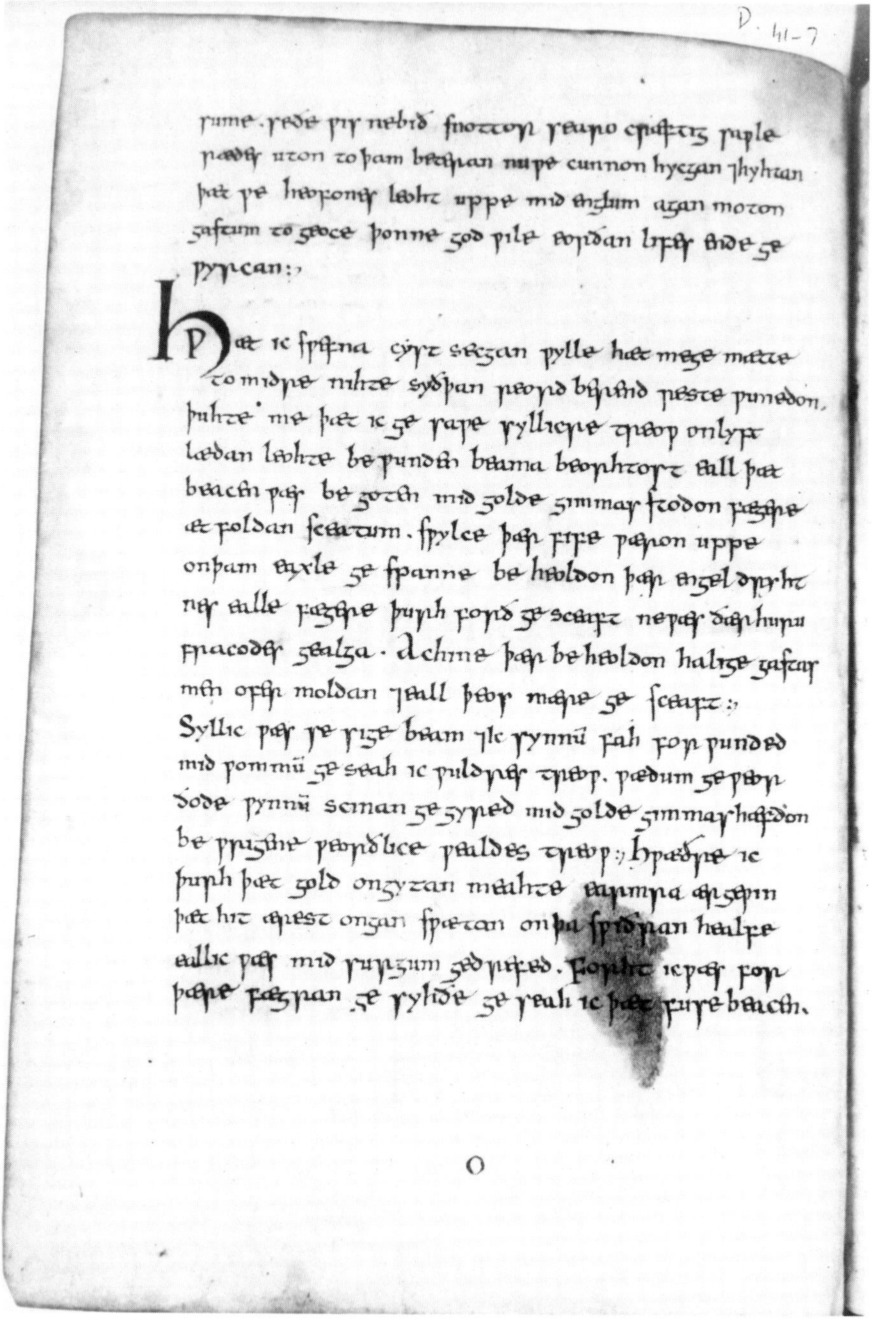

rume . ræde þis ne bið snottor ræswa cristes wyrle
rædes uton to þam betran nu we cunnon hycgan ⁊ hyhtan
þæt we heofones leoht uppe mid englum agan moton
gastum to geoce þonne god wile forðan lifes ende ge
wyrcan :,
HWæt ic swefna cyst secgan wylle hwæt me gemætte
to midre nihte syðþan reordberend reste wunedon .
þuhte me þæt ic gesawe syllicre treow on lyft
lædan leohte bewunden beama beorhtost eall þæt
beacen wæs begoten mid golde gimmas stodon fægere
æt foldan sceatum . swylce þær fife wæron uppe
on þam eaxle gespanne beheoldon þær engel dryht
nes ealle fægere þurh forðgesceaft ne wæs ðær huru
fracodes gealga . ac hine þær beheoldon halige gastas
men ofer moldan ⁊ eall þeos mære gesceaft :,
Syllic wæs se sigebeam ⁊ ic synnum fah forwunded
mid wommum geseah ic wuldres treow . wædum geweor
ðode wynnum scinan gegyred mid golde gimmas hæfdon
bewrigene weorðlice wealdes treow :, Hwæðre ic
þurh þæt gold ongytan meahte earmra ærgewin
þæt hit ærest ongan swætan on þa swiðran healfe
eall ic wæs mid surgum gedrefed . Forht ic wæs for
þære fægran gesyhðe geseah ic þæt fuse beacen.

Plate 9

ceoplæ ðohton moð plonc mæple þ hið onmæ gupeð pæreð
mæ onpiðone penpað mm hæipoð pegeð mæ onpærtth þe
leh pona minte gemotte pehe mæ nturpað piɼpunoth loce
pæt bið þæt thge :7

Me roðinoa rum þæpe berne þeoe populo ropthga binō
pætte riþban orɼoe onpætie oroe þet þonan pette on
runnan þeh ic ɼpiþe be lær hehum þamþe ic hæɼeoe hærpo
mæ riþban rnað rærrɼ æ ge puroþum begiunoth ɼing
par ɼæoban ymæ ruglɼ pen gðono ɼpeo oropum ɼþr
peoe ge næhhe oɼþ brunne brɼro bærn telge ɼprælz
ɼcrurmɼ oæle ɼtor þet onmæ riþaoe yrþur lær mæ
riþban prah hæleð hlð boprorum hyþe beþthe oe zirheoe
mæ mið goloe ɼorþon me gupeoon prætlic prope ymi
þa pipe biɼongth · nuþa gthitho yrepurioa telz yþa puloon
ge rærulo pioe mæþe oyrht polca helm nalɼ ool pite ·
gɼ minbærin pɼua brucan pillað hybæð þrge runo
pan yþryrge pærrian hærtum þr hpærtian yþr hyge
bli þian pɼþe þ ɼrooian habbaþ ɼroinoa þrma ɼþær
ɼia ygeribbna rohria ygoria tilria yge trapria þa
hyria tyr yɼaro ɼrtum ycað yhr ari ɼorpum liɼrum
bilægað yhiluɼan ɼæþmum pɼte cleppað ɼrige
hpæt ic hatte niþum to nytte nama min iɼ mæɼe ·

Plate 10

on þell fættinne· þa liþe þþinc ne þaþ· · lxiii·
ATO noe ⁊þnæc· ncñgiñð uþþ ñi hꝥꝼon þuel
þtiuð· halgan þtuñde· þe iþ eðel þtol ꝥꝥ ge
nymeð liþþe onlunde· lago þiða nꝼꝥ· faþþi
on foldan· gꝼþꝥ onþtuðo gangan· ut oꝼ þan
ce· ⁊on topðan btanm· oꝼ þam hꝥan hoꝼe·
hiþan læd þu· ⁊ꝼallte þa þocne· þe ic þaꝤ þniar on
hlíðe nꝼñede· þñoꝧ lago hæþðe· þnymme geꝼꝥuh
te· þiuðða eðyl· hefꝼñnede þþa ⁊þñtan hynðe·
fꝼuh oꝼꝥñ ⁊þñtuin þtull· þþa him þꝥð þñꝼen bebñuð
luþtum miclum· ⁊alædðe þa oꝼ þaꝤ þele· þnaðna
laꝼe·

Plate 11

Plate 12

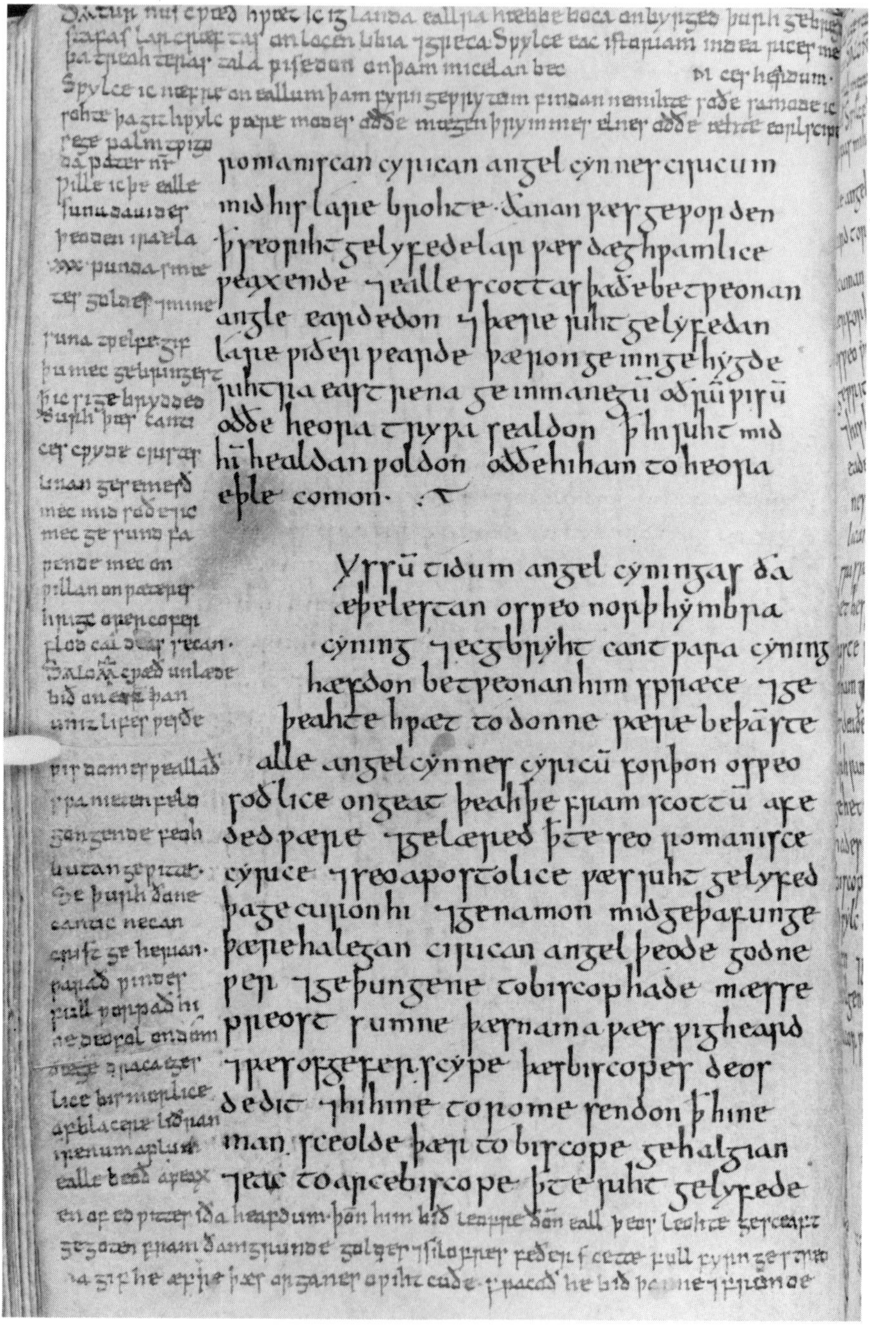

romaniscan cyrican angelcynnes ciricum
mid his lare brohte. Ðanan wæs geworden
þæt seo riht gelyfede lar wæs dæghwamlice
weaxende 7 ealles scottas þa ðe betweonan
angle eardedon 7 þære riht gelyfedan
lare wiðerweard wæron ge inn gehygde
rihtra eastrena ge innanegū oðrū wisū
oððe heora ꞇnyri sealdon þ hi riht mid
hī healdan woldon oððe hi ham to heora
eþle comon. :~

Yssū tidum angelcyningas ða
æþelestan osweo norþhymbra
cyning 7 ecgbryht cantwara cyning
hæfdon betweonan him spræce 7 ge
þeahte hwæt to donne wære be þā state
alle angelcynnes cyricū forþon osweo
soðlice ongeat þeah þe he fram scottū afe
ded wære 7 gelæred þte seo romanisce
cyrice 7 seo apostolice wæs riht gelyfed
þa gecuron hi 7 genamon mid geþafunge
þære halegan cirican angelþeode godne
wer 7 geþungene to biscophade mæsse
preost sumne þæs nama wæs wighearð
7 wes of geferscype þæs biscopes deos
dedit 7 hi hine to rome sendon þ hine
man sceolde þær to biscope gehalgian
7 eac to arcebiscope þte riht gelyfede

Plate 13

c̃.j. angulũ. c̃. m. altaris coopnina. j.j. calacē. c̃
argemeũ. j.ij. paten̄as. alt̃ã aureo parat̃a. alt̃ã
greco ope fabrefactã. j.j. curribulũ argenteũ.
j.j. truce. auro. j ebore arcificiose parata. j.j. re
guī. pillium auro texrī. j.ij. tabulas. auro. c̃
argento fabrefcas. j.ij. candelabra argentea.
auro parata. j.i. mistalē. j.uj. euuangeliorum
texē. auro. j argento ornatos. j.j. scj cuthbti in
tã. mecre. j psace sepram. j.v.ij. pallia. j.uj.
cortinas. j.ujj. tapetia. j.ij. coppas argenteas
cū coopent. j.uij. magnas campanas. j.ij.
coernua. auro. j argento fabrefca. j.ij. uexilla.
c̃.j. lanceã. j.ij. armillas aureas. j meã uil
lã dilectã þypemube, australe cū sius appen
deuciis. idest þexam. uff uppeueiu. þlcer
þyrbe. duas peorhoppar. byrdene. Sehã.
Sectrũ. baturu. daldene. hexeldene. hec oīa
do sub dī. j scj cuthbtj testimonio. u si qsm
alicjd abstulerit: dãpnet indie uidicij cũ
iuda traditore. j iubac uiugnē eternum
q̃ sparac̃ũ diabolo. j angtis ei. Implente
j pcietas cuppas pecunia optima. j uffin
tpius optulit totus exercitus ei scõ cuthbro
xn. hundreb. j eo amplus. frem ū siuī
eadmundū de scdiace. j fidelis patrocinio
scj confessoris diligent pri edoctũ fūne cõ
momnit. u si qd sinistri s̃ in hac expecdi
one euenrec: corp siuū scõ cuthbro refer
ret. j ei illub in die iudicij depsteuandũ
cõmendarec. P ost h̃ abiut. feliceri pugna
uit. pspere reduc. sapient̃ mūtas annis
pea regnauit. taub feliceri obiut. Quo de
fuucto eadmunds fr̃ ei inreguũ successit:
magnū exercitũ rursus cougregauit. j in
scociã sperauit. j neuudo tū oiauoruim
scj cuthbg cluiuc: añ sepulchrij ei genua

flexit. preces fudic. se. j suos deo. j scõ confes
sorj cõmendauit. exercitus sexagiuta li
bras optulit. ipe uero manu ppria. ij.
armillas aureas. j. ij. pallia grea. sup
corpus stm posuit. pace. u. j lege qua
umqm meliore huic: omj tre scj cuth
bti: dedit. dara confirmauit. j frs cõ ait
abraham. q̃ speraus in hostes panē j uj
nū melchisedech obtulit fiuita orõne
multocienf se. j totū exercitũ beato con
fessorj commendaus abiit. De siui du
uelms. & de frai. & chquiis q̃ ibide cou
tinent. carmen compositum.

Is deos buptch. byeorne geoib byeoren
ince steppa ge stabõlab stanas ymbu
tan puudpū. ge pætreu. þeorj ymbeoru
nab. caybtun. honenge. j bep mne þu
nab fola tisca. kj u. onsloba ge moj
sr. jbep pse þexen is þuba bexstem
miteel. þinnab inbem pyxū þilba beon
mouxe inbeopebalum beona uixe
jum. Is inbeþe byntheac bextnum ge
eyõeb. be apfesta eabix cubbexich. jbes
ciene cynuxes heafub osmalbesencle
leo. j aibau bistop. eabbexich. j eabspib.
c̃ bele xexeþeþ. Is beþ mne mubb hcom.
jbelpolb. bistop. j byreorna boteua. be
ha. j bonsil abbot. be ciene cubbexue on
xechebe leube. lusttm. j he prflapa
pel xenom. cayõjec̃d. c̃ tõbem eabixe m
mõem miustpie m ajymeba. þeliqma.
be momia puub puunxe. þiundab. bes
be þyrt. sexxes. cuubb beue bjuluies.
þejibomes. bibes.

Plate 14

Oct. 19. 1725. Tuesday. Given me by Mr. Symbes.
Transcribed by Mr. John Elphinston, late Under Keeper of the Cotton Library, the same that
Num. VII. Vide p. XXV. I have printed transcribed Hearning's Chartulary first printed

Bibl. Cott. Otho. A. XII. 3. Folio 57. this Fragment in the Appendix to John of
Glastonbury.

Fragmentum quoddam historicum

de Eadrico &c.

... brocen wurde. het þa hyssa hwæne horp
for lætan feor afyyan 7 forð gangan hic
gan to handum 7 t hize goðu. þt offan mæz
æþey on funde þ þe eopl nolde yfhðo ze
þolian he let him þa of handon leofne
fleozan hafoc þið þas holtes 7 to þaþe
hilde feop. bo þa man mihte oncnapan
þ þe cniht nolde pacian æt þæ þ ze þa
he to þa þnū fenz. eac hi polde eadpic
hir ealdpe ze laytan fpean to ze feohte
onzan þa fopð beþan zaþ to zuþe he
hafde god ze þanc þa hpile þe he mid han
dum healdan mihte bopð 7 bpad ypupð
beot he ze layte þa he æt fopan hiy fpean
fechtan sceolde.

Ða þap byyhtnoð onzan beopnay typy
mian. pad 7 pædde pincū tæhte hu
hi yceoldon standan 7 þone stede he
aldan 7 bad þ hyþa þandan pihte heol
don faste mid folman 7 ne fophtedon
na. þa he hafde þ folc fazepe ze tpymed
he lihte þa mid leodon þap hū leofyt
þap þæp he his heopð pepod holdoft piste
þap tod on stede ytiðlice clypode pican ga
ap

PLATES

1. The Franks Casket (London, British Museum), front. Poem *Fisc flodu* written in runes.

2. The St Petersburg Bede (St Petersburg, Publichnaya Biblioteka imeni M.E. Saltikova-Shchedrina, Codex Q. v. 1. 18, fol. 107r, lower part). *Cædmon's Hymn* in the lower margin, below the Latin text of Bede's *Ecclesiastical History of the English People*, Book IV, chapter 24. (After Arngart.)

3. The Hatton *Pastoral Care* (Oxford, Bodleian Library, MS Hatton 20, fol. 2v, lower part). The *Metrical Preface* to the Old English *Pastoral Care*.

4. The Corpus Aldhelm (Cambridge, Corpus Christi College, MS 326, p. 5, lower part). Chapter-list for Aldhelm's Latin *Praise of Virginity* in the prose version, followed by *Ealdhelm*, lines 1-10b.

5. The Red Book of Darley (Cambridge, Corpus Christi College, MS 422, p. 5). *Poetic Dialogue of Solomon and Saturn I*, lines 122-53a.

6. The Parker Chronicle (Cambridge, Corpus Christi College, MS 173, Part I, fol. 26r). Annals for A.D. 937-42, with *The Battle of Brunanburh*, lines 57b-73b, and *The Capture of the Five Boroughs*.

7. The *Beowulf* Manuscript (London, British Library, MS Cotton Vitellius A.xv, fol. 145r). *Beowulf*, lines 654-75a.

8. The Vercelli Book (Vercelli, Biblioteca Capitolare, Codex CXVII, fol. 104v). *Homiletic Fragment I*, lines 41a-47, and *The Dream of the Rood*, lines 1-22.

9. The Exeter Book (Exeter, Cathedral Library, MS 3501, fol. 107r). *Riddle* 23, lines 6b-11, and *Riddle* 24, lines 1-27. (After Chambers *et al.*)

10. The Junius Manuscript (Oxford, Bodleian Library, MS Junius 11, p. 73). *Genesis*, lines 1482-96, with an illustration of Noah's Disembarkation from the Ark.

11. The Cambridge Saints' Lives (Cambridge, Corpus Christi College, MS 389, fol. 1v). A monk as scribe: the author Jerome, writing down what the Holy Ghost dictates to him.

12. The Corpus Old English Bede (Cambridge, Corpus Christi College, MS 41, p. 196). *Poetic Dialogue of Solomon and Saturn I*, lines 1-34a, entered in the margins around Bede's *Ecclesiastical History of the English People*, Book III, chapters 28-9.

13. Historical Collection from Sawley (Cambridge, University Library, MS Ff. 1. 27, p. 202). *De situ Dunelmi*, following the Latin *Historia de sancto Cuthberto*.

14. The Maldon Transcript (Oxford, Bodleian Library, MS Rawlinson B. 203, fol. 7r). *The Battle of Maldon*, lines 1-26.

made before its destruction. The range of dates and origins of the many copies attests to the widespread interest in this text transmitted through one of the most popular of Anglo-Saxon authors, Bede.

Most witnesses to Old English poetry were copied by English scribes, but some texts proved of interest also to Continental scribes. For example, the twelfth-century Dijon copy of *Cædmon's Hymn* was made probably at the Abbey of Cîteaux—perhaps in connection with the abbacy of the Englishman Stephen Harding (1109-33). *Bede's Death Song* has fifteen Continental copies (including the earliest witness, a ninth-century copy in Switzerland, St Gallen, Stiftsbibliothek, Cod. 254) alongside the twenty English ones (including sixteenth-century additions to earlier manuscripts, as in Cambridge, Corpus Christi College, MS 359). The *Leiden Riddle*, an early Old English translation of Aldhelm's *De Lorica*, was copied by a Frankish monk at the end of a collection of Latin riddles by Aldhelm (Leiden, Bibliotheek Rijksuniversiteit, Voss. Lat. 4° 106).

Old English language and literature continued in use in England well into the Anglo-Norman period, in the transition to Middle English. Numerous Old English prose texts continued to be copied—mainly collections of legal or homiletic works, as with the *Textus Roffensis* (Rochester, Cathedral Library, MS A.3.5, Part I) and various homiliaries (including Cambridge, Corpus Christi College, MS 303). Certain poetic texts were copied in manuscripts of such date, where they form either original components or early additions. Among them are the late copies of *Cædmon's Hymn*, the text of *William the Conqueror* and the only two copies of the short twelfth-century poem *De situ Dunelmi* which survived into the modern period (Cambridge, University Library, MS Ff. 1. 27: Plate 13; and London, British Library, MS Cotton Vitellius D.xx). The Cotton copy of this poem was destroyed in a fire at Ashburnham House in London in 1731.

Some poetic texts are known only through modern or early modern transcripts and editions made from manuscripts now lost. These include *The Battle of Maldon*, which David Casley (1682-1754 or later) copied by 1725 (Oxford, Bodleian Library, MS Rawlinson B. 203, fols. 7-12: Plate 14) from a manuscript destroyed in the fire of 1731 (MS Cotton Otho A. xii); the *Metres of Boethius*, which Junius copied within the entire *Consolation of Philosophy* (Oxford, Bodleian Library, MS Junius 12) from a manuscript damaged and partly destroyed in the same fire (MS Cotton Otho A.vi); *The Rune Poem*, which Hickes printed in 1705 from Wanley's transcript of a leaf destroyed in the same fire (MS Cotton Otho B.x, fol. 165); and *The Battle of Finnsburh*, which Hickes printed in 1705 from a single leaf which he had found in a collection of Old English homilies (London, Lambeth Palace Library, MS 487), but which has since been lost or mislaid. Hickes likewise printed the text of *De situ Dunelmi* from the

Cotton manuscript before the destruction of its relevant leaf in the fire, which both turned the Cambridge copy (Plate 13) into the sole medieval witness to the poem and endowed Hickes's edition with the status of another primary witness, albeit of very late date. By affecting so many manuscripts with Old English texts, including many which comprised sole or rare witnesses, the fire of 1731 was a pivotal event in Old English studies.[9]

The losses in that fire were accidental, like others inflicted over many centuries through time, strife and wear and tear. Many other losses were deliberate, as texts deemed superfluous or out-of-date came to be discarded or redeployed for other purposes. Such a fate befell Anglo-Saxon manuscripts of many kinds containing Latin, Old English or both. Very many losses occurred during the English Reformation, which included the destruction and dispersal of monastic libraries throughout the realm. Some Old English prose texts are known partly or solely through scraps of leaves cut up for reuse in bindings or as loose wrappings for other texts in the medieval period or later. An important poetic text detached from its former manuscript setting is *Waldere*, which survives as a fragment on two loose leaves of unknown provenance, dating from the late tenth or early eleventh century, recovered in 1860 from bundles of papers and vellum leaves (Copenhagen, Kongelige Bibliotek, Ny Kgl. Samling MS 167b [4°]).

The loss of many Anglo-Saxon objects and works of art has probably reduced the poetic corpus still further.[10] With them many inscriptions may have been lost within genres now represented only by a few objects or monuments including the Ruthwell Cross, the Brussels Cross, the Franks Casket (Plate 1), the Lancashire ring and the Sutton Isle of Ely brooch. Some other inscriptions which survive only in a fragmentary state perhaps originally extended into poetry.[11]

Few witnesses remain in their medieval or early modern homes. The principal exceptions constitute manuscripts in cathedral libraries in England or elsewhere, notably the Exeter and Vercelli Books (Plates 8 and 9), and stone sculptures remaining *in situ*. Yet the dispersal, fragmentation and destruction of libraries, bindings, architectural settings, décors and patterns of life and thought have robbed all the witnesses of their full original contexts.

---

[9] The value of transcripts and editions preceding the fire is assessed by Malone (1951), Rogers (1985), Kiernan (1986), Robinson and Stanley (1991) and Griffiths (1991a) and (1991b).

[10] This process is described by Dodwell (1982).

[11] The corpus of non-runic inscriptions is surveyed in Okasha (1971) and (1983).

Many surviving witnesses themselves have suffered losses. The stone monuments have suffered rubbing, breakage, displacement, faulty reconstruction or, in the case of the Ruthwell Cross, all of these. The Franks Casket has been broken and dispersed, with portions now in London and Florence; all of its former fittings are lost, leaving visible gaps (Plate 1). The Brussels Cross now lacks some portions of plaques, affecting its prose inscriptions. The pages of many manuscripts carry damage making the texts difficult or impossible to read. Corroded pigments have faded, darkened, spread, offset and produced show-through, as in the *Metrical Epilogue* to the Corpus Old English Bede. Liquid or other stains have blurred or lifted the ink or pigment, as in *Andreas* and manuscripts of the *Anglo-Saxon Chronicle*. Handling or exposure has produced rubbing and fading, as in *Waldere* and the *Leiden Riddle*. Scribbles, trials, sketches and other additions in drypoint, ink and pigment have obscured or intruded upon some passages. Mishandling has inflicted multiple damage, as with the large burnt-edged holes in the last leaves of the Exeter Book, which probably resulted from resting a hot poker upon its back, and the cuts and stains which attest to its use as a cutting-board and a beer-mat. Trimmings made to reduce the leaves of some volumes for rebinding or to convert leaves into reused binding material have removed forever some parts of text. Such is the case with *Waldere*, of which only the inner edges of the columns of text on leaves formerly conjoint with the survivors remain. Damp and mould have rotted away parts of some leaves, sometimes removing portions of text. This has affected a copy of the *Metrical Preface* to the *Pastoral Care* (Cambridge, Trinity College, MS R.5.22 [717]) and the *Death of Edward* in MS 'C' of the *Anglo-Saxon Chronicle* (London, British Library, MS Cotton Tiberius B.i). The fire of 1731 charred, fragmented, discoloured and distorted many surviving leaves, as in the *Beowulf* Manuscript (Plate 7) and the Anglo-Saxon copy of the *Metres of Boethius*.

Former bindings have also left marks of many kinds. They include wormholes extending beyond the wooden boards; offsets and stains from the boards or leather turn-ins; and holes and stains made by former sewings of the leaves and the proximity or corrosion of metal mounts or clasps upon the boards (Plates 5 and 11). The text of *Solomon and Saturn I* in the Red Book of Darley is especially badly damaged by rust-burn stains and holes extending into the first six leaves from the metal mounts—probably iron—of a former medieval binding (Plate 5). In other manuscripts mounts made of copper alloy left characteristic green or green-edged stains. Such damage may be lamentable, but it can also be invaluable, as it affords testimony to the history of the manuscript, often otherwise unrecorded. Thus the material evidence can be deciphered as carefully as the texts which it carries, so as to increase knowledge of both.

The destruction or damage of evidence means that later copies, whether of the Anglo-Saxon period or later, frequently preserve invaluable testimony for certain poetic texts. Yet such testimony must be subject to scrutiny to assess its reliability and to recognise the intrusions of its own period and place of production. Sometimes the survival of parts of the damaged original used for the transcript can offer an important control for such scrutiny, as notably with the two Thorkelin transcripts of *Beowulf*. They were made in 1787 by Thorkelin and by his unnamed copyist (Copenhagen, Kongelige Bibliotek, Ny Kongelige Samling, MSS 512 4° and 513 4°) before the edges of the leaves of the Anglo-Saxon copy burnt in the fire of 1731 crumbled away even more (Plate 7). Junius's transcript of the *Old English Boethius* similarly complements the badly burnt and distorted tenth-century copy.

Where the surviving copies are damaged or incomplete, reconstruction of the missing portions is frequently possible only through conjecture, which often remains unprovable. Many attempts have been made over recent centuries to recover damaged passages, variously through textual, palaeographical, linguistic and metrical analysis; chemical applications; and advanced forms of lighting, photography and computer-imaging. In the nineteenth century different forms of chemical reagent were applied to erased, abraded or faded passages in some manuscripts in a misguided attempt to enhance legibility. Such treatment has characteristically stained the surface of the leaves in patches, as in the *Leiden Riddle* and parts of *Solomon and Saturn II* in the Red Book of Darley (Plate 5).

More recently other forms of enhancement, usually non-destructive, have been applied. They include viewing under ultra-violet, infra-red and other spectra of light, sometimes in combination; microscopic examination; microphotography; and digitised manipulation of images from manuscript pages. Such work has led to improved editions, as with the edition of *Waldere* by Arne Zettersten (1979), which drew upon detailed examination of the leaves under ultra-violet light; and the long-term study of the *Beowulf* Manuscript by Kevin Kiernan (1981 and ongoing), which draws extensively upon spectroscopy and computerised imaging. Such developments offer considerable promise for future developments in knowledge of Old English poetry and its context. Other witnesses so far unknown may also survive, awaiting discovery or recognition through archaeological excavation, metal detection, book conservation and scholarly research.

3. The Making of Manuscripts

Recognising the processes which created and affected the material objects can inform and enhance understanding of the texts which they carry.

Throughout the early medieval period manuscripts were made of specially prepared animal skins: parchment or vellum from sheep, goats, calves and cattle (Plates 2-13). Only much later witnesses occur on paper (Plate 14). After removal from the animals the skins had to be soaked, usually in brine or urine, to loosen the hair on one side and the fatty layers on the flesh side. Scraping with a knife and perhaps also a pumice stone cleaned away the hairs and fat, although the leaves of many manuscripts retain fatty patches and hairs or hair-follicles on 'peppered' surfaces attesting to inefficient or incomplete scraping. To obtain the taut surface characteristic of parchment and vellum (as opposed to leather or suède) the skin had to be dried while stretched on a frame. Some scraping of its surfaces could take place in this position.

After drying the skin was trimmed to the required size. The manuscripts ranged from small to very large format, as exemplified by the Red Book of Darley on the one hand (c. 195 x 125 mm) and the Paris and Eadwine Psalters on the other hand (c. 526 x 186 mm and c. 460 x 327 mm). The smallest surviving manuscript with Old English poetry measures c. 130 x 95 mm (London, British Library, MS Cotton Titus D.xxvii, containing *Gloria II*). The four major codices are medium format. Some volumes could be held in the hand, while others required a lectern or support, as with the Corpus Old English Bede (Plate 12). Depending upon the size, some skins yielded only one leaf, but others could produce more, including sheets for double leaves, or bifolia, which would be folded in half lengthways. The leaves would be assembled in groups and sewn together for quires, which frequently consist of four bifolia forming eight leaves, but many other combinations also occur. For example, a quire of eight leaves sometimes incorporates two single leaves, as was the case in four of the seventeen quires of the Exeter Book (Plate 9), although three of them subsequently lost a leaf; the last quire of the Exeter Book now has only five leaves, although originally it may have had at least one more.[12] In many books the quires were numbered or lettered in sequence, with marks in the lower margin at the front or back of the quire (Plate 9).

Leaves prepared in characteristic 'Insular' fashion, according to practices adopted throughout the British Isles in the early Anglo-Saxon period, are rather thick and stiff and have a soft, suède-like surface; in the best-prepared leaves, the hair sides and flesh sides are scarcely distinguishable. Few manuscripts with Old English poetry survive from this period. The St Petersburg Bede is one of the few to possess such characteristics. By the late Anglo-Saxon period the influence of Continental

---

[12] The structure of the Exeter Book and its history are described in Conner (1993:95-147).

practices under the Benedictine reform movement led to the production of
leaves with a yellower hair side and a smoother, whiter flesh side. The
Leiden Riddle occurs in a Continental manuscript exhibiting such characteristics. Up to about the mid tenth century the Anglo-Saxons arranged
quires with hair and flesh sides alternating between adjacent leaves. Thereafter, under Continental influence, the leaves were generally arranged
with hair sides facing hair sides and flesh sides facing flesh sides, to produce a consistent appearance across facing pages.

Before or after folding into quires the leaves had to be laid out for
writing and decorating. This involved pricking and ruling the leaves with
frameworks in drypoint, to guide the lines of script or the edges of frames
for illustrations or other contents. Pricks comprising points, slits or holes
were made with the tip of a knife, awl or stylus, to align the boundaries of
the frames or columns and lines of text. Using these pricks to guide a
straight edge traced with drypoint, vertical and horizontal lines were
drawn in ladder-like frameworks upon the page. The lines were incised
with the tip of a knife or a stylus made of metal, bone or wood. Many
manuscripts retain a row of pricks in the margin at the top, bottom and
one or both sides (Plates 4, 6 and 9). These were used to align the horizontal lines for the top and bottom of the columns as well as the individual
lines of script within them. Sometimes double vertical bounding lines at
both sides of the column produce narrow columns to contain the initials of
lines or sections; only the column on the left-hand side of a column would
function in this way, while the column on the right-hand side could
include normal text. Such practice meant that a single framework could be
prepared for both sides of a leaf and for a series of leaves in succession.
Sometimes the leaves were prepared separately, but frequently the prick-
ings and rulings extend from leaf to leaf in a quire. Increasing faintness
upon leaves farther down in the prepared group meant that the scribes had
to lay out some frameworks anew—occasionally quite differently from the
original version.

In the early Anglo-Saxon period the leaves were usually pricked and
ruled after they had been folded, so the rows of pricks had to stand on
both sides of the page. In the late Anglo-Saxon period pricking and ruling
came to precede folding, so rows of pricks needed to be made only on
both sides of a double sheet, therefore on the outer edges of the leaves. By
the late twelfth century pricking after folding again became widespread.
By the end of the Anglo-Saxon period other materials also came into use,
as graphite or plummet would produce frameworks with grainy greyish
or brownish lines. The patterns visible on the pages of manuscripts reveal
their manner of production, although the subsequently trimmed margins
of some manuscripts have removed many such traces.

Some leaves retain the holes, partly healed holes, scars and welts which the skins acquired while on the animals. The holes vary in size and shape. Sometimes they remain confined to the margins (Plate 10), but sometimes they occur within or extend into the columns of text, which might have to alter its course around them (Plate 4). Most manuscripts contain some such defects. Many contain damage acquired in production, use, abuse, storage, neglect or misguided conservation.

Once laid out the leaves could be written and decorated. The main text would be written in ink, prepared from soot, oak gall or boiled bark. The writing would be made with quill-pens, made from goose or other feathers of varying sizes. Sometimes brushes would be used for painting or outlining, but mostly this too seems to have been carried out with a pen. Initials, headings and other elements might be emphasised by colour, size, embellishment or a combination of these. Among pigments the most common as well as one of the least expensive was metallic red lead (Latin *minium*, hence 'miniature'), sometimes used alongside a vegetable red pigment. Other pigments, derived from the animal, vegetable and mineral kingdoms, included verdigris (green), orpiment (yellow) and folium (purple). Silver and gold would be reserved only for the most luxurious manuscripts, along with leaves dyed purple with shellfish. Such manuscripts would contain sacred texts, mainly the Psalter and the Gospels used for liturgical display. These would be in Latin, although some might also contain Old English, as with the glossed Vespasian Psalter (London, British Library, MS Cotton Vespasian A.i) and the *Codex Aureus* (Stockholm, Kungliga Biblioteket, Cod. A.135), which has an added Old English donorship inscription.

Among manuscripts containing Old English poetry only the Paris and Eadwine Psalters belong to so elevated a category of book. The luxurious layout, elegant script and surviving decoration of the Paris Psalter, along with the traces of much more decoration which has been cut out, indicate that it must have been one of the most magnificent books which the Anglo-Saxons produced. Perhaps some manuscripts with Old English poetry made for important ecclesiastical, aristocratic or royal owners but now lost would have been comparably expensive.

Most manuscripts with Old English poetry belong to the more modest categories of textbooks or library books (as with Plates 2-9). Although some contain initials which now appear silver, as with portions of the Exeter Book, this effect is due to the corrosion of red lead pigment. Some manuscripts carry decoration of some kind, usually in the initials or display lettering. This might be simple, as with the geometric elements in a few initials of *Beowulf* (Plate 7); the quatrefoil, lozenge or cruciform shapes of some *O*s in *Solomon and Saturn II* in the Red Book of Darley; and the foliate terminal of the initial of *Ealdhelm* in the Corpus Aldhelm (Plate 4). The Exeter Book contains many initials modestly decorated with geometric and stylised sub-acanthus foliate ornament. They usually have outlined foliate motifs or lobes with dotted centres or simple veining patterns; some initials have curled tips. The decoration becomes sparser in the latter part of the book (Plate 9), as if the scribal artist lowered the scale and scope of the decorated initials as the work progressed, although the script throughout the volume remains consistently rounded, skilled, clearly legible and a delight to behold.

The Latin text of the Corpus Aldhelm contains many initials which comprise intricate combinations of interlace, foliate and animal ornament characteristic of stylish late Anglo-Saxon textbooks. Initials with such combinations are now known as 'Type I' where full creatures make up the letter and as 'Type II' where it contains only creatures' heads (Temple, 1976:12). Decorated initials of Types I and II open Old English poetic texts in both the Hatton *Pastoral Care* and the Junius Manuscript (Plates 3 and 10). Such initials also occur in *Andreas* in the Vercelli Book and at the beginning of *The Menologium* in MS 'C' of the *Anglo-Saxon Chronicle* (London, British Library, MS Cotton Tiberius B.i).

The Junius Manuscript, the most extensively decorated of all extant Anglo-Saxon manuscripts containing Old English poetry, contains not only twenty-two such initials but also an extensive cycle of biblical illustrations. Derived partly from a late-antique cycle, the illustrations both provide a full-page frontispiece preceding *Genesis*, which comes first in the volume, and accompany its text with full-page and part-page images (Plate 10). The forty-eight original illustrations extend to line 1830 of the poem, leaving spaces for eighty-nine more illustrations never completed, but for a later illustration entered after line 2095. Six sketches in stylus and four ink sketches are entered in some blank areas, as the manuscript apparently served as a sketchbook or model book. The ink sketches provide a bust-length portrait of a beardless man inscribed with the name 'Ælfpine'; and designs for metalwork or openwork plaques in Viking or late Anglo-Saxon style.

Rendered in outline drawing, the original *Genesis* illustrations are the work of two artists. The first drew his illustrations in monochrome ink. The second, considerably more skilful than the first, made his illustrations in multi-coloured ink and pigments: brown, red, green and blue. His accomplished skill must have placed his work in considerable demand and he illustrated another surviving manuscript as well: the Corpus Prudentius (Cambridge, Corpus Christi College, MS 23, Part I), which has some Old English titles and glosses. This artist's contribution to the Junius Manuscript establishes one of the major sources of Old English poetry also as a major witness to English coloured outline drawing, a genre which itself constitutes a major Anglo-Saxon contribution to the history of book-design. The cycle itself is an important witness to the tradition of biblical illustrations in England.

Another important cycle of biblical illustrations accompanies the Eadwine Psalter, which contains many decorated initials with interlace, geometric, foliate and zoomorphic ornament in Anglo-Norman style. Yet the Old English gloss, including the metrical portions, contains no decorated elements.

Only one other Anglo-Saxon manuscript with Old English poetry contains finished illustrations which accompany the poetry as part of the original design. The Paris Psalter includes thirteen small-scale drawings set within the lines of text on its early pages, illustrating parts of Psalms 1-7 in Latin and Old English prose. Formerly it included yet more decoration or illustration on leaves which have been cut out and lost. The bilingual Latin and Old English metrical versions of Psalms 51-150 formerly included elaborate decoration or illustration on full pages preceding the openings of Psalms 51, 68, 80, 97 and 109, while similar pages formerly preceded the openings of Psalms 1, 26 and 38 which have prose versions and of the Canticles following the Psalter. The *Beowulf* Manuscript contains a series of drawn and partly painted illustrations for the *Marvels of the East*, but these do not accompany poetry. Some other poetic manuscripts contain sketches entered in available blank areas but unrelated to the text. These include the ink drawings added to lower margins in *Waldere* and *Andreas* and the drypoint drawings added to outer margins in the Exeter Book. Copies of Old English poetic texts made after the Anglo-Saxon period have little or no decoration (Plates 13-14), although some of them occur in manuscripts in which Latin texts have decorated initials.

Some Anglo-Saxon manuscripts remain uncompleted. Sometimes the headings, decorated initials and lines of display capitals would be entered before the text was written, but frequently scribes left spaces for them, to be entered in a next stage. Some of these spaces remain empty (Plate 12) or came to be filled only by later hands, after the original production had ceased. *The Fates of the Apostles* is a notable case of an Old English poem lacking its opening initial, for which the first five lines of text were indented. Some texts were abandoned midstream, as with *Ealdhelm*.

Few medieval manuscripts containing Old English poetry retain their original or early bindings. The most important of these is the Junius Manuscript, with its plain but serviceable library binding of leather-covered oak boards, perhaps dating from the thirteenth century. The few surviving Anglo-Saxon bindings, parts of bindings and images of bound volumes in Anglo-Saxon illustrations give useful indications of the appearance and structure of the lost bindings which originally enclosed the manuscripts.

There is a wide but disparate body of evidence for methods of

Anglo-Saxon book-production. It comprises images of scribes at work
(Plate 11); the pages, materials and layout of the manuscripts themselves
(Plates 2-12); archaeological material recovered from excavations, metal-
detection and other finds relating to books and literate culture, ranging
from styli and wax tablets to book mounts and clasps; and literary and
linguistic evidence for scribal activities and scribal materials. Notable
accounts of scribal materials, tools, processes and products occur in various Anglo-Latin and Old English riddles. In them a quill-pen, an inkhorn, parchment, a complete book and a book-moth vividly describe their
own experiences, as in *Riddles* 24, 45, 58, 84, 89 and perhaps *Riddles* 49,
65 and 91 in the Exeter Book.[13] Their accounts of the processes which
either transformed them into scribal tools or vehicles of text, or involved
encounters with the written word, illuminate the evidence embedded in the
pages of manuscripts themselves. No recipes as such for preparing manuscripts survive from the Anglo-Saxon period, but *Riddle* 24 (Plate 9) gives
an especially detailed account of the stages of making a book, albeit in oblique or enigmatic terms appropriate to the literary genre.

   This riddle memorably describes the skin being stripped from its
animal by an 'enemy' (*feonda*), soaked in liquid, dried in the sun, scraped
or trimmed with a knife, smoothed perhaps with pumice (*sindrum be-
grunden*), folded by fingers, inscribed by a quill with ink made from
'tree-dye' (*beamtelge*) and covered with gold-decked boards by a 'hero'
(*hæleð*. The speaker's shift from 'enemy' to 'hero' poignantly acknow-
ledges a harmonious outcome of metamorphosis of elements taken from
the animal, mineral and vegetable kingdoms into instruments to serve and
instruct mankind.

   Images of scribes at work occur in numerous Anglo-Saxon manu-
scripts. A few appear in manuscripts containing Old English, as with the
Vespasian Psalter and the eighth-century Lindisfarne Gospels (London,
British Library, MS Cotton Nero D.iv), each of which has an interlinear
Old English gloss added one or more centuries after the book was made.
Yet no Anglo-Saxon manuscript with Old English poetry contains such an
image. Mostly the images show stylised 'portraits' of the authors transcribing their texts: the evangelists, Boethius, St Jerome and others (Plate
11). Some elements in the images manifestly derive from late-antique or
Continental practices, conveyed through their exemplars. Some elements
apparently constitute artistic licence, as when a quill-pen is coloured gold,
which no real bird's feather would be. Some elements probably accurately
reflect everyday practice by Anglo-Saxon scribes.

---

[13] As numbered in Williamson (1977). See also Tupper (1910), Shook (1974) and Göbel
(1980).

The images frequently represent the scribe holding an implement in each hand: a pen in one and a knife in the other, as in the eighth-century Barberini Gospels (Vatican City, Biblioteca Apostolica Vaticana, MS Barb. lat. 570) and the eleventh-century image of Jerome added to the tenth-century Cambridge Saints' Lives by Jerome and Felix (Cambridge, Corpus Christi College, MS 389: Plate 11). This posture is likely to conform with actual practice. The scribe would have found it useful to hold his knife at the ready, variously to prick or rule the leaves, to sharpen the nib of his quill, to correct his mistakes by scraping unwanted ink or pigment from the surface and to steady the page as he wrote upon it. In some images the scribe holds the inkwell in his hand instead, but mostly the inkwell stands alongside him upon his lectern, his throne or the frame enclosing him. The scribes write either within bound books or upon loose leaves or writing tablets.

In early Anglo-Saxon images the writing surfaces usually rest upon their scribes' laps, while in late Anglo-Saxon images they usually rest on lecterns partly covered with drapery. One image shows a wide range of scribal tools, which include a reed-pen, a brush, a compass, a scraper or folder and an ink-bottle, accompanying the Old Testament scribe Ezra in the early eighth-century *Codex Amiatinus* (Florence, Biblioteca Medicea Laurenziana, MS Amiat. 1). The image in the Vespasian Psalter includes a pair of scribes poised to take the author's dictation using a pen with a scroll and a stylus with a pair of writing tablets. The different approaches to representing scribes at work probably reflect varied practices in Anglo-Saxon life as much as they incorporate multiple influences upon Anglo-Saxon book-production from outside sources.

The scripts used for the text, headings and other elements in manuscripts with Old English poetry occur in many styles and degrees of competence, according with the dates, places of origin, training and skill of the scribes who made them.[14] In the early Anglo-Saxon period scripts for Old English as well as Latin centred upon Anglo-Saxon minuscule of various degrees of formality. *Cædmon's Hymn* in the St Petersburg Bede occurs in current Anglo-Saxon minuscule (Plate 2). The Hatton *Pastoral Care*, including its metrical portions, is written in Anglo-Saxon Pointed minuscule (Plate 3). Anglo-Saxon Square minuscule began to emerge during the Alfredian revival in the late ninth centuryand continued in use through much of the tenth century. The poetic texts in both the Red Book of Darley and the Parker Chronicle appear in this script (Plates 5-6). Those in the latter were written by more than one hand according with different

---

[14] The scripts are described and illustrated in Keller (1906), Ker (1957), Bishop (1971), Dumville (1987), Brown (1991) and Hough (forthcoming).

scribal stints.

Continental influence in the tenth-century Benedictine reform movement introduced Caroline minuscule script to England, where it evolved into a distinctive Anglo-Saxon version: English Caroline minuscule, characterised by some special letter-forms (notably of *a*, *f*, *g* and *s*). During the tenth century Anglo-Saxon scribes came increasingly to reserve different text-scripts for different languages, employing English Caroline minuscule for Latin but Anglo-Saxon minuscule for Old English. The main scribe of the Corpus Aldhelm distinguished thus between the poem *Ealdhelm* and the Latin text (Plate 4). Moreover, even within the poem he mostly distinguished between its Old English portions and its Latin or transliterated Greek portions.

Late Anglo-Saxon minuscule emerged by the late tenth century and continued into the twelfth century, alongside Late English Caroline minuscule and proto-Gothic minuscule, which developed in the eleventh century partly through Norman influence. Among the four major codices of Old English poetry, the Vercelli Book and the Exeter Book employ Anglo-Saxon Square minuscule of less or more polished quality; the two scribes of the *Beowulf* Manuscript used a late version of Square minuscule and Late Anglo-Saxon minuscule respectively; and the Junius Manuscript uses Late Anglo-Saxon minuscule (Plates 7-10). The poetic texts in the Corpus Old English Bede also use Late Anglo-Saxon minuscule (Plate 12). Among twelfth-century witnesses, the Cambridge copy of *De situ Dunelmi* uses proto-Gothic minuscule (Plate 13).

Early modern and modern transcripts of Old English texts mainly use revived Anglo-Saxon minuscule or scripts characteristic of their own time and place, as with Casley's copy of *The Battle of Maldon* (Plate 14). These transcripts occur rarely on vellum and mostly on paper leaves.

4. Manuscript Layout and Printed Editions

The manuscripts usually present Old English verse in single columns of long or short lines, which do not correspond to lines of verse. Sometimes the accompanying text occupies double or multiple columns, as with the Eadwine Psalter, the St Petersburg Bede and the Cambridge copy of *De Situ Dunelmi* (Plates 2 and 13). In the first, the interlinear Old English portions share the same column as the Roman version of the Psalter; in the second the verse comprises a marginal addition; and inthe third the Old English verse fits into part of a single column in a double-column layout characteristic of many twelfth-century manuscripts. In a few manuscripts of the Anglo-Norman and later periods the Old English verse spans two columns of a double-column layout. These mostly involve copies of *Cæd-*

mon's Hymn and *Bede's Death Song* embedded within Latin or Old English texts. Sometimes these two poems stand in the margin alongside or below the text, as if they form a gloss upon it (Plate 2). Rarely, in a layout derived from Latin practice, the last lines of a poetic text form a tapered tail of narrowing width. This occurs in both the *Metrical Epilogue* to the Hatton *Pastoral Care* and in *Thureth* (London, British Library, MS Cotton Claudius A.iii). The first three pages of *Judgment Day II* in the eleventh-century Corpus MS 201 have extended ascenders in the first line and extended descenders in the last line, an unusual feature derived from earlier Latin (and perhaps Old English) manuscripts.

Printed editions usually adjust the manuscript texts, both prose and verse, to greater or lesser extents so as to ease comprehension by the non-medieval reader, accustomed to printed books more than to manuscripts. Printing uses fonts with more or less identical repetitions of given letters, contrasting with the subtle or dramatic variety of hand-written texts by one or more scribes frequently working at more than one sitting. The fonts are mostly modern, but the earliest printed editions use revived Anglo-Saxon forms based upon compressed, upright versions of Late Anglo-Saxon minuscule. Some recent editions use a font resembling rounded, upright Square minuscule (Porter, 1991, and Griffiths, 1991b). The use of such a font can seem peculiar, as when representing *The Battle of Maldon* preserved only in eighteenth-century transcript (Plate 14). Here the choice may attempt to reconstruct or emulate the lost Anglo-Saxon copy from which the transcript derives, albeit with a homogenised and partly inauthentic set of letter-forms.

Printed editions make other changes too. In many editions abbreviations are expanded, sometimes without notice. Capitalisation and punctuation are modernised and regularised. This can involve adding punctuation where the original has none or rendering several different marks of punctuation as a single form. Word-division is normalised, as may also be spelling. In an extreme case the forms are changed to standard West-Saxon, in a homogenised or Procrustean approach (Magoun, 1956). Frequently editions render the letter *wynn* (*p*) throughout as *w*, although this can make it difficult for the reader to grasp how readily its shape could be confused with *p* in the transmission of copies, for example in the *Metres of Boethius*. Editions generally ignore line-division in the original, although it could be very helpful to know where line-breaks occur, because medieval scribes frequently made more mistakes than usual when approaching line-endings.

For printing Old English poetry a special form of layout has come to be adopted since the nineteenth century. Metrical units are signalled by setting out the lines of verse in pairs of half-lines separated by a caesura. This layout helps non-native speakers of Old English, which everyone in the modern world must be. Yet it is worth noting that the Anglo-Saxons did not write out Old English poetry in such a way. All their witnesses present Old English poetic texts in continuous lines like prose, in which the line of script may run over to the next at any point within a line of verse. Some Anglo-Saxon manuscripts similarly run together lines of Latin verse, as notably in the Corpus Sedulius (Cambridge, Corpus Christi College, MS 173, Part II); while others set out Latin poetry in lines of verse, following Latin conventions, as in the Corpus Prudentius.

The Anglo-Saxons apparently felt no need to distinguish their own vernacular verse from prose in written layout; presumably they could rely upon their inner ear to recognise its verse form. Yet some scribes marked the lines or half-lines of Old English verse by punctuating points, as with *The Battle of Brunanburh* in the Parker Chronicle, but not *The Capture of the Five Boroughs* in the same manuscript, copied by the same scribe (Plate 6). Most unusually the *Leiden Riddle* is partly set in lines of verse, probably in emulation of the lines of Aldhelm's verse preceding it. Sometimes even the words themselves are written continuously, with no breaks between them, as on the Franks Casket (Plate 1). The modern divisions into lines and half-lines remain subject to dispute, as the prosody of *Beowulf* and other works continues to be studied in detail.

Modern editions also divide poetic texts into distinct units, which might or might not correspond to different poems. Few texts in the manuscripts carry titles; the current names for most Old English poems are the inventions of modern editors. Some copies, as with *Beowulf* and the Junius Manuscript, number the sections of a poem (Plate 10). Yet some manuscripts do little to distinguish between their texts or the parts thereof, which may appear in an extended sequence without initials or other features to demarcate the opening of a new text or section—or even the transition between verse and prose, as at the end of *The Five Boroughs* in the Parker Chronicle (Plate 6). This means that some texts might constitute separate works or parts of the same poem: scholars disagree. The condition notably concerns parts of the Exeter Book. For example, editors have regarded its collection of *Riddles* as comprising between eighty-nine and ninety-five poems and have numbered them accordingly. Becoming familiar with the diverse approaches to presentation and layout exhibited by printed editions on the one hand and the originals on the other can greatly aid the task of assessing and reassessing the character of Old English poetic texts.

A few editions offer or also offer a closer rendition of the manuscript layout by adopting a 'diplomatic' or 'semi-diplomatic' approach. Borrowed from the fields of diplomatics (the study of old documents) and palaeography (the study of old handwriting), this approach aims as faithfully as possible to retain manuscript spellings, capitalisation, punctuation,

abbreviations, line-divisions and so on. For Old English poetry an exemplary case is Alistair Campbell's edition (1938) of the *The Battle of Brunanburh*. It offers both a diplomatic edition of the version found in the
Parker Chronicle, the oldest witness (Plate 6), accompanied by variants
reported from the three other versions; and a critical or normalised edition of the text, provided with expanded abbreviations, added punctuation,
modernised capitalisation and a division into lines and half-lines of verse.
The published facsimile of the Parker Chronicle makes it possible closely
to observe the manuscript layout itself (Flower and Smith, 1941).

Similar observation can accompany the study of the rest of the corpus. Full photographic facsimiles of the known corpus of Old English
poetry have been published, along with some witnesses to rhythmical
prose.[15] These enable students in many centres around the world to examine the manuscript layout of the texts for themselves. Plans are in hand to
produce microfiche or other facsimiles of all manuscripts containing Old
English.

Many major poetic manuscripts have been reproduced in complete
monochrome facsimile at actual size or thereabouts: the St Petersburg
Bede, the *Beowulf* Manuscript, the Vercelli Book, the Exeter Book, the
Junius Manuscript, the Paris Psalter, the Eadwine Psalter, MSS 'A' and 'E'
of the *Anglo-Saxon Chronicle* and the Thorkelin transcripts of *Beowulf*.
Pages from *Beowulf*, the Junius Manuscript and the Eadwine Psalter,
including all the recognised metrical portions of the latter, have appeared
in colour at full or reduced size. The rest of the known corpus, including
media other than manuscripts, is reproduced in monochrome facsimile at
actual size in a single volume edited by Fred Robinson and Eric Stanley
(1991). Although it conveniently gathers together many texts, including all
copies of given texts, the volume ususally crops their pages down to the
poetry alone, thus severing the poetry from its context and making the
ensemble seem like a scrapbook.

Like the transcripts, the photographic reproductions cannot fully replace or replicate the originals, but they offer a powerful tool for deepen-
ing knowledge of Old English poetry, its character and its aims. Through
this and other means an ever-increasing awareness of the presentation, embodiment and material context of the poetic corpus opens a wide horizon
for its study and appreciation.

---

[15] Gollancz (1927), Chambers *et al.* (1933), Malone (1951), Arngart (1952), Whitelock
(1954), Colgrave (1958), Zupitza (1959), Malone (1963), Sisam (1976), Zettersten
(1979) and Robinson and Stanley (1991).

REFERENCES

Adams, E.N. (1917). *Old English Scholarship in England from 1566-1800*. Yale Studies in English 55. New Haven, CT: Yale University Press. (Repr. Hamden, CT: Archon. 1970.)

Alexander, J.J.G. (1978). *Insular Manuscripts, 6th to the 9th Century*. A Survey of Manuscripts Illuminated in the British Isles 1. Ed. J.J.G. Alexander. London: Harvey Miller.

Arngart, O. (ed.) (1952). *The Leningrad Bede: An Eighth Century Manuscript of the Venerable Bede's Historia Ecclesiastica Gentis Anglorum in the Public Library, Leningrad*. Early English Manuscripts in Facsimile 2. Copenhagen: Rosenkilde and Bagger.

Backhouse, J., D.H. Turner and L. Webster (eds.) (1984). *The Golden Age of Anglo-Saxon Art, 966-1066*. London: British Museum Publications.

Baker, P.S. (1984). A Little-Known Variant Text of The Old English Metrical Psalms. *Speculum* 59. 263-81.

Bammesberger, A. (ed.) (1991). *Old English Runes and Their Continental Background*. Anglistische Forschungen 217. Heidelberg: Carl Winter.

Berkhout, C.T., and M.McC. Gatch (eds.) (1982). *Anglo-Saxon Scholarship: The First Three Centuries*. Boston: G.K. Hall.

Bishop, T.A.M. (1971). *English Caroline Minuscule*. Oxford Palaeographical Handbooks. Ed. R.W. Hunt, C.H. Roberts and F. Wormald. Oxford: Clarendon Press.

Bradley, S.A.J. (1982). *Anglo-Saxon Poetry: An Anthology of Old English Poems in Prose Translation with Introduction and Headnotes*. Everyman's Library. London: J.M. Dent.

Brown, M.P. (1991). *Anglo-Saxon Manuscripts*. London: The British Library.

Budny, M. (forthcoming). *Insular, Anglo-Saxon and Early Anglo-Norman Manuscript Art at Corpus Christi College, Cambridge: An Illustrated Catalogue*. 2 Vols. Kalamazoo, MI: Medieval Institute Publications.

Campbell, A. (ed.) (1938). *The Battle of Brunanburh*. London: Heinemann.

Campbell, J. (ed.) (1982). *The Anglo-Saxons*. Oxford: Phaidon Press.

Chambers, R.W., M. Förster and R. Flower (eds.) (1933). *The Exeter Book of Old English Poetry*. London: Percy Lund, Humphries & Co.

Colgrave, B. (ed.) (1958). *The Paris Psalter: MS Bibliothèque Nationale, fonds latin 8824*. Early English Manuscripts in Facsimile 8. Copenhagen: Rosenkilde and Bagger.

Conner, P.W. (1993). *Anglo-Saxon Exeter: A Tenth-Century Cultural History*. Studies in Anglo-Saxon History 4. Woodbridge: Boydell.

Dodwell, C.R. (1982). *Anglo-Saxon Art: A New Perspective*. Manchester Studies in the History of Art 3. Ed. C.R. Dodwell. Manchester: Manchester University Press.

Douglas, D.C. (1951). *English Scholars, 1660-1730*. 2nd rev. ed. London: Eyre & Spottiswoode. (1st ed. 1939.)

Dumville, D.N. (1987). English Square Minuscule Script: The Background and Earliest Phases. *Anglo-Saxon England*. 16. 147-79.

Flower, R., and H. Smith (eds.) (1941). *The Parker Chronicle and Laws (Corpus Christi College, Cambridge, MS 173)*. Early English Text Society, Original Series 208. London: Oxford University Press.

Ford, B. (ed.) (1992). *The Cambridge Cultural History of Britain*, vol. 1: *Early Britain*. Rev. ed. Cambridge: Cambridge University Press. (1st ed. 1988 as *The Cambridge Guide to the Arts in Britain*, vol. 1: *Prehistoric, Roman and Early Medieval*.)

Funke, O. (1962). Some Remarks on Wulfstan's Prose Rhythm. *English Studies* 43. 311-18.

Godden, M. (ed.) (1979). *Ælfric's Catholic Homilies, The Second Series: Text*. Early English Text Society, Supplementary Series 5. London: Oxford University Press.

Godden, M., and M. Lapidge (eds.) (1991). *The Cambridge Companion to Old English Literature*. Cambridge: Cambridge University Press.

Göbel, H. (1980). *Studien zu den altenglischen Schriftwesenrätseln*. Würzburg: Königshausen und Neumann.

Gollancz, I. (ed.) (1927). *The Cædmon Manuscript of Anglo-Saxon Biblical Poetry: Junius XI in the Bodleian Library*. Oxford: Oxford University Press.

Griffiths, B. (ed.) (1991a). *Alfred's Metres of Boethius*. Pinner, Middlesex: Anglo-Saxon Books.

Griffiths, B. (ed.) (1991b). *The Battle of Maldon: Text and Translation*. Pinner, Middlesex: Anglo-Saxon Books.

Hickes, G. (1705). *Antiquæ Literaturæ Septentrionalis Libri Duo*. 2 Vols. Oxford.

Hough, C.A. (forthcoming). *An Introduction to Old English Palaeography*. Ed. M. Budny. Cambridge: Research Group on Manuscript Evidence.

Junius, F. (1994). *Cædmonis Monachi Paraphrasis Poetica Genesios ... Anglo-Saxonice Conscripta*. Ed. P.J. Lucas. Early Studies in Germanic Philology 3. Amsterdam and Atlanta, GA: Rodopi. (1st ed., 1655.)

Keller, W. (1906). *Angelsächsische Palaeographie. Die Schrift der Angelsachsen mit besonderer Rücksicht auf die Denkmäler in der Volkssprache*. Palaestra 43. 2 Vols. Berlin: Mayer & Müller.

Ker, N.R. (ed.) (1956). *The Pastoral Care: King Alfred's Translation of St Gregory's Regula Pastoralis (MS Hatton 20 in the Bodleian Library at Oxford; MS Cotton Tiberius B.xi in the British Museum; MS Anhang 19 in the Landesbibliothek at Kassel)*. Early English Manuscripts in Facsimile 6. Copenhagen: Rosenkilde and Bagger.

Ker, N.R. (1957). *Catalogue of Manuscripts Containing Anglo-Saxon*. Oxford: Clarendon Press.

Kiernan, K.S. (1981). Beowulf *and the* Beowulf *Manuscript*. New Brunswick, NJ: Rutgers University Press.

Kiernan, K.S. (1986). *The Thorkelin Transcripts of* Beowulf. Anglistica 25. Copenhagen: Rosenkilde and Bagger.

Krapp, G.P., and E.V.K. Dobbie (eds.) (1931-53). *The Anglo-Saxon Poetic Records*. 6 Vols. New York: Columbia University Press.

Magoun, F.P., Jr. (1956). *The Anglo-Saxon Poems in Bright's Anglo-Saxon Reader Done in a Normalized Orthography*. Cambridge, MA: Harvard University Press.

Malone, K. (ed.) (1951). *The Thorkelin Transcripts of Beowulf in Facsimile*. Early English Manuscripts in Facsimile 1. Copenhagen: Rosenkilde and Bagger.

Malone, K. (ed.) (1963). *The Nowell Codex: British Museum Cotton Vitellius A.xv, Second MS*. Early English Manuscripts in Facsimile 12. Copenhagen: Rosenkilde and Bagger.

McIntosh, A. (1949). Wulfstan's Prose. *Proceedings of the British Academy* 35. 109-42.

Menner, R.J. (ed.) (1941). *The Poetical Dialogues of Solomon and Saturn*. Modern Language Association of America, Monograph Series 13. New York: Modern Language Association of America.

Mitchell, B., and F.C. Robinson (1992). *A Guide to Old English*. 5th Ed. Rev. with Prose and Verse Texts and Glossary. Oxford: Blackwell. (1st ed. 1964.)

Moffat, D. (1992). Anglo-Saxon Scribes and Old English Verse. *Speculum* 67. 805-27.

Nicholson, L.E., and D.W. Frese (eds.) (1975). *Anglo-Saxon Poetry: Essays in Appreciation for John C. McGalliard*. Notre Dame, IN: University of Notre Dame Press.

O'Brien O'Keeffe, K. (1990). *Visible Song: Transitional Literacy in Old English Verse*. Cambridge Studies in Anglo-Saxon England 4. Ed. S. Keynes and M. Lapidge. Cambridge: Cambridge University Press.

Ohlgren, T.H. (1992). *Anglo-Saxon Textual Illustration: Photographs of Sixteen Manuscripts with Descriptions and Index*. Kalamazoo, MI: Medieval Institute Publications.

Okasha, E. (1971). *Hand-List of Anglo-Saxon Non-Runic Inscriptions*. Cambridge:

Cambridge University Press.

Okasha, E. (1983). A Supplement to *Hand-List of Anglo-Saxon Non-Runic Inscriptions*. *Anglo-Saxon England* 11. 83-118.

O'Neill, P.P. (1988). Another Fragment of the Metrical Psalms in the Eadwine Psalter. *Notes and Queries* 233. 434-6.

Page, R.I. (1987). *Runes*. London: British Museum Publications.

Pope, J.C. (ed.) (1967-8). *Homilies of Ælfric: A Supplementary Collection*. 2 Vols. Early English Text Society, Original Series 259-60. London: Oxford University Press.

Porter, J. (transl.) (1991). *Beowulf: Text and Translation*. Pinner, Middlesex: Anglo-Saxon Books.

Robinson, F.C., and E.G. Stanley (eds.) (1991). *Old English Verse Texts from Many Sources: A Comprehensive Collection*. Early English Manuscripts in Facsimile 23. Copenhagen: Rosenkilde and Bagger.

Rogers, H.L. (1985). *The Battle of Maldon*: David Casley's Transcript. *Notes and Queries* 230. 147-55.

Shippey, T.A. (1972). *Old English Verse*. London: Hutchinson.

Shook, L.K. (1974). Riddles Relating to the Anglo-Saxon Scriptorium. In: *Essays in Honour of Anton Charles Pegis*. Ed. J.R. O'Donnell. Toronto: Pontifical Institute of Mediaeval Studies. 215-36.

Sisam, C. (ed.) (1976). *The Vercelli Book: A Late Tenth-Century Manuscript Containing Prose and Verse (Vercelli, Biblioteca Capitolare CXVII)*. Early English Manuscripts in Facsimile 19. Copenhagen: Rosenkilde and Bagger.

Sisam, K. (1953). *Studies in the History of Old English Literature*. Oxford: Clarendon Press.

Stanley, E.G. (1984). Alliterative Ornament and Alliterative Rhythmical Discourse in Old High German and Old Frisian Compared with Similar Manifestations in Old English. *Beiträge zur Geschichte der deutschen Sprache und Literatur* 106. 184-217.

Temple, E. (1976). *Anglo-Saxon Manuscripts, 900-1066*. A Survey of Manuscripts Illuminated in the British Isles 2. Ed. J.J.G. Alexander. London: Harvey Miller.

Tupper, F., Jr. (ed.) (1910). *The Riddles of the Exeter Book*. Boston: Ginn.

Webster, L., and J. Backhouse (eds.) (1991). *The Making of England: Anglo-Saxon Art and Culture, A.D. 600-900*. London: British Museum Press.

Wheloc, A. (1643). *Historiæ Ecclesiasticæ Gentis Anglorum Libri V*. Cambridge.

Whitelock, D. (ed.) (1954). *The Peterborough Chronicle (The Bodleian Manuscript Laud Misc. 636)*. Early English Manuscripts in Facsimile 4. Copenhagen: Rosenkilde and Bagger.

Williamson, C. (ed.) (1977). *The Old English Riddles of the* Exeter Book. Chapel Hill, NC: University of North Carolina Press.

Wilson, D.M. (1984). *Anglo-Saxon Art from the Seventh Century to the Norman Conquest*. London: Thames and Hudson.

Zettersten, A. (ed.) (1979). *Waldere (Edited from Royal Library, Copenhagen, Ny Kgl. S. MS. 167 b)*. Old and Middle English Texts, ed. G.L. Brook. Manchester: Manchester University Press.

Zupitza, J. (ed.) (1959). *Beowulf: Reproduced in Facsimile from the Unique Manuscript, British Museum MS Cotton Vitellius A.xv, with a Transliteration and Notes*. 2nd ed. Early English Text Society, Original Series 245. London: Oxford University Press. (1st ed., 1882.)

A NATIVIST APPROACH TO *BEOWULF*:
THE CASE OF GERMANIC ELEGY

JOSEPH HARRIS

Anyone who reads *Beowulf* in the original accompanied by Klaeber and the older commentaries will realize that understanding the poem is, in large part, a matter of understanding its intertextuality.[1] This explains the essential failure of the New Critical or *werkimmanent* approaches, so common since World War II, to make the poem historically meaningful for contemporary readers who have only their reading in modern literature to contextualize this strange survivor of lost textual worlds. Although close reading should have made the poem count emotionally, its membership in the "canon" seems more than ever nominal. Add to this the difficulties of integrating it into a "literary history" where even the barest date and social context are lacking. Theorists of such conventional modern fusions of history with literary criticism cannot agree on the possibility of literary history itself (see, for example, Perkins, 1992); they would have to be all the more skeptical—or dismissive—of the feasibility of literary history for a body of poetry of ultimately oral character and, as we write in shorthand, of a basically "traditional" nature. But these barriers can be enabling, making archaic oral-derived poetry—where the "death of the author" occurs long *avant la lettre*—more relevant to contemporary students of literature; without the distraction of date and local habitation students go directly to the really literary part of the task of literary history, the search for what Northrop Frye called an "order of words" (Barthes, 1977; Frye, 1970: 17). In particular the obstacle posed to literary-historical understanding by "tradition" comes to seem only apparent.

Tradition is here best understood as the vast network of discourses behind the poem and ultimately constituting it—sources known to "the poet" certainly, but just as vitally the performances of countless speakers, only some of them actual artistic ancestors, in every discourse genre (Culler, 1981:100-18).[2] Tradition or intertextuality in this broad interpretation is theoretically limitless, but in its application to a limited lit-

---

[1] *Beowulf* will be cited here from Klaeber's edition with occasional reference to the important editions, commentaries, and translations of Wrenn-Bolton and Chickering; no attempt has been made to check every edition, article, and commentary.

[2] For a more detailed application of "intertextuality" to traditional oral literature, and for references, see Harris (1990). See Vésteinn Ólason (1985) for a suggestive and earlier formulation of this point in the realm of the traditional ballad.

erary history might be compared to "hypertext" in current computer usage, both in the sense of a series of nodes leading through a network of related discourses and in the sense that, although any given "user" may not know the limits of a work's intertextuality, those limits are set by the handiwork of makers. As literary historians of early Germanic traditional literature, our task is both to make the intertextual connections and to interpret them. The circularity of this process, oscillating unprovably between particular and general, is not unlike the celebrated "philological circle" of Spitzer (1967:23-6). All this means that the student of a "traditional" *Beowulf*, an open work if there ever was one, has nothing to fear from postmodern gaps and discontinuities, which Old English scholars must acknowledge having in spades.

Armed with these reassurances and with tools of the contemporary study of literature, today's students of *Beowulf* would do well to return to pre-war masters such as Heusler, Schneider, Baesecke, and de Vries and to the idea of the common heritage, "tradition", of early Germanic oral literature—not in ignorance of the considerable non-Germanic "tradition" of relevance to the poem, but in the effort to revive and extend what was good in the old masters' understanding of the native side of its intertextuality. The post-war uneasiness with anything Germanic and hereditary, and its frequent condemnation as "romantic", is conditioned, like any point of view, by its own historical moment and need not detain contemporary students.[3] The "Germanic background" has, of course, been extensively mapped, but unknown areas continue to be filled in, even in our day, and despite a long history of scholarship, nativist work on *Beowulf*, work conceived inside that generous matrix of "traditional" intertextuality, has much that is new to contribute.[4]

Earlier generations of scholars generally favoured *history* and *story* in relating the poem to the Germanic background. The former teaches us, for example, to place and trace the kings, clans, and "nations" that people the poem, while the latter gives a place in the world of Germanic story to allusions to "heroes"; but the categories of story and history often overlap. One might instance Chambers and Malone as students of history and story, but they are only two conspicuous high points of the Anglo-American tradition of scholarship. From the beginning *Beowulf* scholars were also cognizant of the Germanic continuity in *institutions* and in *poetics*. Among the former one might instance feud, the *comitatus*, the family, and reli-

---

[3] Stanley's classic (1975) exposes much nationalistic, pan-germanist wishful thinking in nineteenth- and early twentieth-century Old English scholarship, but in its turn does not escape the law of historical relativity. More recently cf. Frantzen (1990).

[4] For example, Fulk (1989). The term "nativist" in the present essay is deliberately coloured by the current debate in Celtic studies (cf. McCone, 1990).

gion. The latter refers to the total organization of the Old English verbal artifact in the context of poetry that is not merely comparable but related through tradition; it includes verse structure and rhetoric, and also performance and audience in so far as they are immanent in the work. *Literary history* for poetry like *Beowulf* would seem to require the combination of poetics with the other three realms of comparison just mentioned; for example, the names of Heusler (esp. 1905) and Schneider (esp. 1928-34 and 1955) are famously attached to the argument that the mode of existence and distribution of certain stories, *Heldensagen*, was intrinsically connected with certain literary forms, *Heldenlieder*, and that insight, though overstated, allowed a relatively firm construction of developmental sequences in literary history. Or again, the theory of evolution from lay to epic, principally associated with Heusler, does not operate entirely within poetics, as might appear, but in combination with history, story, and institutions, and Heusler's *Die altgermanische Dichtung* remains the single most successful outline of a literary-historical "order of words" based on poetics, especially genre structure, in different combinations with the external factors I have tried to capture as history, story, and institutions. Recently poetics has more frequently been combined with audience, performance, and the growth of literacy, factors which can go beyond the Germanic context in the sense given above, but contemporary exercises in the spirit of Heusler, involving comparative reconstruction of a presumably antecedent pattern and the (circular) demonstration of devolution to extant works, have also been attempted, especially for parts of *Beowulf* (for example, Harris, 1979; Clover, 1980).

Such, in bare bones, are some principles for relating *Beowulf* to its Germanic tradition. I hope in the following pages to flesh out these notions with a new but brief study.

***

Beowulf begins the series of speeches that constitute his last words or "death song" with a reference to his childhood that has parallels in similar elegiac poems in Old Norse (Harris, 1992). He progresses quickly to his youth at the court of his uncle, the Geatish king Hrethel, along with the princes "*Herebeald ond Hæðcyn oððe Hygelac min.*" The account of Hæthcyn's accidental slaying of Herebeald follows, a passage with an urgent echo of a myth best preserved in the Icelandic eddic material where the god Hǫðr (cf. *Hæth*-cyn) accidentally shoots his brother Baldr (cf. Here-*beald*). Klaeber takes an uneasy position on the significance of the myth parallel, ultimately rejecting it in his Introduction (p. xli), but in his notes tentatively citing Neckel (1920:141-3) in lieu of a literary-historical explanation of his own (note to ll.2435f.). I would subscribe to Neckel's idea that the English poet's ultimate source is a Swedish heroic poem in which events in Hrethel's family have been assimilated to the mythic pattern. The question of the Baldr myth in these lines and in other secular reflexes deserves a fresh discussion,[5] but on this occasion I wish instead to focus on the following "digression", often called the Old Man's Lament (ll.2444-62).[6]

Opened and closed with *swa* ('so', 'thus'), these lines constitute something like a Homeric simile, the only one of its kind in *Beowulf*. The Lament, however, is surely an example of what Mikhail Bakhtin (had he written about Old English!) might have called the heterogeneous voices of *Beowulf*, a paraphrase of an elegy, not unlike several in Old English and Old Norse and as beautifully integrated into the epic as the similar elegy known as the Lament of the Last Survivor (ll.2247-66 and context). Let us first examine the passage and its integration:

> Swa bið geomorlic   gomelum ceorle
> to gebidanne,   þæt his byre ride
> giong on galgan;   þonne he gyd wrece,
> sarigne sang,   þonne his sunu hangað
> hrefne to hroðre,   ond he him help*e* ne mæg
> eald ond infrod   ænige gefremman.
> Symble bið gemyndgad   morna gehwylce
> eaforan ellorsið;   oðres ne gymeð
> to gebidanne   burgum in innan
> yrfeweardas,   þonne se an hafað
> þurh deaðes nyd   dæda gefondad.
> Gesyhð sorhcearig   on his suna bure
> winsele westne,   windge reste
> reote berofene,—   ridend swefað,
> hæleð in hoðman;   nis þær hearpan sweg,
> gomen in geardum,   swylce ðær iu wæron.

---

[5] Materials for such a discussion should include such older works as Detter (1894:82-8), Schück (1909:28-9), Nerman (1913:69-73), Björkman (1920:24-34), Neckel (1920:141-2), Malone (1923:156-8; 1934:160-61), and Olsen (1924:164-8), as well as standard modern discussions such as de Vries (1956:ii.220-21), who is neutral, and Turville-Petre (1964:120-21), who is skeptical. Dronke (1969:322-3) notices the parallel without skepticism, convincingly integrating it into her admirable discussion of Germanic myth as reused by the Christian *Beowulf* poet; and Frank (1982:10-11) observes an apparent nordicism in Beowulf's use of a genitive object with the verb *missan* in the epic's euhemerization of the Baldr myth (*miste merceles*, l.2439a)—one of many pieces of evidence in her brilliant argument for a tenth-century *Beowulf* poet in touch with contemporary Norse poetry.

[6] The classic literary study of the "digressions" is Bonjour (1950).

Gewiteð þonne on sealman,   sorhleoð gæleð
an æfter anum;   þuhte him eall to rum,
wongas ond wicstede.   Swa Wedra helm ...   (2244-62)

('So it is sad for an old man to live to experience that his son ride young on
the gallows; that he then utter a poem, a sad song, when his son hangs as a
joy to the raven, and he, old and wise with years, cannot give him any
help. Every morning, again and again, his son's journey elsewhere is
remembered. He does not care to await another heir within his strongholds
now that the one and only has completed his experience of events through
death's compulsion. Suffering from grief he sees in his son's dwelling—a
wasted wine-hall, a wind-swept resting place deprived of joy: riders are
sleeping, warriors in the grave; the sound of the harp is not there, no
amusements in the courts, such as once were there. Then he goes to his
bed; alone he sings a sorrow-song after the one and only; all seems to him
too spacious, fields and dwellings. Thus did the ruler of the Weder-Geats
...')

The simile, brief as it is, has suggestions of ring-structure, a compositional
device that is frequently associated with oral and oral-derived poetry; the
ideal is a chiastic ordering of elements, of the form ABB'A'.[7] In the Old
Man's Lament the sequence is slightly freer, and the answering elements
seem to shift from a more metaphorical to a more literal realization. The
initial image of poetic lament (*gyd, sarigne sang wrecan*) is probably
metaphorical for a simple utterance of grief; the proper place of a formal
poetic dirge is not while the son is hanging (*þonne*) but after the
experiences of memory and in the exhaustion of hope described in the
body and close of the passage (*sorhleoð*). Similarly the conspicuous repetition of the verb "to ride" at beginning and end seems to shift from metaphorical to literal; riding the gallows is almost certainly an old ritual
metaphor, but the reference near the end of the passage to riders sleeping
(in death) seems to be an elegiac topos.[8] The repetition of the half-line *to
gebidanne* functions in the ring-structure in much the same way; a common but nonetheless extended sense of the verb ('to experience') is followed in the ring by an instance of basic usage ('to await'). The ultimate
pattern here, then, is not the perfect mirror-imaging of classic ring com-

---

[7] For discussion of ring-structure, references, and appropriate caveats on the orality of
the device see Niles (1983:153-62).

[8] Yggdrasill, literally probably "horse of Yggr/Odin", is the cosmic tree of Norse mythology, on which the god himself was hanged, a sacrifice to himself; the gallows is Odin's
steed, "Sleipnir of ropes." "The metaphor is carried further. Men swing on the gallows,
and the verb *ríða* means both 'to swing' and 'to ride'. Therefore, [the eleventh-century
skald] Sigvat said in his lay in memory of St Ólaf, 'men ride to the world of death on
Sigar's horse' (*ríða ... til Heljar Sigars hesti*)" (Turville-Petre, 1964:48). In addition to
Turville-Petre's discussion and notes, see de Vries (1956: esp. §§271, 284, 376). On the
elegiac topos, see n. 10 below and Harris (1982b).

position, but a looser form that can be schematized as follows:

A (*to gebidanne*), B (*ride*), C (*sang*), A' (*to gebidanne*), B' (*ridend*), C' (*sorhleoð*).[9]

My translation attempts to clarify one feature of the passage that has been obscure to commentators who wonder that *bur*, normally a small attached "room" or unattached "cottage", should here have to refer very broadly to a dwelling place that itself contains a wine-hall and a wind-swept resting place. The proposed solution is that on a visit to his son's "room" (*on his suna bure*) the troubled mind of the father (*sorhcearig*) experiences a vision (*gesyhð*) of traditional elegiac scenery, and the passage modulates into generalized elegiac wording suggestive of the actual *sorhleoð* to be mentioned a few lines later.[10]

The Old Man's Lament differs from typical Homeric similes in that the comparanda are drawn from the same class of beings and are in fact so close that early students of *Beowulf* explained what we now understand as a simile as instead a continuation of the story it illustrates.[11] In the juxta-position the grief of two fathers, the Geatish king Hrethel and the un-named *gomel ceorl*, after the death of sons is compared; the hidden third term of comparison is the unavengability of the deaths. When one Geatish prince accidentally killed the other it was a *feohleas gefeoht* (l.2441a)—a

---

[9] Perhaps we should add a reference to the death itself as element D (*sunu hangað hrefne to hroðre*), repeated in chiastic position as D' (*eaforan ellorsið*); in that case the entire structure would turn around an unmirrored central element E: namely, the father's frustration (*helpe ne mæg ... gefremman*). On the stable central element of a ring, see Niles (1983:153). With these additions the whole pattern would be ABCDED'A'B'C'. Cf. Lord (1991) for a very similar case in the Old English *Battle of Maldon*.

[10] Klaeber's note to ll.2455-9 points in this direction for the plural "dead warriors", and I have taken Klaeber's generalized reference to "a typical motive of elegiac poetry" further in Harris (1982b). Wrenn and Bolton (note to l.2455) agree with Klaeber that *bur* is used "in the general sense of 'dwelling-place'." Chickering's translation ("Miserable, he looks upon his son's dwelling, deserted wine-hall, wind-swept bedding ... The rider sleeps ...") seems unacceptably to make the accusatives *winsele westne* and *windge reste* objects of the verb *seon on*, which would take a dative object in *bure*; there are also metrical objections to this interpretation. His choice of a singular rider is clearly conscious but should entail emendation of *swefað* to *swefeð*; Chickering's valuable commentary (366-7) could mislead with the remark that "singular and plural forms are mixed" here: both words are plurals, but in the noun the inflection is ambiguous.

[11] The older scholarship (e.g. Nerman 1913) was concerned to integrate the passage set off by *swa*'s into the Hrethel frame; by Klaeber's time the other view had prevailed, and he treats the question as closed and the *swa*-passage straightwardly as a simile. More recently Taylor (1952) returned to the early view according to which the *swa*-passage is not a simile and deals with Hrethel himself. For complete references consult the indices in Fry (1969).

phrase that seems to carry the weight of an oxymoron, thus a "'feud' that could never be settled by wergeld" (or, of course, by blood)—and Dorothy Whitelock (1939) showed that the *gomel ceorl*, if the father of a legally executed son, similarly had no recourse to revenge. In some features, however, the simile and its narrative matrix in the story of Hrethel stand in complementary relationship: for example, the legendary-historical Hrethel of Beowulf's memory dies of grief and frustration, but the *gomel ceorl* is simply last seen taking to his bed; Hrethel is not given the elegiac vision or a poem comparable to that of his *semblable*. Because the material of the simile is so close to what it is supposed to illuminate, we may be tempted, where they do not conflict, to merge the two images in imagination: to see the *ceorl* as moribund, and to attribute elegiac feelings and song to Hrethel. Filling out their stories in this way borders on a classic critical fallacy (the girlhood of Shakespeare's heroines), but if we find that both are part of a more pervasive pattern, we may be justified in regarding both as reflexes of something much deeper, fundamental to elegy and to this section of *Beowulf*.

A significant analogue of both stories has gone unnoticed in the literature on *Beowulf*, an analogue from the genetically related sister literature in Old Norse. About 961, Bǫðvarr, the beloved son of the aging Icelandic poet Egill Skalla-Grímsson drowned on what should have been a routine voyage; this tragedy followed close on the loss of another son to sickness. Bǫðvarr's ship and the bodies washed up on the shore, and Egill rode out to find the corpses. He carried the dead son out to the promontory of Digranes and laid him in the family burial mound beside Egill's father. In the evening he rode home to the farm at Borg, went straight to his bed-closet, lay down and locked himself in. For three days he took no food or drink. On the third day his wife Ásgerðr sent for one of Egill's favourite children, Þorgerðr. When she arrived Þorgerðr announced her intention to die with Egill, and he admitted her to the bed-closet. But Þorgerðr tricked her father into taking a drink from a horn, which turned out to contain milk, thus spoiling his fast.

> Then Þorgerðr said: "What course shall we take at this point, now that this plan of ours is cancelled? It would be my wish now, father, that we two extend our lives so that you can compose a funeral lament for Bǫðvarr—and I will carve it on a wooden tablet[12]—but that after that we two die, if it seems right to us. I think that your son Þorsteinn will be slow to compose the poem in memory of Bǫðvarr, but it will not be

---

12 On the slim, ruler-like *(rúna)kefli* see, for example, Page (1973:96-7).

fitting if he is not given this honour of the dead, for I do not
think that you and I will be sitting at the funeral feast when he
is honoured."[13] Egill said that it was not to be expected that
he would be able to compose poetry just then even if he tried
—"but I can attempt it," he said.

The poem follows.[14]

At its conclusion the saga continues its sketch of the occasion:

Egill starting getting more and more vigorous as he went on
working on the poem, and when the poem was finished, he
recited it to Ásgerðr and Þorgerðr and his household. Then
he got up out of his bed and seated himself in his high seat. He
called that poem *Sonatorrek*. Afterwards Egill had [both] his
sons honoured with the funeral feast as ancient custom
required.   (*Egils saga* 242-57 [Ch.78])

The poem—the title probably means "Difficult Avenging of Sons", but is
usually translated as "Lament for Sons"—is the most beautiful and revealing human document of the last decades of Norse paganism; but the saga
scene is a brilliant literary creation of the thirteenth century. The late date
of the saga (1200-30) and the writerly aspect of the scene rightly set off
alarm bells for an historian of actual events instead of literary truth. But

---

[13] Þorgerðr is playing on Egill's prejudice against his surviving son Þorsteinn and seems
further to imply that the traditional funeral (or memorial) feast can only be performed
properly if a memorial poem has been composed. With this assumption a difficulty in the
translation of the latter part of her sentence can be explained: "... but/and it will not be
fitting if he is not given the funeral feast (*at hann sé eigi erfðr*). [However, if Egill can
compose the necessary poem in advance, perhaps even Þorsteinn will be able to manage a
funeral feast.] For I do not believe that we two will be [still alive for the occasion, will be]
sitting at the drinking when he is given the funeral feast (*at hann er erfðr*)." Recent
translations which apparently do not make the assumption of this relationship between the
poem and the wake are forced either to generalize the first occurrence of *erfðr*, as in my
translation in the text, into something like "daß er nicht die gebührende Totenehre erhält"
(Schier, 1978:233) or else to give *erfðr* a strict translation but twist the meaning of *því at*
("Nor will it do if Bodvar isn't honoured with a funeral feast, though I don't expect ...";
Pálsson and Edwards, 1976:204). Fell (1975:146) solves the problem by carrying the
relation between poem and feast so far as to replace the latter with the former and translate
sé eigi erfðr as "to die unsung".
[14] Full copies of the poem (twenty-five stanzas) are found only in closely related copies
of the saga from the seventeenth century, but they stem ultimately from a lost fourteenth-
or fifteenth-century vellum; the preserved fourteenth-century copy in the saga collection
Möðruvallabók has only the first stanza; one and a half stanzas are also preserved in the
versions of *Snorra Edda*. See Nordal (*Egils saga*: xcv-xcvii, 245-56) and Turville-Petre
(1976:27-8).

the saga-writer is evidently in touch with a deep oral-literary past, and significant analogies to *Beowulf* pervade both the late prose and the relatively early verse. As in the overlapping narratives of paternal bereavement in *Beowulf*, an old man grieves for a lost son who cannot be avenged, takes to his bed to die, and composes a funeral elegy: *erfikvæði eftir Bǫðvar: sorhleoð … an æfter anum*. Egill does not die, however, and the contrast with Hrethel establishes a life-giving aspect of lament which is supported in other early Germanic sources.

Further realizations of the pattern of paternal grief and lament in *Beowulf* and *Sonatorrek* are to be found in Old Norse literature, especially earlier in *Egils saga* itself when the poet's grandfather "took to bed, overcome by sorrow and old age" and the hopelessness of avenging his slain son against a king. As in the events following Bǫðvarr's death, a sibling of the dead youth stimulates the old man to live on, and he responds with an elegy (*Egils saga* 60 [Ch. 24]). A third saga analogue is harder to interpret. Hávarðr Ísfirðingr is an old man who takes to his bed with grief, evidently determined to die, after learning of the killing of his only son; but Hávarðr is also shaken out of his decline by a relative, his wife, who puts the old man on the path to executing an appropriate vengeance. The first two stanzas attributed to Hávarðr in the saga are clearly elegies and show some of the same themes as *Sonatorrek*.[15] In a fourth such incident narrated in the saga literature *Landnámabók* reports on an early settler of Iceland named Vǫlu-Steinn who had two sons, Ǫgmundr and Egill. When Ǫgmundr was killed in a feud, the surviving son sought out the wise man Gestr Oddleifsson "and asked Gestr to make a plan to cure the mortal grief [*helstríð*] which his father bore for his son Ǫgmundr. Gestr composed a beginning for the *Ǫgmundardrápa* [Lament for Ǫgmundr]" (*Landnámabók* [Benediktsson, 1968:184, 186] 159-6). Elsewhere two fragments of an elegy for a lost son are attributed to Vǫlu-Steinn, and it is usually assumed (see Nordal, 1924) that Gestr had succeeded in his intention that Vǫlu-Steinn should complete the poem—and so live on. A full examination of these realizations of the pattern and a detailed comparison between the motifs and language of *Sonatorrek* and the other Norse elegies and those of the *Beowulf* passages is material proper to a longer study, but one shared idea must be mentioned because it suggests the cultural depths of Germanic elegy.

In stanza 17, then, Egill says:

---

[15] The literature on the questionable authenticity of Hávarðr's poetry and on the problematic transmission history of the saga would lead too far afield in the present context; but see de Vries (1964-67:i.259-60; ii.383-5).

Þat er ok mælt
at engi geti
sonar iðgiǫld
nema sialfr ali
enn þann nið
er ǫðrum sé
borinn maðr
í bróður stað.

Turville-Petre (1976:36-7) translates this as: "This is also said that no one
may get recompense for his son unless he himself begets yet another
descendant who will be for others (?) a man born in place of his brother."
Compare *Beowulf* where the old man "*oðres ne gymeð / to gebidanne
burgum in innan / yrfeweardas þonne se an hafað / þurh deaðes nyð dæda
gefondad*" (ll.2451b-54).[16] The sentiment of the Old English seems simple:
the bereaved father does not care to wait for another heir in his courts
now that the special one has experienced death.

The difficulties with Egill's stanza are greater; the text is possibly
damaged, and the poet is clearly alluding to some subtext, probably a proverb or gnomic sentiment, as the line "this is also said" strongly suggests.
Egill is not saying simply that having a son is recompense for losing a son;
like Hrethel, Egill did have a surviving son at the time the poem was
composed. Instead he means that the only recompense for a son lost is
another who is specifically engendered and born to replicate or at least to
replace the first. Magnus Olsen must have understood the stanza in this
way when he proposed (1936:239-40) the attractive emendation of *ǫðrum*
to *endr* to give, by tmesis, *endr-borinn maðr* "a man born again". Even
without emending, the odd *ǫðrum* and the emphatic *í bróður stað* could
carry this meaning, and we may correct Turville-Petre's translation to:
"no one may get recompense for a son unless he himself begets again *the*
descendant who will be a man *born for the other one, in the place of his
brother*." The thought, then, leads into a submerged archaic religious
mental world of rebirth within the family.[17] The poetic point in *Sonatorrek*, however, is that the context of this bit of traditional wisdom shows

---

[16] Klaeber (note to l.2454) interprets the last phrase here as "(has) experienced [evil]
deeds", and he is followed by Hoops (1932:262); but there seems to be a modern consensus for relying on the perfective sense of the verb to give something like "has
completed his trial of deeds in the compulsion of death" (Swanton, 1978:151; cf. Wrenn-
Bolton, 1973:187). I have not seen it noted that this language is closely paralleled by
gesawon seledream (or perhaps *-dreamas*)) in the similar elegiac language of the Last
Survivor (l.2252), "[they] saw the last of joys in the hall" (Swanton, 1978:143); cf. the
similar usage in ll.2726f.

[17] On this topic see, among others, Eckhardt (1937) and de Vries (1956:i.182, 218).

that the so-called compensation is being rejected. Later in the poem the other compensations of Odin cited in stanzas 23-4 lead to a final consolation, but according to the dictum of stanza 17 they cannot constitute a genuine recompense for a son, which can only come with a dedicated fraternal replacement. Yet this *iðgiǫld* ('recompense') shows up as unrealistic in Egill's stanza 17. Egill did not see himself as about to engender a new Bǫðvarr; according to the prose, Egill was bent on dying, and according to the poem itself, he foresees death for himself. Perhaps the sapiential source itself was already half ironic.[18] Probably, however, it is Egill who treats his subtext, the proverbial wisdom about rebirth, with bitter irony.

The Old English may be much closer in meaning to Egill's poem than appears at first glance. A text which reports one intentional action is of course repressing at least one alternative; so the fact that the old man "does not care to await another (or second) heir" means that someone imaginable to the poet would have chosen to await one. The implicit reason for awaiting a new heir to replace the lost one is recompense, an exchange in a literal sense. The imaginable someone who would care to accept this exchange could not be unique, but would be representative of a class with respect to the decision to "await" or not. Awaiting or not awaiting surely refers to life on this earth (cf. *in geardum*) as opposed to a life after death. Thus the text presents the decision of the *gomel ceorl* in opposition to the opinion of a class of people who would wait in this life, and a general knowledge of religion would favour the idea that not "waiting here" for a replacement son is equivalent to a decision to join the family on the Other Side. (This last point cannot be proven from the passage, but no educated reader would expect the consequences of not waiting at the time and place of the text to be anything else, for instance some modern or oriental oblivion.) We cannot know whether the *gomel ceorl*'s decision for suicide—for that is what it amounts to—is a common one, though the isolation of his figure (*an æfter anum*) and the centrality of the decision in the episode imply that it was not, that it was unusual enough to be worth the telling; but the fact that the old man rejects life and the recompense of another heir carries with it the certainty that he knew of a belief—probably a belief held by a large class, a common belief—similar to that cited by Egill, that a new male heir is a recompense for a lost son. Again, we cannot know with certainty the form such a common belief was imagined as taking; but if it was common *Lebensweisheit* (a double sense

---

[18] Cf. *Hávamál* 72: "*Sonr er betri / þott sé síð of alinn / eptir genginn guma*" ('a son is better, though he be born late, after the death of the man'); the *Poetic Edda* is cited from Neckel (1983).

would be appropriate here), then it could have been encoded in an apothegm like the one cited by Egill.

Admittedly a laboured analysis of a beautiful passage, but ferreting out its presuppositions justifies a free paraphrase of the Old English which can fill in background and thought gaps, as follows: the old father knows, on the basis of traditional wisdom, perhaps wisdom embodied in gnomic verse or proverb, that the world offers no recompense for the death of a son except a new male heir; from the Icelandic we can perhaps add that the heir must be specifically engendered for the purpose and a rebirth of the dead son. In any case the *gomel ceorl* rejects this doubtful consolation. He will not wait but wishes to die. Egill takes a similar position over against the same or a similar traditional idea, but while the Old English text states the father's negative decision and leaves the maxim implicit, Egill quotes the maxim sarcastically and leaves its rejection unspoken.

If the *Beowulf* poet really is in touch not only with a profoundly native elegiac pattern but also with an archaic religious proverb like that cited by Egill, it should be worthwhile looking again, even if very briefly, at *Beowulf*'s connection to Germanic myth as represented in the Baldr story. In discussions of the domestic tragedy of Herebeald/Baldr and Hæthcyn/Hǫðr, the role of Hrethel has been overlooked. He corresponds structurally to Odin, the bereaved father, who according to Snorri grieved most of all the gods and whose revenge was made problematical by the fact that the accidental killer was also his own son (Snorri *Edda* [Faulkes, 1982:45-8] Ch. 49). In the simile the father is a *gomel ceorl*; in Old Norse literature Odin is so often refered to as old, *gamall*, that it seems unnecessary to collect the evidence, but he is also frequently a *karl*, the cognate of *ceorl*, including an instance where the slain Baldr is "the churl's son" (*karls sonr*; Snorri *Edda*, Faulkes, 1982:48). In *Beowulf* the son died by hanging; Odin was the lord of the gallows, god of the hanged, and hanging was a sacrifice to Odin. The father in Old English is both old and *infrod* 'wise'; so is Odin. The son is hanging to the joy of Odin's bird, the raven, while the father is a poet, and Odin god of poetry. Finally (apparently a central religious irony of late Norse paganism)[19] the son is dead, and Odin lord of the dead. Odin's recompense for the death of the beloved Baldr is no more satisfactory than that of Hrethel (who got none), but it involves *both* the revenge contemplated by Hrethel and the Norse fathers in the saga passages *and* the idea of a specially engendered replacement for a brother, just the notion on the minds of the *gomel ceorl* and Egill (in stanza 17), who elsewhere in *Sonatorrek* also dwells on his helpless desire

---

[19] Cf. the memorial poems *Eiríksmál* (c.950) and *Hákonarmál* (c.961) edited in *Skjaldedigtning* [Jónsson, 1908-15], 1B: 164-6; 57-60).

for revenge: this new son of Odin, Váli, must be especially sired for and dedicated to the task of avenging his brother Baldr (de Vries, 1956:ii.277-80).

* * *

These ideas and narrative patterns could be pursued further through the intertextual labyrinth of the surviving Old Germanic monuments, but I hope enough has been said to suggest—and only suggestion, not proof, is possible—some less obvious aspects of the relationship of *Beowulf* to Germanic tradition, its position in this particular ethnic web of words. Specifically, I hope I have been able to suggest the cultural depth of the elegiac tradition in *Beowulf,* its religious and ritual overtones, and its ultimate grounding in myth—though not necessarily the Baldr myth exactly as we know it from the Viking Age sources. The Old English poem, whatever its date, seems, in short, to maintain a subterranean contact with the world of ideas, the poetic language, and the oral-literary forms of the tribes and nations that spoke Germanic tongues.

Obviously not everything in *Beowulf,* a poem certainly by a Christian poet for a Christian audience, comes from this tradition. Above all the long epic form itself seems, according to Heusler (1905) and many others (Buchloh, 1966; Andersson, 1987:3-29), to be ultimately of Virgilian inspiration. As the dramatic native lay underwent expansion mental space was gained, or so Walter Haug (1975) has argued,[20] for something more like self-conscious reflection. In *Beowulf* the newly won "space" is occupied with the religious and social problems of coming to terms with pre-Christian ancestors and with proper conduct, especially royal conduct, in the archaic period preceding that of writer and audience—by implication conduct that still had relevance for their descendants. But I think the poet is also consciously occupied with the "burden" of the poetic past and implicitly asks what these old forms—elegy, flyting, heroic lay—may still mean in (for example) the age of Offa the Great. That is why he makes his epic, among other things, a *summa litterarum* that looks back to traditional genres, and why he packs it with his versions of a great deal of traditional narrative (Harris, 1982a and 1985).

It would be impossible in the short compass of this chapter even to outline the materials, primary or secondary, for a comparative Germanic approach to *Beowulf.* Heusler's *Die altgermanische Dichtung,* differentiating "Old Germanic" from "Proto-Germanic" (*urgermanisch*) and "Common Germanic" (*gemeingermanisch*), defines its key concept negatively:

---

[20] But see Andersson (1988).

"Old Germanic is for me a cultural concept without chronological boundaries: Germanic culture in so far as it was not tangibly shaped by the
Church and by classical education, its poetic traces extending far into the
Middle Ages" (Heusler, 1941:8). Though it is easy to see self-contradic-
tory features in this brief definition (in the matter of chronological
boundaries) and some problematic aspects even in the more flexible definition constituted by the whole book, the concept of an "Old Germanic"
cultural matrix within which literary comparisons are charged with
genetic-historical, and not merely with esthetic, significance is a durable
one. Among the extensive primary materials the most important for *Beowulf* are Scandinavian, and the bibliography attached to this article attempts within its limits to give titles of some reference books and readers'
guides in this field.

   The problem of spatial and temporal disjuncture in the comparative
context deserves a further, closing comment. Comparative literature typically deals either with contiguity—movements (Symbolism), near contemporaries (Dickens and Dostoyevsky), influence (of Poe on the French;
Virgil on Dante)—or else with discontinuous similarity—genres (satire),
structures (*style indirect libre*), or social relations (courtly literature in
France and Japan). Neither of these standard approaches precisely coin-
cides with the kind of comparison open to students of *Beowulf*'s Germanic
background. *Sonatorrek*, our example, is dated about 961 mainly on the
testimony of a thirteenth-century saga; both are Icelandic; the epic is
English and may have been in writing earlier than the ninth century.[21]
Our justification for making the kinds of comparison indulged in in this
paper even across such stretches depends on faith in the strength of
"tradition". Though an understanding of the tradition cannot be arrived at
without logical circularity, tradition itself is not a mystical concept. Germanic tradition, like any ethnic tradition, is essentially enduring talk;
language, and communication sustained over time, are its essence, and its
concrete expression in (oral) literature is the intertextuality that we invoke
in the comparative enterprise.

---

[21] The dating is, of course, inconclusively debated; cf. Chase (1981); Fulk (1982);
Andersson (1983); Niles (1983:96-117). If Frank (1982) is right, the special brand of
"traditional" comparatism I am arguing for is unnecessary (cf. note 5 above).

REFERENCES

Andersson, Theodore M. (1981). The Lays of the Lacuna of *Codex Regius*. In: *Speculum Norroenum: Norse Studies in Memory of Gabriel Turville-Petre*. Ed. U. Dronke *et al*. Odense: Odense University Press. 6-26.
Andersson, Theodore M. (1983). Review Article: The Dating of *Beowulf*. *University of Toronto Quarterly* 52. 288-301.
Andersson, Theodore M. (1986). Beyond Epic and Romance: *Sigurðarkviða in meiri*. In: *Sagnaskemmtun: Studies in Honour of Hermann Pálsson*. Ed. R. Simek *et al*. Vienna, Cologne, Graz: H. Böhlau. 1-12.
Andersson, Theodore M. (1987). *A Preface to the Nibelungenlied*. Stanford, CA: Stanford University Press.
Andersson, Theodore M. (1988). Walter Haug's *Heldensagenmodell*. In: *Germania: Comparative Studies in Old Germanic Languages and Literatures*. Ed. Daniel G. Calder and T. Craig Christy. Wolfeboro, NH: Brewer. 127-42.
Barthes, Roland (1977). The Death of the Author. In: *Image, Music, Text: Essays*. Sel. and tr., Stephen Heath. New York: Hill and Wang. 142-8. (Originally in *Mantéia* 5 [1968].)
Benediktsson, Jakob (ed.) (1968). *Landnámabók*. In: *Íslendingabók [and] Landnámabók*. Íslenzk fornrit 1, pt. 1. Reykjavík: Hið íslenzka fornritafélag.
Björkman, Erik (1920). *Hæðcyn* und *Hákon*. *Englische Studien* 54. 24-34.
Bonjour, Adrien (1950). *The Digressions in "Beowulf"*. Medium Ævum Monographs 5. Oxford: Blackwell.
Buchloh, Paul G. (1966). Unity and Intention in Beowulf. *English Studies Today* 4. 99-120.
Chambers, R.W. (1912). *Widsith: A Study in Old English Heroic Legend*. Cambridge: Cambridge University Press. (Rpt. New York: Russell & Russell. 1965).
Chambers, R.W. (1959). *Beowulf: An Introduction to the Study of the Poem with a Discussion of the Stories of Offa and Finn*. 3rd ed. with a Supplement by C.L. Wrenn. Cambridge: Cambridge University Press.
Chase, Colin (ed.) (1981). *The Dating of Beowulf*. Toronto: University of Toronto Press.
Chickering, Howell D., Jr. (ed. & tr.) (1977). *Beowulf: A Dual-Language Edition*. Garden City and New York: Anchor.
Clover, Carol J. (1980). The Germanic Context of the Unferth Episode. *Speculum* 55. 444-68.
Clover, Carol J. and John Lindow (eds.) (1985). *Old Norse-Icelandic Literature: A Critical Guide*. Islandica 45. Ithaca, NY, and London: Cornell University Press.
Culler, Jonathan (1981). *The Pursuit of Signs: Semiotics, Literature, Deconstruction*. Ithaca, NY: Cornell University Press.
Detter, Ferdinand (1894). Zur Ynglingasaga. 2. Der Baldrmythus; König Hygelac. *Beiträge zur Geschichte der deutschen Sprache und Literatur* 19. 496-516.
Dronke, Ursula (1969). Beowulf and Ragnarǫk. *Saga-Book of the Viking Society* 17. 302-25.
Eckhardt, Karl August (1937). *Irdische Unsterblichkeit: Germanischer Glaube an die Wiederverkörperung in der Sippe*. Weimar: H. Böhlau.
Faulkes, Anthony (ed.) (1982). *Snorri Sturluson: Edda. Prologue and Gylfaginning*. Oxford: Clarendon.
Fell, Christine (tr.) (1975). *Egils Saga*. [Poems tr. by John Lucas]. London: Dent.
Frank, Roberta (1982 [for 1979]). Old Norse Memorial Eulogies and the Ending of *Beowulf*. In: *The Early Middle Ages*. Ed. William H. Snyder. Acta 6. Binghamton, NY: Center for Medieval and Early Renaissance Studies. 1-19.
Frantzen, Allen J. (1990). *Desire for Origins: New Language, Old English, and Teaching the Tradition*. New Brunswick, NJ: Rutgers University Press. 1990.

Fry, Donald K. (1969). *Beowulf and The Fight at Finnsburh: A Bibliography*. Charlottes-ville, VA: University of Virginia Press.
Frye, Northrop (1970). *Anatomy of Criticism: Four Essays*. New York: Atheneum. (1st ed. Princeton, NJ: Princeton University Press. 1957.)
Fulk, Robert D. (1982). Review Article: Dating Beowulf to the Viking Age. *Philological Quarterly* 61. 341-59.
Fulk, Robert D. (1989). An Eddic Analogue to the Scyld Scefing Story. *Review of English Studies*, N.S. 40. 315-22.
Gippert, Stefan, Britta Laursen, and Hartmut Röhn (1991). *Studienbibliographie zur Älteren Skandinavistik*. Berliner Beiträge zur Skandinavistik 1. Leverkusen: Norden.
Harris, Joseph (1979). The *senna*: from Description to Literary Theory. *Michigan Germanic Studies* 5. 65-74.
Harris, Joseph (1982a). *Beowulf* in Literary History. *Pacific Coast Philology*. 16-23. (Rpt. in *Interpretations of Beowulf: A Critical Anthology*. Ed. R.D. Fulk. Bloomington, IN: Indiana University Press. 1991. 235-241.)
Harris, Joseph (1982b). Elegy in Old English and Old Norse: A Problem in Literary History. In: *The Vikings*. Ed. R.T. Farrell. London and Chichester: Phillimore. 157-64. (Repr. in *The Old English Elegies: New Essays in Criticism and Research*. Ed. Martin Green. Rutherford, etc.: Fairleigh Dickinson University Press; London and Toronto: Associated University Presses. 1983. 46-56.)
Harris, Joseph (1985). Die altenglische Heldendichtung. *Neues Handbuch der Literaturwissenschaft*. Vol. 6: *Europäisches Frühmittelalter*. Ed. Klaus von See. Wiesbaden: AULA-Verlag. 237-76.
Harris, Joseph (1990). Reflections on Genre and Intertextuality in Eddic Poetry (with special reference to *Grottasǫngr*). In: *Atti del 12ᵉ Congresso internazionale di studi sull'alto medioevo: The Seventh International Saga Conference, Spoleto 4-10 settembre 1988*. Ed. Teresa Pàroli. Spoleto: Centro italiano di studi sull'alto medioevo. 231-43.
Harris, Joseph (1992). Beowulf's Last Words. *Speculum* 67. 1-32.
Haug, Walter (1975). Andreas Heuslers Heldensagenmodell: Prämissen, Kritik und Gegenentwurf. *Zeitschrift für deutsches Altertum und deutsche Literatur* 104. 273-92.
Heusler, Andreas (1905). *Lied und Epos in germanischer Sagendichtung*. Dortmund: Ruhfus. (Rpt. Darmstadt: Wissenschaftliche Buchgesellschaft. 1956.)
Heusler, Andreas (1941). *Die altgermanische Dichtung*. 2nd ed. rev. Potsdam: Athenaion. (Rpt. Darmstadt: Gentner. 1957.)
Hoops, Johannes (1932). *Kommentar zum Beowulf*. Heidelberg: Winter.
Jónsson, Finnur (ed.) (1908-15). *Den norsk-islandske skjaldedigtning*. Vols. 1A-2A (diplomatic texts) and 1B-2B (critical texts). Copenhagen: Gyldendal. (Rpt. Copenhagen: Rosenkilde & Bagger. 1967 (A) and 1973 (B).)
Klaeber, F. (ed.) (1953). *Beowulf and the Fight at Finnsburg*. 3rd ed. Boston: D.C. Heath. (1st ed., 1922).
Lord, A.B. (1991). Ring Composition in *Maldon*; or, a Possible Case of Chiasmus in a Late Anglo-Saxon Poem. In: *The Ballad and Oral Literature*. Harvard English Studies 17. Ed. Joseph Harris. Cambridge, MA: Harvard University Press. 233-42.
Malone, Kemp (1923). *The Literary History of Hamlet. 1. The Early Tradition*. Heidelberg: Winter.
Malone, Kemp (ed.) (1936). *Widsith*. London: Methuen.
Malone, Kemp (ed.) (1962). *Widsith*. 2nd ed. rev. Anglistica 13. Copenhagen: Rosenkilde and Bagger.
McCone, Kim (1990). *Pagan Past and Christian Present in Early Irish Literature*. Maynooth: An Sagart.
Neckel, Gustav (1920). *Die Überlieferung vom Gotte Balder dargestellt und vergleichend untersucht*. Dortmund: Ruhfus.

Neckel, Gustav (ed.) (1983) *Edda: Die Lieder des Codex Regius nebst verwandten Denkmälern*. I: *Text*. 5th ed. rev. Hans Kuhn. Heidelberg: Winter.

Nerman, Birger (1913). *Studier över Svärges hedna litteratur*. Uppsala: Appelberg.

Niles, John D. (1983). *Beowulf: The Poem and Its Tradition*. Cambridge, MA: Harvard University Press.

Nordal, Sigurður (1924). Völu-Steinn. *Iðunn* 8. 161-78. (Rpt. in his *Áfangar*. 2 vols. Reykjavík: Helgafellsútgáfan [Víkingsprent]. 1943-44. ii.83-102. Also rpt. in his Ritverk: Mannlýsingar. 3 vols. Reykjavík: Almenna Bókafélagið. 1986. i.297-311.)

Nordal, Sigurður (ed.) (1933). *Egils saga Skalla-Grímssonar*. Íslenzk fornrit 2. Reykjavík: Hið íslenzka fornritafélag. 1933.

Olsen, Magnus (1924). Om Balder-digtning og Balder-kultus. *Arkiv för nordisk filologi* 40. 148-75.

Olsen, Magnus (1936). Commentarii scaldici. I. Sonatorrek. *Arkiv för nordisk filologi* 52. 209-55.

Page, Raymond I. (1973). *An Introduction to English Runes*. London: Methuen.

Pálsson, Hermann and Paul Edwards (tr.) (1976). *Egil's Saga*. Harmondsworth: Penguin.

Perkins, David. (1992). *Is Literary History Possible?* Baltimore and London: The Johns Hopkins University Press.

Robinson, Fred C. (1985). *Beowulf and the Appositive Style*. Knoxville, TN: University of Tennessee Press.

Schier, Kurt (tr.) (1978). *Die Saga von Egil*. Saga 1. Düsseldorf: Diederichs.

Schneider, Hermann (1928-34). *Germanische Heldensage*. 2 vols. Grundriss der germanischen Philologie, 10. Berlin: de Gruyter. (Rev. ed. of vol. 1, 1962.)

Schneider, Hermann (1955). Einleitung zu einer Darstellung der Heldensage. *Beiträge zur Geschichte der deutschen Sprache und Literatur* (Tübingen) 77. 71-82. (Rpt. in: *Zur germanisch-deutschen Heldensage: Sechzehn Aufsätze zum neuen Forschungsstand*. Ed. Karl Hauck. Wege der Forschung 14. Darmstadt: Wissenschaftliche Buchgesellschaft. 1961. 427-49.)

Schück, Henrik (1909). *Studier i Beowulfsagan*. Uppsala Universitets Årsskrift 1909. Uppsala: Almquist and Wiksell.

Short, Douglas D. (1980). *Beowulf Scholarship: An Annotated Bibliography*. New York and London: Garland.

Spitzer, Leo (1967). Linguistics and Literary History. In: *Linguistics and Literary History: Essays in Stylistics*. Princeton, NJ: Princeton University Press. 1-39. (1st ed. 1948.)

Stanley, E. G. (1975). *The Search for Anglo-Saxon Paganism*. Cambridge: Brewer. (Originally a series of articles in *Notes & Queries* 1964-65.)

Swanton, Michael (ed. & tr.) (1978). *Beowulf*. Manchester Medieval Classics. Manchester: Manchester University Press.

Taylor, A.R. (1952). Two Notes on Beowulf. *Leeds Studies in English* 7-8. 5-7.

Turville-Petre, E.O.G. (1964). *Myth and Religion of the North: The Religion of Ancient Scandinavia*. New York: Holt, Rinehart and Winston; London: Thames and Hudson.

Turville-Petre, E.O.G. (1976). *Scaldic Poetry*. Oxford: Clarendon.

Vésteinn Ólason (1985). Tradition and Text. In: *The Concept of Tradition in Ballad Research: A Symposium*. Ed. Rita Pedersen and Flemming G. Andersen. Odense: Odense University Press.

de Vries, Jan (1956). *Altgermanische Religionsgeschichte*. 2 vols. 2nd ed. rev. Grundriss der germanischen Philologie 12. Berlin: de Gruyter. (Rpt. 1970.)

de Vries, Jan (1964-67). *Altnordische Literaturgeschichte*. 2 vols. 2nd ed. rev. Grundriss der germanischen Philologie 15. Berlin: de Gruyter.

Whitelock, Dorothy. (1939). *Beowulf* 2444-2471. *Medium Ævum* 8. 198-204. (Repr. in her *From Bede to Alfred: Studies in Early Anglo-Saxon Literature and History*. London: Variorum Reprints. 1980.)

Wrenn, C.L. (ed.) (1973). *Beowulf, with the Finnesburg Fragment*. Rev. ed. W.F. Bolton. London: Harrap. 1973. (1st ed., 1953).
Þórólfsson, Björn K. and Guðni Jónsson (eds.) (1943). *Hávarðar saga Ísfirðings*. In: *Vestfirðinga sögur*. Íslenzk fornrit 6. Reykjavík: Hið íslenzka fornritafélag.

THE CHRISTIAN LANGUAGE AND THEME OF *BEOWULF*

THOMAS D. HILL

One of the traditional topics of medieval English literary criticism is the question of "paganism and Christianity" in *Beowulf*. There have been a number of articles and even books concerned with the problem; recently E. B. Irving and Fred C. Robinson have devoted respectively a major article (Irving, 1984) and a significant portion of a book (Robinson,1985) to re-examining it. If after over a century of learned discussion and commentary on *Beowulf*, it continues to be necessary to discuss an issue, there must be something rather problematic about it. And there is—most comparable early medieval epic texts are either emphatically and militantly Christian (like the *Chanson de Roland*) or unapologetically pagan or secular in their viewpoint (like the *Táin Bó Cúalnge* or *Egils saga*). *Beowulf* is neither. Klaeber has spoken of "the problem of finding a formula which satisfactorily explains the peculiar spiritual atmosphere of the poem," (1953:cxxi, n.2) and this question remains an important issue in modern *Beowulf* criticism.

Obviously any issue which has received as much attention as this one is difficult and the "solution" or, to be more precise, the way of understanding this issue which I am proposing will inevitably be somewhat controversial. To put the matter succinctly, I think the *Beowulf*-poet is presenting a radical synthesis of pagan and Christian history—which is without parallel in Anglo-Saxon or Anglo-Latin literature (so far as I am aware). There are, however, parallels in Old Irish and Old Norse-Icelandic literature; it is a fascinating although perhaps unresolvable question whether there was any direct intellectual or literary influence between these literatures in the early Middle Ages.

It is necessary first to define the ideological problem which the *Beowulf*-poet (and reflective Anglo-Saxons throughout the era) faced. To begin with, the Anglo-Saxons (like most archaic peoples) were deeply conservative and venerated antiquity. The evidence for this proclivity is massive and pervasive. Good swords in *Beowulf*, for example, are inevitably "old"—ideally a sword is "the work of Weland" the archetypal, oldest and thus the best smith. Anglo-Saxon ideas about—their legal definition of—aristocracy and kingship are obscure to some degree, but it is clear that Anglo-Saxons venerated "old" families and that the ideal of an ancient royal line extending far back into the past was an important ideological concern shared even by a Churchman as hostile towards Germanic antiquity as Alcuin.[1] As far as Anglo-Saxon secular literature is concerned, there is ample evidence of its deliberately archaic and archaizing character. Leaving aside *Beowulf* itself, *Widsith* and *Deor* reflect remarkable and extensive knowledge of the Germanic past.[2] There is also evidence within and without *Beowulf* that Anglo-Saxon poets knew and recited poems now lost about the heroes of the major cycles of Germanic heroic legend as they are known to us from the the extant heroic literature preserved in Middle High German and Old Norse-Icelandic.

Anglo-Saxon Christians, however, had to deal with a problem which all European Christians of the first millennium faced, the simple and unarguable historical fact that Christianity itself, and in particular their Christianity, was not particularly old. The date of *Beowulf* is much controverted, but there are no conclusive arguments against dating the poem to the age of Bede, a date which was favoured by a majority of *Beowulf* scholars of the last generation, and which is still perfectly posible and plausible. Indeed the arguments for a late dating of the poem are motivated in part by a quite understandable scholarly concern that the reasonable guess—that *Beowulf*, is relatively early rather than relatively late —should solidify into a secure "fact" by dint of much repetition.[3] I should perhaps add that while I myself am agnostic about the dating of *Beowulf*, I find the arguments for an early dating suasive and the possibility congenial.

At any rate whether we accept the early or the late dating of *Beowulf*, it is clear that a reflective Anglo-Saxon must have been aware that the roots of his nation and culture were pagan and Germanic and that Christianity was a relatively recent innovation among a people to whom antiquity was precious and innovation suspect.

One of the ways in which medieval authors dealt with the problem of paganism and its consequences was to pretend that the history of their nation began with the conversion to Christianity and that nothing of real consequence happened before that momentous date. Bede is a conspicuous exemplar of this tradition of historiography—the pagan Anglo-Saxons receive very muted treatment in the *Historia Ecclesiastica*. The sins of the Christian Britons receive much more emphasis than the heroic accomplishments of the pagan Anglo-Saxons and Jutes. But a secular Anglo-

[1] On the Anglo-Saxon genealogies see Sisam (1953), and Hill (1988). For an interesting comment by Alcuin reflecting his belief in the *gæfa* (victory bringing luck) of a Woden descended king, see Epistola 129 (Duemmler, 1895:129).

[2] The editions of those poems by Kemp Malone (1933/1962) provide a useful and illuminating compendium of information which graphically illustrates the extent of the Germanic learning of these poets.

[3] On this problem see the essays collected in Chase (1981).

Saxon aristocrat, whose claims to prestige and authority depended in part on an ancient and therefore necessarily pagan lineage, would be much less inclined to ignore the achievements of his pagan ancestors than a monk cut off from his own family and culture.

Some literary histories address the "pagan" heritage of the Anglo-Saxons as if that heritage was limited to the few references to Woden in the poetic corpus and the Anglo-Saxon charms—which are almost always treated as if magic was as marginal and "low" in Anglo-Saxon society as it is in ours. If we had a fuller corpus of Anglo-Saxon secular poetry we might well have more material about the Anglo-Saxon pagan pantheon rather than having to depend so heavily on Old Norse-Icelandic texts for information about Germanic paganism in England. Certainly we would know more about "pagan" heroic legend since there is ample evidence in the surviving literature that the Anglo-Saxons were deeply and abidingly interested in Germanic heroic legend—legends whose heroes were after all pagan. But leaving aside the literary evidence of interest in the pagan past in Anglo-Saxon England, this heritage was of interest to Anglo-Saxons in ways much more immediate than in their choice of songs and stories to listen to. The Anglo-Saxon state—the kingdom itself (or for most of this period the various Anglo-Saxon kingdoms)—was founded by pagans. The kings ruled by virtue of a claimed descent from Woden. And if royal descent and royal genealogies were presumably rather remote from the daily experience of most Anglo-Saxons, the genealogies of the lords of the shires were of more immediate concern. Every Anglo-Saxon freeman was expected to have a lord whose claim to aristocratic status was based on aristocratic descent extending into the far past. And in the age of Bede (a perfectly possible milieu for the composition of *Beowulf*) no Anglo-Saxon could claim more than three or four Christian ancestors. Modern historians would of course insist that most if not all of these claims to genealogical antiquity were fraudulent or exaggerated and that powerful men simply adorned their present power with fantastic claims that their ancestors had been similarly powerful in the remote past. For the purposes of the literary historian, however, it is not the truth or falsehood of these claims which is at issue, but rather the ideology implicit in such claims and the fact that royal and aristocratic authority—no matter how devout a Christian a given Anglo-Saxon might be—had to have pagan roots. Anglo-Saxon law was similarly Germanic and pagan in origin, and in so far as it was law based on the idea of personal vengeance, could be reconciled with Christian ideals of forgiveness and universal justice with difficulty.

I would submit that a young Anglo-Saxon warrior who was schooled in Germanic heroic legend, whose claim to aristocratic status extended far into the pagan past, whose law was the old law confirmed by his people since time immemorial, whose homeland had been won by pagan warriors, who bore on his person ancient pagan ornaments, who defended himself with an old sword purportedly made by Weland and certainly made by pagan craftsmen, and whose landscape was dominated by magnificent burial mounds in which the great men (and women) of his race were buried in pagan splendour, had much reason to respect the pagan heritage of his people no matter how pious he was and no matter how deeply he venerated the Church and the priests, the monks, and the nuns who served it. Such a young (or old) aristocrat faced a deep cultural conflict since the dominant authoritities in the Church in this period would not, or to put the case more accurately, could not accept the claim that the paganism was a legitimate mode of religious and cultural self understanding. If paganism was legitimate, if pagans too could be saved, what was the point of Christian faith and Christian ascesis?

This cultural problem of how to reconcile Christian faith with an appreciation for the cultural achievements of the pagan past is an issue which recurs throughout the history of Western European thought—this was after all a central concern of that complex intellectual movement we call Renaissance humanism. And there have been different responses to this problem at different places and times in the history of Christian thought. The spectrum of these responses varies from Augustine's statement that the virtues of the ancient Romans were splendid vices, to Erasmus's invocation of Socrates as a saint. Roughly speaking, we may say that Christian thinkers who felt relatively secure about their own culture and faith have tended to be receptive to the merits of pagan past whether it be classical Latin and Greek or Celtic or Germanic, paganism and those who felt themselves threatened by it have harshly rejected "paganism" and pagan culture. Certainly in the history of Western European Christianity the humanists won their case and the classical pagan authors became central in the tradition of Christian European education. The beautiful quotation from Leo XIII with which E. K. Rand concludes his magisterial review of this problem is the utterance of a man supremely confident in his own faith and Christian culture:

> Quarum rerum utilitate perspecta Ecclesia Catholica quemadmodum cetera quae honesta sunt, quae pulchra, quae laudabilia ita enim humanarum litterarum studia tanti semper facere consuevit quanti debuere in eisque provehendis curarum suarum partem non mediocrem perpetuo collocavit.

> Perceiving, then, the usefulness [of the literatures of Greece and Rome,] the Catholic Church, which always has fostered whatsoever things are honest, whatsoever things are lovely, whatsoever things are of good report, has always given to the study of the humanities the favor that it

deserves, and in promoting it, has expended no slight portion of its best endeavor.[4]

The point is that while there is a tradition of Christian hostility and suspicion towards the pagan past, there has also been a more positive and receptive attitude which is clearly recognisable in the high Middle Ages and later and which seems to be reflected in *Beowulf*. Hostility towards pagan culture was based in part on the historical situation of any given Christian author, but it was also based in part on individual temperament. The teaching of the Catholic Church is not univalent and unequivocal concerning this problem. It is perfectly true that a famous clause from the Athenasian creed states that "extra ecclesia nullus salvus est", but even for the rigorous theologians who constructed this creed, the term "ecclesia" must include the patriarchs and such righteous gentiles as Melchesidech and Job. Dante's equivocation suggests something of the complexity of the problem. In accordance with the austere tradition of Catholic rigorism, he situates such pagans as Virgil and Aristotle in a pleasant but sad limbo situated before Hell, but Cato who is as much a pagan as any other is a guardian of Purgatory, and a certain Rifeo—known only from two lines in the *Aeneid* as the "iustissimus unus / qui fuit in Teucris et servantissimus aequi" (II. 426-27) is, according to Dante, in heaven. Dante, like the *Beowulf*-poet seems to have thought that some gentile "pagan" heroes could be saved, but unlike the *Beowulf*-poet, he is very cautious and hesitant about this possibility.

There are of course various solutions to the problem of the "peculiar spiritual atmosphere" of *Beowulf* and indeed it is possible to ignore the problem altogether, but it seems to me that the most consistent way to read the poem as we have it is to assume that the *Beowulf*-poet had thought long and hard about the problem and had arrived at (or had been taught) an essentially "humanistic" reading of his forefathers' paganism. He seems to have believed that the best and greatest of these men knew about God, creation, and natural moral law, and that when they died their souls went to heaven.[5] All of these beliefs can be explicitly supported from the text, but there are two problems which must be faced before we can simply define the *Beowulf*-poet as a Germanic humanist and turn to other problems. One is internal—the other and more serious one—external.

From the point of view of the literary historian concerned with "the peculiar spiritual atmosphere of the poem", *Beowulf* is a remarkably con-

---

[4] Quoted from Rand (1928:68, 299).

[5] For a magisterial study of Christian ideas and Christian language in *Beowulf*, see Klaeber, 1911-12. For a recent discussion of the salvation of the heathen in *Beowulf*, see Hill (1988).

sistent text in that the religious language of the poem reflects the religious knowledge of those patriarchs who lived before the covenants and the creation of Israel. It is useful to have a term to define the religion of Beowulf, Hrothgar, and the good Germanic heroes in the poem and I would suggest that we define them as Noachites, that is, as gentiles who share the religious heritage and knowledge of Noah and his sons without having access to the revealed knowledge of God which was granted to Abraham, Isaac, and Jacob, a tradition culminated by the revelation of the Law to Moses and continued by the charismatic tradition of prophecy in Israel. Every reference in the poem which touches on religion can be understood in these terms except for one—lines 179-83 in which the poet apparently condemns Hrothgar and the Danes for idol worship.

There can be no question that this passage presents a major difficulty for those of us who would argue that the *Beowulf*-poet is consistent and careful in depicting the good pre-Christian heroic figures in the poem as monotheistic Noachites. One simple solution to this difficulty is to assume that these lines are an interpolation by a scribe who was offended by the "humanistic" depiction of pre-Christian heroes and heroines in the poem. This solution was favoured (with some reservations) by Tolkien (1936:294, n.34) and Whitelock (1951:78). We have only one manuscript of the poem and there are a number of junctures in the poem in which lines or entire passages have been lost. Interpolations are easily understandable from a paleographical and codicological point of view; and the motivation for an interpolation at this point is also readily understandable. The usual criterion for determining whether a given passage is integral or an interpolation in a given text is whether the suspect passage differs either stylistically or conceptually from the text in which it occurs as a whole. If it is in some way markedly different from its immediate context, then one can reasonably argue that it was not part of the original text.

In this instance there is an immediate discrepancy between this condemnation of paganism in *Beowulf* and the remainder of the poem. The poet who is responsible for this passage states unequivocally that pagans such as the Danes do not "know" the identity of the true God, "*metod hie ne cupon, / dæda demend, ne wiston hie drihten god / ne hie herian ne cupon, / wuldres waldend.*" (ll.180-83: 'They did not know the Lord, the Judge of deeds nor did they know of the Lord God, not did they know how to praise the Ruler of Glory.) This claim is of course generally true of "real" "historical" Germanic paganism. Germanic pagans, like the Romans and the Greeks, worshipped a variety of gods and did not know either the appropriate names for God or the formulas of worship which were current in Christian Latin tradition. In *Beowulf*, however, such historically pagan figures as Beowulf and Hrothgar know, worship and thank the one God of Judeo-Christian faith for the blessings of their lives, know

that God judges deeds, and if we accept the straightforward literal significance of the formulas which characterise their deaths, ascend to heaven
after their deaths. Indeed, forty-five lines or so after the flat assertion that
the pagan Danes do not know how to worship the Lord, the *Beowulf*-poet
speaks of how the equally pagan Geats gave thanks to God after their successful sea voyage: "*gode þancodon / þæs þe him yðlade eaðe wurdon.*"
(ll.227-8; 'They gave thanks to God since the sea passage had been easy
for them.') Beowulf and his men cannot be Christian, but their prayer is
characterised by a Christian formula and they are praying at an appropriate time and in an appropriate manner from a Christian perspective.
And there are numerous other passages in the poem in which characters
who would have been "historically" pagan, speak about God and religious
issues from a "Noachite" perspective. The discrepancy between the poem
as a whole and the condemnation of the Danes' idol worship is absolute;
either the *Beowulf*-poet forgot for a moment to maintain the careful bal-
ance which he maintains elsewhere in the poem—in which the admirable
heroic figures in the poem speak about religious matters from a monotheistic perspective, but know nothing of revealed religion—or someone
else added that passage to the poem.

This condemnation of the idol worship of the Danes is in itself a
problem for this argument, but one which can be dealt with by the simple
assumption that the text of *Beowulf* is corrupt at this point. A larger
problem, however, which bears on this argument, and which has led a
great many distinguished scholars to be very hesitant about accepting what
the simplest and most direct understanding of what the language of the
poem would seem to imply, is that no other Anglo-Saxon or Anglo-Latin
authors who deal with the pagan past of the Germanic peoples seem to
have been at all sympathetic to paganism or to any other aspect of the
culture of the ancient Germanic peoples. At various times in the history of
Christian thought, Christian authors have been more or less sympathetic
towards the excusable ignorance of those who lived before the advent of
Christianity, but in the Latin west in the early Middle Ages Christian Latin
authors were univocal in their condemnation of the pagan past. Alcuin's
famous remarks about the monks at Lindisfarne who listened to heroic
poetry are so frequently quoted that Anglo-Saxonists are weary of them
and yet the passage is worth citing because of the clarity, force, and
directness of Alcuin's language:

> Verba Dei legantur in sacerdotali convivio. Ibi decet lectorem
> audiri, non citharistam; sermones patrum, non carmina gen-
> tilium. Quid Hinieldus cum Christo? Angusta est domus:
> utrosque tenere non potuit. Non vult rex cęlistis cum paganis
> et perditis nominetenus regibus communionem habere; quia

rex ille aeternus regnat in caelis, ille paganus perditus plangat
in inferno.

Let the words of God be read at the meal of the clergy. There it is proper to
listen to the lector, not a harp-player; the sermons of the Fathers not the
songs of the people. For what has Ingeld to do with Christ? Narrow is the
house; it cannot hold both.The King of Heaven wants nothing to do with
so-called kings who are pagan and damned. For the eternal King reigns in
heaven; the damned pagan laments in hell.[6]

The *Beowulf*-poet is even more anomalous in the context of early
medieval Christian thought in that the admirable characters in *Beowulf* are
not strictly speaking pagans, but rather monotheists, Noachites, as I have
chosen to call them. In this respect we may begin by observing that the
Beowulf-poet is (as far as we know) historically wrong since the pre-
Christian Germanic peoples were in fact pagans who worshipped a number of different gods and there is no historical evidence that any of these
peoples anticipated the distinctive Judeo-Christian claim that there is one
God, who created the heavens and the earth (*Beowulf* lines 90-98) and
who governs the course of history (*Beowulf* lines 696-702). In a strict
sense the *Beowulf*-poet is not being particularly sympathetic to pagans—
with the problematic exception of lines 175-88 he does not even mention
pagans or pagan worship. (He does mention pagan burial practices, but
that is another and a special topic.)

In this respect the *Beowulf*-poet seems wholly *sui generis*; no other
Anglo-Saxon author seems to have made such claims and since most
medievalists are very reluctant, and generally rightly so, to accept any
feature of a medieval poem as essentially original, many *Beowulf* scholars
are not inclined to accept the implications of the Christian language of the
poem at face value. Thus when Beowulf says of his grandfather Hrethel
that when he died *"godes leoht geceas"* (line 2469) 'he chose God's light'
—language which in a Christian context would clearly imply that the person who died went to heaven—many scholars implicitly assume that the
poet is more or less thoughtlessly using Christian formulas without careful
attention to their implications. If there were only a few instances of this
kind of usage, or if there was more in the poem which reflected conventional Christian hostility to the pre-Christian past than one suspect
passage, then one would, in my judgment, be justified in assuming that the
Beowulf-poet was conventional or muddled in his thinking about these
problems. The poet is, however, quite careful and consistent in his treatment of religious issues and his use of religious language, and I would

---

[6] Alcuin, "Epistola 124" (Duemmler, 1895:183).

argue that it is necessary to view this aspect of the poem from a somewhat broader perspective than Anglo-Saxonists generally do and to consider the poet's depiction of the religion of such figures as Beowulf and Hrothgar in the context of Celtic (particularly Old Irish) and Old Norse-Icelandic literary history as well. In so doing I am following the suggestions of J.R.R. Tolkien and in particular the arguments of Charles Donahue (Donahue, 1949-51).

We may begin by observing that Anglo-Saxon literature is preserved in fragmentary form in that we only have a small portion of what was once a very extensive corpus. Almost every Anglo-Saxon poem, for example, is preserved in a single manuscript copy. Even the much more extensive corpus of Anglo-Latin literature is only a portion of what once existed. Did the abbot or monks at Lindisfarne, for example, defend themselves against Alcuin's attack? This raises another problem which needs at least to be noted. Alcuin's works were preserved because he was an eminent and orthodox Catholic authority. The protest of a secularised abbot would have received much less respectful attention. This is not to raise again the fantasy of narrow minded monks erasing the remembrance of a religiously "incorrect" past, but simply to observe that the preservation of the texts which we have occurred in a particuar religious and social milieu, and that the character of that milieu affected what was preserved. For better or worse, *Beowulf* is the only lengthy secular poem preserved in Old English and it is preserved in one manuscript which was nearly lost. By contrast there are over thirty manuscripts of Aelfric's second series of *Catholic Homilies*. It is hardly a novel observation that secular texts, even secular texts written by Christian authors, reflect a significantly different perspective than specifically Christian literary texts, particularly so if the latter are written by clerics or monks. If we had more Anglo-Saxon secular literature, *Beowulf* might seem much less anomalous than it does when compared with rest of the Old English poetic corpus which is almost all specifically religous.

Again it is important to remember that much of the Christian Latin literature which deals with the conversion of the Germanic pagans, was written generations after the actual conversion process and the authors of these texts had an obvious interest in depicting the conversion as a straightforward and relatively quick one in which the missionaries had no occasion to make compromises and in which their new converts understood and accepted their new faith without hesitations or doubt. The actual process of conversion must inevitably have involved many ambiguities and complexities, and even willing converts could only have acquired a relatively sophisticated understanding of their new faith after years of instruction and worship. In fact, on the level of popular Christianity there is ample evidence for the existence of semi-Christian magic and folk-belief as exemplified most clearly in the Anglo-Saxon charms which were current for generations after the conversion. Thus if the *Beowulf*-poet seems to exhibit anomalous views about such topics as the salvation of unbaptised Germanic kings and heroes, we must remember that there is a great deal of evidence for other "unorthodox" religious ideas being current in Anglo-Saxon literary culture, even if this particular unorthodox idea seems unique to *Beowulf*.

If the *Beowulf*-poet's ideas about the existence and salvation of Germanic Noachites cannot be paralleled in Old English or Anglo-Latin literature as such, these ideas can be paralleled readily enough in the two vernacular literatures which are geographically and culturally closest to Old English literature. Both Old Irish and Old Norse-Icelandic literature are "insular" literatures in that both languages were spoken as native languages in England and Scotland during the Anglo-Saxon period. Again, both Old Irish and Old Norse-Icelandic literature possessed a rich literary tradition which was originally pagan. One of the immediate contrasts between Old French epic tradition and the heroic literature of the Anglo-Saxons, the Norse and the Irish is that the heroic literature of these insular peoples is much more archaic and looks back to the pagan roots of these nations. For linguistic and historical reasons the historical memory of the romance speaking peoples of Europe simply did not extend before the advent of Christianity; their "pagan" epics were the classical Latin epics.

In Old and (early Middle) Irish secular literature the *ollaimh, ollaves* and the bards faced an ideological problem quite similar to that which the *Beowulf*-poet faced in that the traditional heroic literature of the Irish peoples concerned heroes born long before the advent of Christianity. It seems clear, however, that the learned secular authors of Ireland were willing to argue that their great heroes were saved and are now in heaven although the ways which the authors of these texts devised to achieve this happy result reflect a bold and imaginative effort on their part. Thus in the death tale of Conchobar, Conchobar is wounded (the solidified brain of a slain enemy is embedded in his skull) and only partially healed—any excitement will kill him. He remains seven years in this parlous state until he is told of the passion of Jesus, leaps up to lead an onslaught of the Ulstermen to avenge this crime, and dies as an Irish martyr to the faith (Cross and Slover,[7] 1969:346). According to "The Phantom Chariot of Cu Chulainn" Cu Chulainn was summoned out of hell by Saint Patrick in order to convince the high king of Ireland of the merits of Christianity, and Cu Chulainn persuaded Patrick to arrange for his salva-

---

[7] The 1969 reprint of this anthology contains a bibliographical supplement which directs the reader to the Irish editions of these texts.

tion during this process (Cross and Slover, 1969:354). The death tale of Cu Chulainn concludes with Christian prophecy by the spirit of Cu Chulainn and in "The Colloquy of the Old Men" Patrick's guardian angels specifically assure him that it is appropriate for him to listen and to record the stories of the *fian* and so Patrick himself and his clerics record the stories from the lips of Ossin (Cross and Slover, 1969:464). It is difficult for someone who is not a specialist in the field to evaluate and interpret the complex narrative strategies by which the authors of these texts reconcile—at least on a formal level—the conflicting world views of Old Irish heroic legend and Christianity. A broad generalisation does seem appropriate however —the Irish bards and *ollaves* were sure enough of themselves and their literary and cultural traditions to claim that their great "pagan" heroes and kings were saved and rejoicing in the Christian heaven—heaven itself would be a poorer place without them.

In some ways Old Norse-Icelandic literary tradition is more directly relevant to *Beowulf* than Old Irish secular heroic prose. Old English and Old Norse-Icelandic are cognate languages and can be defined as cognate literatures. There are many striking parallels between the two literary traditions and there was much contact and mutual infuence between the two. Hence the treatment of "paganism" or to be more precise, pre-Christian religious ideas in the family sagas is important for students of *Beowulf* in that Icelandic secular literature provides the closest approximation of the lost secular literature of Anglo-Saxon England which still exists. Obviously we cannot treat Icelandic texts of the high middle ages as if they could provide direct evidence of what we have lost, but Icelandic literature is an important resource for the Anglo-Saxonist and indeed has long been recognised as such.

For the purposes of the present discussion, one immediate problem with the issue of the presentation of the conversion from Germanic paganism to Christianity in Old Norse-Icelandic literature is that this literature is so rich that one could write extensively about the problem without even beginning to treat it adequately. For two relatively recent discussions see Lönnroth (1969) and Harris and Hill (1989). In the context of this paper I wish to concentrate on one particular literary text which is strikingly similar to *Beowulf* in its treatment of "pagan" heroes who are nonetheless committed monotheists set apart from their pagan surroundings. *Vatnsdœla Saga* is an interesting text of considerable literary merit, but no one would claim that it is one of the great literary monuments of the period. The saga is a family saga concerned with the history of a given family over generations and the author of the saga makes several quite distinctive claims about the early history of this family. One is that unlike the other great founding families of Iceland who were at odds with Harald the Fairhaired, the leading men of this family were actually on good terms with him and emigrated to Iceland because of the power of fate as articulated by the disappearance of a magic amulet and its reappearance in Iceland. Again the family had their own distinctive form of religous commitment. When the first bishop arrives to convert the Icelanders Thorkel krafla demurs:

> Þorkell kvazk eigi vilja aðra trú hafa—"en þeir Þorsteinn Ingimundarson hǫfðu ok Þórir fóstri minn; þeir trúðu á þann, er sólina hefir skapat ok ǫllum hlutum ræðr."
>
> (*Vatnsdœla saga*, kap. 46 [Sveinsson, 1939:125])

(But Thorkell said he did not want a faith different from that Thorsteinn Ingimundarson and the rest of them had held—and Thorir my foster father. They believed in Him who made the sun and ruled all things.)

The bishop, of course, quickly explains that this faith is perfectly compatible with Christianity and Thorkel and his family, after some hesitation, are converted. The monotheistic and ethical principles of the pre-Christian Vatnsdœla dwellers are mentioned repeatedly throughout the saga. These men not only knew that one God had created the sun and ruled all things but that aggressive behaviour was morally wrong (cap. 11) and that God would punish or reward men according to their deeds (cap. 23) and the theme of the one god who made the sun recurs repeatedly. In terms of historical plausibility the edifying moral monotheism of the Vatnsdœla family before the conversion is historically unlikely and since there is much magic and fantasy woven into the saga, one might be tempted to dismiss this aspect of the saga as simply late pious fantasy projected into the far past. It is important, however, to distinguish between *Vatnsdœla saga* as an aesthetic success or failure and its literary historical interest as an attempt to bridge the gulf between the pagan Germanic past and the Christian present. The author of *Vatnsdœla saga* like the *Beowulf*-poet was attempting to reconcile pious antiquarian sympathy for the Germanic past and the claims of Christian truth. The kind of dogmatic hostility to the Germanic past reflected in Alcuin's letter about the monks of Lindisfarne was as current in thirteenth century Europe and Iceland as it was in Anglo-Saxon England, but it did not prevent the author of *Vatnsdœla saga* from depicting noble monotheistic pre-Christian Germanic heroes just as the *Beowulf*-poet had done before him. To summarize then, the peculiar spiritual atmosphere of *Beowulf* looks a good deal less peculiar and unique if one compares the poem to the other heroic literaures of Northern Europe whose poets and learned men faced the kind of ideological problem which the *Beowulf*-poet faced. There are other similar depictions of the pagan past current in Old Irish and Old Norse-Icelandic literature and a simple solution to the problem of Christianity in *Beowulf* is to assume that the *Beowulf*-poet approximated the solution that these other authors arrived at either independently or as the result of the influence of poems and histories now lost.

This discussion of the Christian context of *Beowulf* is necessarily controversial and partial; there are a number of smaller problems which could receive fairly extended discussion in their own right. Thus, for example, the poet alludes to the practice of sortilege in lines 202-04; this is a "pagan" practice but one sanctioned by the precedent of Old and New Testament practice. Again, there is the problem of lines 589-90 in which Beowulf apparently threatens Unferth with hell-torment, an anomoly convincingly explained by Fred C. Robinson (1974:129-30). These smaller problems lead us to a larger issue, however, which is that there is no received answer to the question of the "peculiar spiritual atmosphere of *Beowulf*" and eminent and well respected Anglo-Saxonists have offered quite divergent interpretations of this problem in the poem. Of the most recent discussions of the issue I particularly recommend that by Fred C. Robinson in *Beowulf and the Appositive Style*; Robinson's conclusions are quite different than mine, but they merit careful attention. Again, E.B. Irving has reargued the more traditional view that the *Beowulf*-poet was bound by and committed to the traditions of Germanic poetry and simply was not concerned with theological consistency. In a sense both these scholars are arguing for a more traditional and "orthodox" view of the Christianity of the *Beowulf*-poet than my argument would imply. Robinson is arguing that the *Beowulf*-poet was deeply concerned about the paganism of his characters, but had to accept the harsh traditional views of churchmen such as Alcuin, whereas Irving simply thinks that the poet was unconcerned with theological issues. In contrast, I am arguing that on this crucial ideological issue the *Beowulf*-poet was willing to question the authority of what must have been the majority opinion of the church of his time. The language of the poem can be most readily understood in these terms, but many scholars are reluctant to grant that an Anglo-Saxon poet could have challenged the authority of the church so directly. There are other Old English and Anglo-Latin texts which reflect the tension between a natural respect for traditional Germanic culture and the radical and exclusive claims of Christian faith; but there are none which so clearly affirm the positive, admirable, spiritual dimension of Old Germanic culture as the *Beowulf*-poet does. (It may also be added that the *Beowulf*-poet was keenly aware of the problematic features of the Germanic heroic ethic, but that would have to be the occasion for another paper or monograph.) When one considers the problem in a somewhat broader perspective, however, both the achievement and the ideological perspective of the *Beowulf*-poet come into sharper focus. We can see more clearly if we broaden our perspective.

I would be suprised if the problem of the "peculiar spiritual atmosphere" of *Beowulf* did not continue to be the occasion of scholarly controversy, but I do think it is important that the "humanistic" sympathy which the *Beowulf*-poet exhibits towards the best of the pagan past is not "heretical" even if it was (apparently) a minority view in the Anglo-Saxon church. As time passed and the western church emerged from the trauma of the destruction of the Roman empire, "high" medieval and renaissance philosophers and theologians began to reconsider the ramifications of the contempt for the pagan past implicit in such texts as Alcuin's letter to the monks at Lindisfarne, and a much more nuanced and appreciative view of the achievements of the pagan past became possible. The question of the salvation of the heathen became an important issue for poets such as Langland and Dante and the philosophy of Thomas Aquinas is based upon the recovery and assimilation of Aristotle's thought. Great poets often see more deeply than their contemporaries; and if the *Beowulf*-poet seems to have anticipated by generations the humanism and tolerance of thinkers like Erasmus, we need not be surprised. Irish *ollaves* and Icelandic sagamen and women learned to recognise the spiritual validity of their own heritage and its essential compatibility with Christianity. This tradition of tolerance and respect for the past is as much part of the heritage of early medieval Europe as the rigid and bigoted contempt for the pagan past which we commemorate in school handbooks. We could even argue that this was the better way, and we may hope that it will be the more enduring part of that heritage.

REFERENCES

Chase, Colin (1981). *The Dating of Beowulf.* Toronto: University of Toronto Press.
Cross, Tom Peete, and Clark Harris Slover (1969). *Ancient Irish Tales.* Rev. bibliography by Charles W. Dunn. New York: Barnes and Noble.
Donahue, Charles (1949-51). Beowulf, Ireland and the Natural Good. *Traditio* 7. 263-77.
Duemmler, Ernestus (ed.) (1895). *Alcuin: Epistolae Karolini Aevi II.* Monumenta Germaniae Historica. Berlin: Weidmann.
Harris, Joseph and Thomas D. Hill (1989). Gestr's 'Prime Sign': Source and Signification in *Norna-Gests Þáttr. Arkiv för Nordisk Filologi* 104. 103-22.
Hill, Thomas D. (1988a). The 'Variegated Obit' as an Historiographic Motif in Old English Poetry and Anglo-Latin Historical Literature. *Traditio* 44. 101-24.
Hill, Thomas D. (1988b). Woden as 'Ninth-Father': Numerical Patterning in Some Old English Royal Genealogies. In: *Germania: Comparative Studies in Old Germanic Languages and Literatures.* Ed. Daniel G. Calder and T. Craig Christy. Exeter: D.S. Brewer. 161-74.
Irving, Edward B. Jr. (1984). The Nature of Christianity in Beowulf. *Anglo-Saxon England* 13. 7-21.

Klaeber, Fr. (1911-12, 1912). Die christlichen Elemente im *Beowulf. Anglia* 35. 111-36, 249-70, 453-82; 36. 169-99.

Klaeber, Fr. (ed.) (1953). *Beowulf and the Fight at Finnsburg.* 3rd ed. Boston: D.C. Heath.

Lönnroth, Lars (1969). The Noble Heathen: A Theme in the Sagas. *Scandinavian Studies* 41. 1-29.

Malone, Kemp (ed.) (1962). *Widsith.* Anglistica 13. Copenhagen: Rosenkilde and Bagger.

Malone, Kemp (ed.) (1966). *Deor.* 2nd ed. New York: Appleton-Century-Crofts.

Rand, E.K. (1928). *Founders of the Middle Ages.* Cambridge, MA: Harvard University Press.

Robinson, Fred C. (1974). Elements of the Marvellous in the Characterisation of Beowulf: A Reconsideration of the Textual Evidence. In: *Old English Studies in Honour of John C. Pope.* Toronto: University of Toronto Press. 119-37.

Robinson, Fred C. (1985). *Beowulf and the Appositive Style.* Knoxville, TN: The University of Tennessee Press.

Sisam, Kenneth (1953). Anglo-Saxon Royal Genealogies. *Publications of the British Academy* 39. 287-348.

Sveinsson, Einar Ol. (ed.) (1939). *Vatnsdœla saga.* Íslenzk Fornrit VIII. Reykjavík: Hið Íslenzka Fornritafélag.

Tolkien, J.R.R. (1936). *Beowulf:* The Monsters and the Critics. *Publications of the British Academy* 22. 245-95.

Whitelock, Dorothy (1951). *The Audience of Beowulf.* Oxford: Clarendon Press.

THE SHORTER HEROIC VERSE

GRAHAM D. CAIE

There is a tendency to view the shorter 'heroic' verse in Old English as a rare window through which we can catch a glimpse of the lost world of pre-Christian, common Germanic life and values. Tacitus' propaganda piece *Germania* (Mattingly, 1948), written in the first century A.D., is still considered by many critics as a touchstone for what is commonly called 'the heroic code' of Anglo-Saxon society with its values of honour, courage and loyalty: a retainer fights loyally for and protects his lord who in turn rewards the thane and sets an example of heroism in war.

Students coming to Old English are equally keen to find the early pagan, mythological world of the Anglo-Saxons and are sometimes disappointed by the fact that nearly all the verse is Christian. Some critics, such as George Anderson, praise the heroic verse as it paints a world of Germanic values "before any Christian allusion comes in to mar the picture" (Anderson, 1949:155), while Eric Stanley in *The Search for Anglo-Saxon Paganism* highlights critics' shameless attempts to decipher pagan Germanic elements in much of the poetic corpus. For example, Barend Symons in 1900 considered that "the development of heroic song and of the epic was interrupted by Christianity" (Stanley, 1975:9). Such views presuppose that there was a wealth of heroic literature censored or at best filtered by the Christian missionaries who held the key to literary survival.

The image of Anglo-Saxon society that is often presented is that of constant battle, acts of heroic bravery, supernatural feats of individual strength, of solemn pledges by the lord to give treasure to the thane in return for military loyalty, of heroic boasts and proud speeches, mead-hall drinking and of the *scop* narrating heroic lays. There are few women or children around and society seems to function without the need of farmers, merchants and tradesmen, while the only craftsman in sight is the smith, creating famous swords. This picture is gleaned from scanty information in the very early *Germania* and the very late heroic poems such as *Brunanburh* and *Maldon* (cf. O'Keefe, 1991).

However, recent critics, such as Roberta Frank (1991), warn us about over-reliance on the *Germania,* a work written with the propagandist aim of praising the morality and fighting spirit of the barbarian Germanic tribes in order to shame the lax and immoral Romans:

> The *Germania* appears, like a fairy godmother, to mark and
> legitimize the birth of a Germanic consciousness, conceived

by kings and scholars in emulation of the Caesars. The imagination of the Anglo-Saxons was stirred by this tradition,
vague and unformed, of something majestic out of the past, of
a golden age when men were taller, bolder, freer and more
glorious. ... Poets of Germanic legend, too, conjured up for
their contemporaries a magnificent, aristocratic descent, a
proud history embodying current hopes and fears, a pleasant
dream transmuting the desert of daily existence into a landscape rare and strange.   (Frank, 1991:104)

There are relatively few works extant that might be called "heroic"—
really only five—and many are fragmentary, no longer extant in an Old
English manuscript, or written very late in the Old English period. Critics
are inclined to consider this tiny group of fragments as the tip of the ice-
berg and that once there must have been vast amounts of heroic lays or
epics in circulation, but we have no proof of this at all (cf. Wilson, 1952:
Chapter One, 'Heroic Legend').

Roberta Frank (1991:88) suggests that the Anglo-Saxons "tried
harder and harder in each passing century to establish a Germanic identity." The later verse such as *Brunanburh* reflects a growing sense of
nationality, a need to have roots and to cast a nostalgic glance at a period
that never existed. At a time when Alfred and his successors were uniting
England, it was politically astute to claim a northern heritage and to be
descended from the legendary kings of Denmark. It is not by chance that
the *Beowulf*-poet chose an archetypal Scandinavian as his hero, because it
was becoming increasingly popular to cultivate a sense of Anglo-Danish
community and find a continuity from the initial Saxon invasions. The
Brunanburh-poet, for example, concludes with a backward glance at the
great Saxon and Anglian invasions.

Much of our concept of heroic society comes, therefore, from a
literary genre which is aristocratic and which presents an idealised code of
behaviour and life-style. The heroes, akin to our modern James Bond, are
individuals who stand out as perfect examples of the code to which they
adhere. A parallel might be made with the idealised heroes of the chivalric
code who lived only in courtly literature and who were used politically
and nationalistically to conjure up a time that never was.

It is perhaps the Christian poetry of saints' lives and biblical heroes
and heroines that best illustrates what we call the heroic spirit. Here the
battles are both spiritual and physical, as in *Judith*, *Guthlac* and *Andreas*
with the protagonists enacting courageous deeds against demonic enemies,
being true to their Lord who rewards them with the promise of living in
the perfect *comitatus* in the after-life (cf. Hill, 1981).

Poems such as *Beowulf, Widsith* and *Deor* demonstrate that the Anglo-Saxon reader was well aware of heroic legends such as that of Finn, Ingeld, Sigemund and Eormanric. Many heroic poems use them as illustrative material or briefly allude to them without refreshing their audiences' memories. Many of the allusions are lost to us today, just as references to popular television programmes or singers will be lost to future generations. It would appear, however, that the *Deor* and *Widsith* poets *expect* us to know the many allusions to the names of ancient rulers and legends, although the poems are not about these characters (cf. Eliason, 1969).

Deor and *Widsith* are to be found in the Exeter Book amidst elegies, lyrics, riddles, wisdom verse and homiletic prose; *Deor* might well be classed as philosophical or wisdom poetry rather than heroic for its only claim to being "heroic" lies in the five examples used to illustrate the message. The refrain, an unusual stylistic device in Old English poetry, recurs after the allusion to some tragedy and suggests the poet's theme: "*Þæs ofereode, þisses swa mæg*" ('That passed away, so can this'). "*Þæs*" refers to the preceding event that passed, while "*þisses*" hints at the poet's own predicament which is only explained at the conclusion. In this sense the poem has also affinities with the riddle tradition. The explanation of his personal tragedy is that he, Deor of the Heodening tribe, has been replaced by Heorrenda who has also been given his land. Fate has struck and his fortune reversed, but there appears to be no bitterness, as he calls his rival "*leoðcræftig mann*" (1.40: 'a man skilled in song'). There might, however, be irony in his final "*Þæs ofereode, þisses swa mæg*", if it implies that Heorrenda's fate will also change. The fact that the previously listed tragedies were of mammoth proportions in comparison also puts his present unemployment in perspective.

The first episode alludes to the fate of Weland the smith, famous in Germanic mythology as the Vulcan figure, the smith of the gods and heroes. He appears in *Beowulf,* is depicted on the Franks Casket (8th century) and is mentioned by Alfred in his translation of Boethius's *De Consolatione Philosophiae*. In *Deor* we just hear of his sorrow and and exile and are expected to know the nature of his suffering, namely, that he was captured by King Nithhad, who had his hamstrings cut to keep him in his service as a blacksmith. In the second episode we are told of the tragedy of Beadohild, Nithhad's daughter, caused by Weland's revenge, but the details we have to glean from Norse sources. Weland killed Nithhad's sons and raped Beadohild, who in *Deor* is described as pregnant and grieving for her lost brothers. Perhaps the audience is meant to know that Weland and Beadohild were eventually reconciled and married and their child became the hero Widia mentioned in *Widsith* and *Waldere*. So their suffering apparently passes and so also could that of Deor.

The other allusions are more obscure to us today. Mæthhild, wife of Geat, is described as being miserable, distressed and deprived of sleep, but, although it has been suggested that it might refer to a Northern Orpheus and Eurydice myth, the origins of the legend and the outcome of her sorrow are unknown. There is perhaps a link with Beadohild in that both are about a woman's suffering.

The next two characters, however, appear to be oppressors rather than oppressed. The Theoderic mentioned might either be Theoderic the Goth, responsible for the death of Boethius, whose philosophy of mutability and consolation permeates the poem, or Theoderic the Frankish ruler (511-534) who spent much of his life in exile. Perhaps he, like Eormanric, the next character in the catalogue, was chosen as someone who inflicted tragedy on the lives of others. Eormanric, 4th-century king of the Ostrogoths, was infamous for his cruelty and treachery: in *Beowulf* Hama is said to have fled from him, and we know from the 13th-century *Þiðrekssaga* that he also treated his wife and son treacherously and exiled his uncle Theoderic, another candidate for the Theoderic of this poem.

After having given specific examples of bullies and sufferers, the poet turns to the general situation of the sorrowing man who thinks there is no solution. The poet offers the Christian consolation that the wise God will bring about change and show him grace, then concludes with his own predicament and personal tragedy. The effect of keeping the reference to the "this" of the refrain a secret to the end, both highlights his problem, elevating it to epic proportions, and also puts it in perspective: if such major, world-known tragedies were resolved, so also could his. But if his audience were aware of the story of Heorrenda, the usurping *scop,* they might know that he assisted his lord, Heoden to elope with Hild and this led to an eternity of hostilities. The choice of myths is therefore rather curious if the theme is one of "this too shall pass", as for some the happy ending is highly suspect and for others, like Eormanric, they themselves were the agents of suffering. It would be nice to see the poem as an imaginative presentation of the Boethian philosophy of consolation, but one is left wondering if it is not intended to be ironical.

Widsith and *Deor* have both been preserved in the Exeter Book, are both about *scops* and are classed as 'catalogue poems' by Nicholas Howe (1985:169): "These poems, especially *Widsith*, represent in catalogue form the core of those narratives which would together constitute a poetic encyclopedia of early medieval Germania." *Widsith* seems to serve the function of a mnemonic poem that might help a poet remember the major figures of heroic legend. There is no evidence to prove that this is a very early poem, although many would like to think that it reflects the life and work of a pre-Christian *scop* (cf. Greenfield and Calder, 1986; Rollman, 1982; Malone, 1962).

According to S.A.J. Bradley (1982:336), *Widsith* "enshrines much of their [the Anglo-Saxons'] cultural identity and collective ethic. ... It is surely a poet's poem." There is also an educational and entertainment value in such lists, as they contain all that one needs to know about the major heroic figures and provide a game of "spot the hero" in the same way as football champions or teams can be rattled off by some today. It is clear that no single man could have lived long enough to have been with all the rulers that the *Widsith*-poet claims to have served, and that we are dealing with a fictional character. He certainly lived up to his name, Widsith or "far-journey(er)", as he claims to have travelled from as far afield as Persia and India to Frisia and the land of the Picts. The story-line is sparse with the list of rulers and countries only held together by the fact that they are known to Widsith. Some are still known, such as Alexander, Caesar, Attila the Hun and Offa, others come to us through early medieval texts such as *Beowulf* from where we recognize Hrothgar, Hrothulf, Finn, Ingeld, and Ongentheow, while others have been lost in the depths of the Dark Ages but must be assumed to form part of the *scop*'s repertoire.

After a brief introduction by the narrator who describes how Widsith received treasure and held high estate in his own tribe of the Myrgingas and how he accompanied his first patron, Ealhhild, to Eormanric's court, Widsith himself "unlocks his word-hoard" and begins his catalogue. First comes a series of rulers and their lands in the form of "Attila ruled the Huns, Caesar ruled the Greeks", and so on. He pauses to praise the powerful and heroic Offa of the Angles before alluding to the well-known uncle and nephew team, Hrothgar and Hrothulf, in the same enigmatic way as the *Beowulf*-poet does. Neither poet spells out the events of the later feud, leaving all to our knowledge of the legend and to our imagination. It seems to represent the fact that peace in heroic society is only a veneer and that enmity might break out, even within a family, at any moment.

The second section largely comprises a list of the tribes he has been with and the rulers who have been generous to him in the style of "I have been with the Burgundians who gave me a collar; Guthhere gave me bright treasure as a reward for a song". This time he dwells on the largesse of Eormanric and has only good to say of this benefactor with whom he spent some time and who gave him a magnificent collar. Just as Beowulf hands over the priceless collar he received from the Danes to his lord, Hygelac, so Widsith passes on Eormanric's gift to the ruler of the Myrgingas, Eadgils, who in return gave him land. His generous patroness Ealhhild, daughter of Eadwine, is known throughout many lands, he claims, because of his songs, thus demonstrating the social function of the *scop* as one who spreads the fame of those who give him gifts. In fact, he modestly states, people in the know say they have never heard better singing:

þonne monige men,   modum wlonce,
wordum sprecan,   þa þe wel cuþan,
þæt hi næfre song   sellan ne hyrdon. (106-8)

(Then many men, proud in mind, those who had expert understanding,
said that they never heard a better song.)

The final catalogue lists the places and people he has visited rather than
served, and Widsith's monologue concludes with the maxim that the best
ruler is the one that God appoints. The narrator rounds off the poem with
a brief but illuminating description of the function of the *scop*: his life is
one of travelling through many lands, yet he will always find a ruler:

se þe fore duguþe wile   dom aræran,
eorlscipe æfnan,   oþþæt eal scæceð,
leoht ond lif somod;   lof se gewyrceð,
hafað under heofonum   heahfæstne dom. (140-3)

(who in the presence of veterans wishes to exalt his glory, show his dig-
nity, until all passes away, light and life together. He gains praise and will
have lofty glory under the heavens.)

This is the traditional function of the Germanic *scop*—one who creates
immortality for his patron in this earth, giving him the ultimate gift of
dom through his songs in exchange for treasure. It is not surprising that
the trademark of the *scop,* namely the lyre, should be found in the Sutton
Hoo burial ship amidst all the essential items for the hero in the afterlife.
Poets were more than mere entertainers, they could make or break one's
reputation and give or withhold immortality. *Widsith,* therefore, is not
about one *scop*—it provides us with inside information about the repertoire, the mnemonic tricks, the social function and the journeyings of this
important trade. For a price the church would ensure one's *dom* 'glory' in
the next world, but the *scop* would keep one's memory and deeds of
valour alive in this life.

Another important and recurring figure in Germanic myth is Walter of Aquitaine. The legend appears in its most extensive form in the
early 10th-century Latin poem *Waltharius,* while other versions are to be
found, for example, in Italy (11th century) and Germany (13th century)
and there are references to this tale, obviously well-known in the Germanic world, in *Þíðrekssaga* and the *Niebelungenlied.* The traditional
legend is about how Walter of Aquitaine and Hildegyth, held hostage by
Attila the Hun, manage to escape and in so doing take treasure with them.
This treasure attracts the attention of Guthhere (or Guntharius), King of
the Franks, and Hagena, a fellow hostage, who attack them in a bloody

battle in which Walter loses an arm, Guthhere a leg and Hagena an eye. Walter and Hildegyth manage to escape and return home where they marry; Walter becomes King of Aquitaine and the story has a happy end.

The Old English version, called *Waldere*, is incomplete, preserved in two vellum fragments of the late 10th century that are themselves damaged (Zettersten, 1979). The 63-line fragment was discovered in 1860 in the Royal Library, Copenhagen, and its physical state poses many problems: who is speaking when and which leaf comes first? One of the fragments contains a speech of heroic encouragement to Waldere, probably by Hildegyth, to fight bravely and trust in his sword Mimming, made by the famous Weland. The speech contains traditional heroic exhortations to fight bravely, for example:

> ... is se dæg cumen
> þæt ðu scealt aninga   oðer twega
> lif forleosan   oððe l[..]gne dom
> agan mid eldum,   Ælfheres sunu. (8-11)

(The day has come when you must do one of two things: lose your life or achieve lasting(?) glory amongst men, son of Ælfhere.)

He must never falter or show cowardice, but honour himself with good deeds. She also warns him against being too rash (*"to fyrenlice"*) and there is an echo of the proud behaviour of Byrhtnoth of *The Battle of Maldon* in the fears she has of his pride tempting him to give an advantage to his opponent. "Fight bravely, but don't be too rash" is her advice.

The initial section of the second fragment might be spoken by any of the four protagonists, as it discusses the history of the treasure that has been taken from Attila. Waldere's remarks to Guthhere conclude this fragment: he challenges Guthhere and boasts of the power of his famous armour, Ælfere's legacy; he who trusts in God will win the day. The highly rhetorical and conventional speeches suggest that the poem was an original Old English version of the myth, but from this meagre material we cannot tell the length or genre of the poem. We have then by pure chance a tiny fragment of a genuinely heroic Old English poem, the type of poetry, perhaps, that Alcuin of York criticised the clerical community for listening to.

The stylized, heroic speeches of *Waldere* echo those of the two great battle poems in Old English: *The Battle of Brunanburh* and *The Battle of Maldon*, both of the late 10th century. Just as Hildegyth encourages Waldere to gain eternal glory by valiantly fighting, so the *Brunanburh* poet states that King Æthelstan and his brother Eadmund

```
                    ealdorlangne tir
  geslogon æt sæcce  sweorda ecgum
  ymbe Brunanburh              (3-5)
```

(won life-long glory by their swords' edges at the battle round Brunanburh.)

Brunanburh (Campbell, 1938) appears in four manuscripts of the Anglo-
Saxon Chronicle at the date 937 and begins "*Her*" ('here' or 'in this year')
just like the chronicle's prose entries. There are six poems in versions of
the Chronicle: *The Capture of the Five Boroughs*, which honours Edmund's victory over the Norse in 942, *The Coronation of Edgar* (973 and
14 years after his accession), *The Death of Edgar* (975), *the Death of
Alfred* (1036), about the murder of Æthelred's son by Earl Godwine, and
The Death of Edward (1066). There are other late Old English entries in
annals that might be termed poetic, but have often been called "degener-
ate" late Old English verse. Michael Alexander (1983:209) states that
"each of these pieces is more feeble in content than the last, and the verse
itself finally crumbles into prose adulterated with rhyme." It should be
noted, however, that there is no clear-cut difference visually or audibly
between the alliterative and rhetorical prose such as one finds in the sermons of Ælfric and Wulfstan and what is traditionally considered poetry
and we have no evidence that the authors of these works were deliberately
seeking to write traditional poetry.

　　Unlike the other poems we have looked at, the events in *Brunanburh*
appear to be historically accurate. The poem relates how King Æthelstan
of Wessex and his sixteen-year-old brother Eadmund, grandsons of
Alfred, led the armies of Wessex and Mercia against the joint forces of the
Scots under Constantine, the Strathclyde Britons under Owen and the
Vikings from Dublin under Olaf, son of the king of Dublin. The English
success was decisive for the West Saxons, as it led to greater unification of
England under the leadership of Wessex. Alfred's dream of a unified
country was now being fulfilled by his illustrious grandsons. It is clearly a
work that contains strong patriotic feelings and it makes excellent propaganda.

　　The location of the battle is uncertain, but it is thought to be near
the Irish Sea, anywhere from Chester to Dumfries in Scotland, but possibly near the estuary of the Mersey. *Dingesmere* (line 54) is however still
unlocated. The fact that such a battle did indeed take place is supported by
other annals and, as the poem found its way into the Chronicle around
955, it must have been written soon after the event. Whether it was meant
for inclusion in the Chronicle is uncertain, as the initial "*her*" is not
metrically essential. John Pope (1966:55) suggests that the poem's

ardor suggests that the battle had occurred very recently; its self-sufficiency, that it was designed as an independent piece; yet its perspective and its concerns are not far removed from those that govern the Chronicle.

The poem begins with the routing of the enemy: five young kings lay dead, Olaf (Anlaf) was put to flight over the sea again and Constantine, whom the poet generously calls 'wise', fled back to the north, having lost his son and kinsmen in battle. "He had little cause to boast about that battle" (ll.44-5). The poet then returns to the fighting of the day which he describes in stock phrases of spears clashing, weapons contending and banners meeting on the field of battle, not to mention the ubiquitous beasts and birds of battle:

> Letan him behindan   hræ bryttian
> saluwigpadan,   þone sweartan hræfn,
> hyrnednebban,   and þane hasupadan,
> earn æftan hwit,   æses brucan
> grædigne guðhafoc,   and þæt græge deor,
> wulf on wealde.   (60-5)

(They left behind them corpses for the black-coated, horny-beaked black raven to share, and the dun-plumaged white-tailed eagle to enjoy the carrion, that greedy war-hawk, and the grey beast, the forest wolf.)

The poem abounds in metaphor and kenning such as "*hamora lafan*" (l.6) 'the remnants of the hammer' for 'sword', but, although it has been called "a tissue of heroic formulaic cliché, themes and stylistic variation" (Greenfield and Calder, 1986:148), it functions well as a poem that celebrates a great national victory in traditional language. Malcolm Godden comments on resemblances between *Brunanburh* and the battle of Abraham against Lot's enemies in *Genesis A*, for here the northern enemies are defeated by the heroic force that had God on their side. (Godden, 1991: 210). The deliberately archaic style of *Brunanburh* is fitting in a poem that wishes us to compare this 'modern' victory with those of the first Germanic invaders. Æthelstan and Eadmund's success in managing to remove their joint opponents from English soil is significantly compared at the conclusion to the great victory when the Angles and Saxons came across the sea and defeated the Welsh:

>   Ne wearð wæl mare
> on þis eiglande   æfre gieta
> folces gefylled   beforan þissum
> sweordes ecgum,   þæs þe us secgað bec,

> ealde uðwitan,   siþþan eastan hider
> Engle and Seaxe   up becoman,
> ofer brad brimu   Brytene sohtan,
> wlance wigsmiþas,   Wealas ofercoman,
> eorlas arhwate   eard begeatan.   (65-73)

> (Nor has there ever been greater slaughter of folk in this island before this,
> felled by the sword's edge, as books tell us, ancient authorities, since
> hither from the east the Angles and Saxons arrived over the wide sea to
> seek the land of Britain, the proud war-smiths, conquered the Welsh, and,
> keen for glory, gained the land.)

There is also a sense of excitement about the poet's enthusiasm for the great victory. This was an age when it was politically expedient for the West Saxons and Mercians to associate themselves with their Saxon and Anglian forefathers. The poet seems to imply that the English are now claiming their rightful inheritance from the same Celtic peoples whom their forefathers defeated. The stereotype imagery evokes the heroic period of the great Germanic victories and thereby links past and present. It is, as John Pope claims, "a royal panegyric".

One passage that shows the poet's originality also demonstrates his desire to underline the magnitude of the victory in a setting even greater than the national:

> Feld dænnede
> secga swate,   siðþan sunne up
> on morgentid,   mære tungol,
> glæd over grundas,   godes condel beorht,
> eces drihtnes,   oð sio æþele gesceaft
> sah to setle.   (12-17)

> (The field was wet with the blood of men, from the time in the morning
> when the sun rises, that glorious star, glided over the earth, the bright
> candle of God, the eternal lord, till the noble creation sank to rest.)

This victory, he implies, should be seen in a cosmic and spiritual context, while the elevated and archaic style, deliberately artificial, stresses the importance of the occasion and raises this victory to the heroic stature of the immortal battles of Old Testament narrative and heroic epic. There is, however, no attempt made to create a hero of flesh and blood, who has choices to make and is subject to fate and the tensions of life. In this way *Brunanburh* is a fitting chronicle poem.

Another great battle that mirrors the heroic resistance of the English against invasion is *The Battle of Maldon* (Gordon, 1937; Scragg, 1981; Scragg and Deegan, 1991). There is only brief mention of it in a few versions of the Chronicle for the year 991: they mention that an ealdorman of Essex, Byrhtnoth, was killed by Vikings at Maldon and that thereafter tribute or Danegeld was paid to the Danish invaders. At face value it does not look promising material for a great heroic poem to honour the English, as not only are they defeated, but the dreaded Danegeld that drained the country of much of its revenue seems to have been initiated as a consequence. Yet it has become the most popular Old English battle poem and, with its millennium in 1991, the centre of much scholarly activity.

It is again by pure chance that *Maldon* survives, as its unique manuscript, Cotton Otho A xii, was badly burned in the fire of 1731 and the poem totally destroyed. The fire in Ashburnham House, Westminster, severely damaged Sir Robert Cotton's great collection of manuscripts, including *Beowulf*. A transcript of the poem had been made in just a few years before the fire by either John Elphinston or David Casley and printed by Thomas Hearne in 1725. It would appear that the poem was incomplete when transcribed, with both the beginning and end missing.

From this poem and two Latin prose works, *The Life of Oswald* and *The Book of Ely*, it would appear that Byrhtnoth achieved the stature of a local martyr and great hero in East Anglia (see Blake, 1978; Clark, 1968; Doane, 1978). The facts surrounding the event, as far as one can determine from other sources, are as follows. The Viking Olaf, probably Olaf Tryggvason, later King of Norway, came with a large fleet of ships to Folkestone and worked his way round the coast and eventually up the Blackwater estuary, called the Panta in the poem, disembarking on the island of Northey. The island has a narrow, tidal causeway linking it to the mainland, but the ealdorman Byrhtnoth stopped the Vikings leaving the island by blocking the causeway. This is the point at which the poem begins. A Viking messenger taunts the English by demanding tribute, which Byrhtnoth heroically refuses. Three of Byrhtnoth's men easily block the causeway even at low tide and the first "pirate" who sets foot on it is killed.[1] Then comes the much disputed section:

> ongunnon lytegian þa   laðe gystas,
> bædon þæt hi upgang   agan moston,
> ofer þone ford faran,   feþan lædan.
> Ða se eorl ongan   for his ofermode
> alyfan landes to fela   laþere ðeode.
> Ongan ceallian þa   ofer cald wæter
> Byrhtelmes bearn   (beornas gehlyston):

---

[1] As Christine Fell (1986) has demonstrated, OE *wicing* probably means 'pirate'.

"Nu eow is gerymed,   gað ricene to us,
guman to guþe;   god ana wat
hwa þære wælstowe   wealdan mote." (86-95)

(The hateful strangers began to use guile, they demanded that they should
have access to come over the ford, to lead the infantry over. Then the earl
[Byrhtnoth] in his pride yielded too much land to the hateful people. The
son of Byrhthelm [Byrhtnoth] called over cold water (the soldiers listened):
"Now is space made for you, come quickly to us, men to battle. God alone
knows who will control the battlefield.")

The two disputed phrases are "*ongunnon lytegian*" and "*for ofermode*".
The former implies that the Vikings used some kind of trick, treachery or
guile, but it could just be that they taunted the English into giving them
more room to fight by saying that the English could only win if the
Vikings were trapped on the island, and never in an equal fight. Byrhtnoth's decision to grant them this request comes from his *ofermod* a word
which is generally translated as 'pride' in the negative sense as it is used
elsewhere in the poetic corpus to translate the *superbia* of Lucifer. Critics
have tried to excuse him by calling it "extreme or excessive courage",
"over-confidence", but there are no other examples in Old English of this
word used in a morally positive sense (cf. Gneuss, 1976b; Robinson,
1979). We might recall Hildegyth's fear in *Waldere* that her hero might
show off in battle: "You have too outrageously searched out battle on the
other man's premises", she exclaims. Exactly the same might be said about
Byrhtnoth and his predicament reflects a central problem for the Germanic hero. In order to achieve fame and everlasting glory he must perform feats of bravery that will go down in history. The temptation must
be great to do the outrageous, to take incredible chances in the hope of
astounding all and creating heroic possibilities. Had Byrhtnoth refused to
allow the Vikings access to the mainland, thereby beating them by starving
them out, his name would not go down in history. But this act of outrageous pride that was to lead to the English defeat is indeed an act of personal heroism, akin to Beowulf's decision to fight the dragon on his own.
In any century some of the most memorable deeds in wartime might well
be classed as verging on the mad and irresponsible (cf. Swanton, 1968 and
1977; Gneuss, 1976a).

At no other point is there the slightest suggestion from the poet that
the hero was to blame. Far from it; this act of *hubris* provides an opportunity for him and his loyal men to show text-book heroic behaviour. In
order to highlight their exemplary prowess, the poet paints the other side
of the coin in the shape of the cowards who forget their promises of
loyalty, fail their leader and flee to the woods. Just as the *Beowulf*-poet
praised the magnanimity of Hrothgar by comparing him with the nig-
gardly Heremod, or the valour of Beowulf by contrasting him with the

ignominious Unferth, so also the loyal retainers of Byrhtnoth appear all the more valiant when contrasted with Godric. The characters are very much types and their speeches are text-book examples of legendary heroes proclaiming their loyalty. It is otherwise difficult to imagine leaderless men about to be slaughtered having the time in the turmoil of the battle field for such set speeches.

Byrhtnoth is initially successful, hacking down Danes and encouraging his men to concentrate on the battle, those "*þe on Denon wolde dom gefeohtan*" (l.129), 'who wished to gain glory by fighting the Danes' (cf. Woolf, 1976). Even when struck by a spear he manages to kill his assailant and laugh:

> Se eorl wæs þe bliþra,
> hloh þa, modi man,   sæde metode þanc
> ðæs dægweorces   þe him Drihten forgeaf. (146-8)

(The earl [Byrhtnoth] was the happier; he laughed, the courageous man, and gave thanks to the Lord for the day's work that the Lord had granted him.)

After his death Godric and his brothers Godwine and Godwig flee, forgetting the gifts and favours Byrhtnoth had given them. Even worse, Godric fled on his lord's horse, causing confusion in the battle, as many thought it was Byrhtnoth escaping. In contrast, the remaining thanes encourage each other one by one by moving speeches of loyalty. Leofsunu will avenge his lord and friend, and even a Northumbrian hostage pledges allegiance to the cause. They will fight to the death, avenge their lord, keep their word and encourage others to do likewise. The veteran Byrhtwold's exhortation is often quoted as the epitome of heroism (see Caie, 1976):

> "Hige sceal þe heardra,   heorte þe cenre,
> mod sceal þe mare,   þe ure mægen lytlað.
> Her lið ure ealdor   eall forheawen,
> god on greote.   A mæg gnornian
> se ðe nu fram þis wigplegan   wendan þenceð.
> Ic eom frod feores;   fram ic ne wille,
> ac ic me be healfe   minum hlaforde,
> be swa leofan men,   licgan þence." (312-19)

("The mind must be the tougher, the heart the keener, the courage must be greater, as our strength diminishes. Here lies our leader slaughtered, the good man in the dust. He who is considering leaving this battle will forever regret it. I am aged; I will not go away, but I intend to lie beside my lord, by so dear a man.")

In addition to the Germanic sentiments expressed in *Maldon* the poet is equally at pains to stress Byrhtnoth's Christian faith, a faith that in the later Latin works mentioned above places him on a level with martyr saints.

Many critics indeed have interpreted *Maldon* as a Christian allegory of the battle between good and evil with Byrhtnoth sacrificing himself. It is true that Wulfstan and other homilists cast the Danes in the role of the devil's party, come to afflict the wayward English. The Danes here, for example, are "heathens", "slaughterous wolves", "hellish assailants" and "fiends" (cf. Cross, 1965). The same spirit and language is found in the description of the heroes and heroines of the religious verse who risk all to fight for nation and religion. And Byrhtnoth does indeed achieve immortality by his sacrifice, while the virtues he and his men display are both heroic and Christian—courage in the face of adversity, love of one's lord and a willingness to fight for him, loyalty, and a desire for *dom*, the heroic reputation and Christian glory. Byrhtnoth's final speech might well be that of a dying martyr:

"Geþancie þe,   ðeoda waldend,
ealra þæra wynna   þe ic on worulde gebad.
Nu ic ah, milde metod,   mæste þearfe
þæt þu minum gaste   godes geunne,
þæt min sawul to þe   siðian mote
on þin geweald,   þeoden engla,
mid friþe ferian.   Ic eom frymdi to þe
þæt hi helsceaðan   hynan ne moton."   (173-180)

("I thank you, Ruler of nations, for all the joys that I have enjoyed on earth. Now my greatest need, merciful Lord, is that you grant to my spirit the grace that my soul may journey to you, into your power and come forth with peace. I beg you not to let the devils harm it.")

S.A.J. Bradley (1982:519) sums up the central tensions in the poem thus:

this strategic defeat of the English was a victory of the national spirit. Byrhtnoth testifies to his oneness with his people, with his land, with his lord the king; he witnesses to his Christian faith in defiance of heathendom and, dying, commends his soul to God. His men in turn testify to their oneness with him and thereby witness to their participation in the same total integrity of secular and spiritual values. ... But though, perhaps for calculated propagandist reasons, the poet appeals to the heroics of Germanic antiquity—and thus sends scholars looking to the *Germania* of Tacitus—he is even more strikingly forward-looking, even medieval, in his integration of these heroics with the motives of Church, Crown and country.

Almost as long a period of time separates Tacitus and Byrhtnoth as divides Byrhtnoth from us, and the late 10th- and 11th-century audiences must have realized that the bloody skirmishes with marauding Danes were a far cry from the heroic Germanic ideals of *Maldon*. But in times of national disaster, as this indeed was, such propaganda is necessary to promote values such as national pride and Christian belief, the determination to oust intruding forces and to combat heathenism. Modern propaganda at the time of war—the nationalistic songs and flag-waving—is no less crude. There will always be the foolhardy who gain a posthumous medal, those who gain glory by dying young at the moment of great personal bravery or fame, and those who flee.

We have, then, scraps and fragments of what we call heroic verse in Old English, and yet we think of it as containing the quintessential spirit of Anglo-Saxon times. We will never know if the paucity of material is because the earlier secular verse was never written down, if it was deliberately destroyed or whether it never existed to any extent in England. It is curious that the best known examples of what we like to call the Germanic ideal occur at the end of the Anglo-Saxon period, just before the Conquest. Its emergence in the 10th century, as witnessed in *Brunanburh*, is undoubtedly connected with political needs of the Saxon rulers to create a united kingdom by claiming a common Germanic heritage with a great past and ideals of loyalty to God and the king. It nourished a sense of nostalgia for a time of fixed beliefs when men could be heroes and heroes were immortal. A time that never was—yet will be forever.

REFERENCES

Alexander, Michael (1983). *Old English Literature*. Macmillan History of Literature. London: Macmillan.
Anderson, George K. (1966). *The Literature of the Anglo-Saxons*. Princeton, NJ.
Blake, Norman (1978). The Genesis of *The Battle of Maldon*. *Anglo-Saxon England* 7. 119-29.
Bradley, S.A.J. (tr. & ed.) (1982). *Anglo-Saxon Poetry*. London: Dent.
Caie, Graham D. (1976). *The Judgement Day Theme in Old English Poetry*. Copenhagen: Nova.
Calder, D.G. *et al.* (1983). *Sources and Analogues of Old English Poetry*. II. *The Major Germanic and Celtic Texts in Translation*. Cambridge: D.S. Brewer, and Totowa, NJ: Barnes and Noble.
Campbell, A. (ed.) (1938). *The Battle of Brunanburh*. London: Heinemann.
Clark, G. (1968). *The Battle of Maldon:* A Heroic Poem. *Speculum* 43. 52-71.

Cross, J.E. (1965). Oswald and Byrhtnoth: A Christian Saint and a Hero who is a Christian. *English Studies* 46. 93-109.

Doane, A.N. (1978). Legend, History and Artifice in *The Battle of Maldon. Viator* 9. 39-66.

Dobbie, E. Van K. (ed.) (1942). *The Anglo-Saxon Minor Poems.* The Anglo-Saxon Poetic Records, vol. VI. New York: Columbia University Press.

Eliason, Norman E. (1969). *Deor* — A Begging Poem? In: *Medieval Literature and Civilisation: Studies in Memory of G.N. Garmonsworthy.* Ed. Derek Pearsall and Ronald Waldron. London: Athlone Press. 55-61.

Fell, Christine (1986). Old English *wicing*: A Question of Semantics. *Proceedings of the British Academy* 72. 295-316.

Frank, Roberta (1991). Germanic Legend in Old English Literature. In: Godden and Lapidge, 1991:88-106.

Gneuss, H. (1976a). *Die Battle of Maldon als historisches und literarisches Zeugnis.* Bayerische Akademie der Wissenschaften, Philos.-hist. Klasse, Sitzungsberichte 1976, no. 5. Munich.

Gneuss, H. (1976b). *The Battle of Maldon* 89: Byrhtnoth's *ofermod* Once Again. *Studies in Philology* 73. 117-37.

Godden, Malcolm, and Michael Lapidge (eds.) (1991). *Cambridge Companion to Old English Literature.* Cambridge: Cambridge University Press.

Gordon, E.V. (ed.) (1937). *The Battle of Maldon.* Methuen's Old English Library. London: Methuen.

Greenfield, S.B., and Daniel Calder (1986). *A New Critical History of Old English Literature.* New York: New York University Press.

Hill, Joyce (1981). Soldiers of Christ in OE Prose and Poetry. *Leeds Studies in English* 12. 57-80.

Howe, Nicholas (1985). *The Old English Catalogue Poems.* Anglistica 23. Copenhagen: Rosenkilde and Bagger.

Howe, Nicholas (1989). *Migration and Mythmaking in Anglo-Saxon England.* New Haven, CT: Yale University Press.

Malone, Kemp (ed.) (1962). *Widsith.* Copenhagen: Rosenkilde and Bagger.

Mattingly, H. (tr.) (1948). *Tacitus: On Britain and Germany.* Harmondsworth: Penguin.

O'Keefe, Katherine O'Brien (1991). Heroic Values and Christian Ethics. In: Godden and Lapidge, 1991:107-125.

Pope, John C. (ed.) (1966). *Seven Old English Poems.* The Library of Literature. Indianapolis: The Bobbs-Merrill Co.

Robinson, Fred C. (1979). God, Death, and Loyalty in *The Battle of Maldon.* In: *J.R.R. Tolkien, Scholar and Storyteller.* Ed. M. Salu and R.T. Farrell. Ithaca, NY, and London: Cornell University Press. 76-98.

Rollman, David (1982). *Widsith* as an Anglo-Saxon Defence of Poetry. *Neophilologus* 66. 431-439.

Scragg, D. (ed.) (1981). *The Battle of Maldon.* Manchester: Manchester University Press.

Scragg, D. (ed.) (1991). *The Battle of Maldon A.D. 991.* Oxford: Blackwell.

Shippey, T.A. (1972). *Old English Verse.* London: Hutchinson.

Stanley, E.G. (1975). *The Search for Anglo-Saxon Paganism.* Cambridge: D.S. Brewer, and Totowa, NJ: Rowman and Littlefield.

Swanton, Michael J. (1968). *The Battle of Maldon:* A Literary Caveat. *Journal of English and Germanic Philology* 67. 441-50.

Swanton, Michael J. (1977). Heroes, Heroism and Heroic Literature. *Essays and Studies by members of the English Association.* 30. 1-21.

Wilson, R.M. (1952). *The Lost Literature of Medieval England.* London: Methuen.

Woolf, R. (1976). The Ideal of Men Dying with their Lord in the *Germania* and in *The Battle of Maldon. Anglo-Saxon England* 5. 63-81.

Zettersten, Arne (ed.) (1979). *Waldere.* Manchester: Manchester University Press.

SNAKES AND LADDERS:
AMBIGUITY AND COHERENCE
IN THE EXETER BOOK RIDDLES AND MAXIMS

WIM TIGGES

In a very interesting and compellingly coherent account of Old English poetry, *The Guest-Hall of Eden*, Alvin Lee cogently illuminates the thesis that "most old English poetry reflects, in varying degrees, an imaginative unity—not a uniformity or a monotony—that is at once heroic, Germanic, didactic, *and* Christian" (Lee, 1972:6). "The Old English poetic records", he concludes, "are best approached as an environment of images" (156), whereby "a firmly established Old English poetic image for God's earthly Creation is that of the world as a dryht-hall" (142).

Although Lee covers a wide area of Anglo-Saxon poetry, including not only the Biblical narratives, saints' lives, elegies and *Beowulf*, but also representatives of the so-called "Wisdom poetry", he is almost entirely silent about the maxims or gnomes, and to the Exeter Book Riddles (henceforth EBR) he does not refer at all. This is curious, because the riddles and maxims are not only arguably heroic, Germanic, didactic, and Christian, they are, if anything, *the* environment of images *par excellence*. I suspect a major reason why Lee left them out of account is their apparent lack of unity. In this essay, I intend to introduce the reader to the riddles and maxims, which together cover about 1630 lines of verse, i.e. more than 5 percent of the extant corpus, by concentrating on their structural and individual coherence. In section I below, I will discuss the EBR in terms of their unity-in-variety, and individual texts will be briefly elucidated with an eye to the special problems caused by their inherent riddling ambiguity in arriving at viable solutions. Section II will deal more succinctly with the associative devices of the maxims, concentrating on those in the Exeter Book.

I

"*Is þes middangeard missenlicum / wisum gewlitegad, wrættum gefræt-wad*" (ll.1-2: 'This middle-earth has been variously beautified, splendidly adorned'; EBR 29 [31] and 30 [32]).[1] Thus the riddlers of the Exeter Book

---

[1] Numbering of all riddles as in Williamson (1977), followed by the traditional numbers as in Krapp-Dobbie (1936) between square brackets. All quotations are as in Williamson's standard edition, and translations are my own.

begin two consecutive items, the first of which proceeds to describe what
is apparently a bagpipe, the second what may apply to a ship but also to a
wheelbarrow. Unlike with Aldhelm's collection of Latin *ænigmata*, no
answers are provided for the Old English compilation. Hence, the very
diversity of the solutions suggested and argued in fairly modern times may
remind the reader of poor Hamlet's inability to distinguish a hawk from a
handsaw unless the wind was southerly, or else of the mad confusion of
items such as shoes and ships and sealing-wax, or cabbages and kings, in
Alice's adventures in the wonderlands of nonsense. If a single text of a
mere fourteen lines already causes scholars to disagree as to whether it
describes a ship or a wheelbarrow (or a mill-stone!), what method is there
in this madness of some ninety-odd Anglo-Saxon poems that individually
invite guesses about such various topics as swans and swords, shirts and
ships, onions and oysters, kings and crosses, books, bells, buckets, bul-
locks, beehives and barnacles? As to the individual riddle 30 [32], it might
perhaps be helpful to reformulate the riddle as a conundrum: why is a ship
like a wheelbarrow (or a mill-stone)? But if Alice, with her Victorian
addiction to riddles, was unable to find the answer to the Mad Hatter's
question "Why is a raven like a writing-desk?", to which the Hatter
himself confessed he did not know the answer either, who are we to play
word-games devised by Anglo-Saxon rune-masters in the eighth century,
and apparently still appreciated in the late tenth, when the Exeter Book
was compiled, and still later by Bishop Leofric of Exeter, who is assumed
to have bequeathed the codex to his Cathedral Library when he died in
1072?[2]

The list of Leofric's donations contains a reference, most likely to
our codex, as "*.i. mycel Englisc boc be gehwilcum þingum on leoðwisum
geworht*" ('one big book in English on various matters, composed in
verse'; Williamson, 1977:3). This clearly suggests the miscellaneous nature of the Exeter Book, which contains such "various matters" as the Advent lyrics of *Christ I*, a saint's life (*Guthlac*), the heroic *Widsith*, the

---

2 For a more extensive description of the Exeter Book, see the Introductions to Krapp-
Dobbie (1936:ix-lxxxviii, esp. ix-xvi) and Williamson (1977:3-28, esp. 3-12). An early,
extensive discussion of the riddles which is still generally acclaimed can be found in three
articles by Trautmann in *Anglia* (1914), which also provide detailed information on the
language of the poems in question. A more general introduction, providing linguistic
information as well, is Hacikyan (1966:1-41). Hacikyan also includes a list of proposed
solutions (1966:63-72). For more updated lists, see Fry (1981) and Göbel (1980:57-65).
Extensive bibliographies are to be found in Williamson (1977:467-82) and Pinsker &
Ziegler (1985:404-19), and see the relevant sections in the *Old English Newsletter*. Williamson and Pinsker & Ziegler present comprehensive and argumentative commentaries on
individual riddles. For sources and analogues, see Calder & Allen (1976: 162-74). Göbel
(1980:12-16) gives the solutions to the Latin riddle collections of Symphosius, Aldhelm,
Tatwine and Eusebius.

major elegies, and lots of bits and pieces concerning human gifts, fortunes and wisdom. The riddles are found in three groups near the end of the codex: numbers 1-57 (in Williamson's numbering) are on fols. 101a-115a, a variant of riddle 28 and riddle 58 on fols. 122b-123a, and numbers 59-91 on the unfortunately badly damaged fols. 124b-130b. With the exception then of the middle group of two items (but see note 3 below), the riddles were placed together in sequences rather than being randomly scattered over the manuscript. As some folios are clearly missing (as can be ascertained from gaps in the text), and as the Latin riddle collections tended to comprise round numbers of 100, 60 or 40 items, it may not be too speculative to assume that at some stage in the compilation an "editor" was trying to either eke out an existant collection from the smaller to the greater number, or to make up a native collection by culling items from the native (oral?) as well as from the learned Latin (written) tradition, until an orderly figure of one hundred was reached. The final group in particular has a few mysterious one- and two-liners (Krapp-Dobbie 66, 67, 75, 76 and 79) and an item in Latin (86 [90]), which may be evidence of hurried half-recollection as the compilation neared its completion. Since we do not know exactly how many leaves are missing, and as the riddles differ greatly in length (the longest ran to at least 108 lines, the average length is about 15 lines), we cannot be certain of all the facts.[3]

Taking into account Williamson's remarks (1977:23-4) that there is

---

[3] Krapp-Dobbie (1936:xii) indicate gaps between fols. 105 and 106 and between 111 and 112 "of one or more folios". They also state there that gatherings XV, XVI and XVII "appear never to have had more than their present number of folios", i.e. 7, 7 and 5 respectively. A complete gathering would normally contain eight folios. No gap occurs between gatherings XV and XVI, which would have shown in the text of the poem *Resignation*. As gathering XIV (fols. 106-111) has only six folios, a loss of two sheets would account for this shortage, and gathering XV would remain one short. Williamson (1977:336-8) has convincingly demonstrated a gap in the text of riddle [70], which he renumbers as 67 and 68. This would account for gathering XVI. Gathering XVII, which ends the manuscript, may have lost up to three final folios, but then these might have contained a new text.

Riddles which are textually deficient because of such missing folios are 18 [20] (19 [21] appears to be complete at its beginning), 38 [40] and 39 [41], and 67 and 68 [70]. I assume, with Goldsmith (1975), that item 58 [60] is not a riddle at all, but serves to introduce *The Husband's Message*, which follows it in the manuscript. To her arguments, which are shared by Pinsker & Ziegler (1985:283-4), I would add the point that the dual used in ll.15 and 17 of the poem would exceptionally include the reader as addressee, whereas all other instances of the dual in riddles express the togetherness of two aspects of the riddle-topic (cf. e.g. riddles 61 [63].5b, 70 [72]. 4b, 81 [85].2b and 7a, 84 [88].11bff.). So, if Williamson's numbering is correct, and with riddle 58 [60] discarded, we have 85 complete and five incomplete riddles; fols. 94-130 contain 22 ruled lines (Krapp-Dobbie, 1936:xii), with an average of 32.5 verses per page or 65 per folio. If four folios are missing, this would account for the loss of some 260 lines to represent five completions and ten missing riddles, to make up a total of 100.

no evidence of an Anglo-Saxon tradition of "social riddling", that the Latin riddles are "a far cry" from the Old English ones, and that there is very
little influence from the Latin riddles upon the Old English, a superficial
glance at the "organisation" of such collections as those by the Italian
Symphosius and the West-Saxon Aldhelm (see Göbel, 1980:12-16) shows
that there is a fairly close resemblance with that of the EBR. Aldhelm, for
instance, although he starts out, after a clever double acrostic preface in
praise of the "Arbiter" who ordains all of Creation, by describing such
large and general phenomena as Earth, Wind, Cloud, Nature, Rainbow,
Moon and Fate (I-VII), soon comes down to earth and collocates such
diverse topics as a dog, a bellows and a silk-worm (X-XII), salt, a bee and
a file (XIX-XXI), or a stork, writing-tablets and a cuirass (XXXI-III)[4]. In
fact, Aldhelm's *Ænigmata*, written around 700 in the late Latin tradition
which F.H. Whitman (1970:179-80) ascribes to "a gradual degeneration in
poetic sensibility", are organized according to length rather than subject-
matter: most of the first twenty items run to four hexameters, increasing
to five for the next 18, and gradually lengthening to some ten lines or
more in most of the final fifteen items; a lengthy (83-line) *ænigma* C on
Nature (*Creatura*) concludes the collection.

In the EBR too, there are some very lengthy items, each of which
comprehensively describes Nature, Creation or "the creative principle"
(water?). Riddle 1 [1-3] is solved as Storm and runs to 104 lines; 38 [40],
solved as Creation or Water, breaks off at line 108, and 80 [84], Water,
although heavily mutilated by its opposing element burning a hole into the
manuscript, amounts to 56 lines. Pinsker & Ziegler (1985:246) refer to
such poems as "*Lehrgedichte*" (didactic poems) rather than riddles proper,
but of course this would be equally valid for Aldhelm's hundredth. All
three of them contain various references to the Creator. Riddle 1 [1-3] in
fact opens with the challenge "*Hwylc is hæleþa þæs horsc ond þæs hyge-
cræftig / þæt þæt mæge asecgan, hwa mec on sið wræce ...*" ('Who, of
men, is so clever and so wise that he can tell who drives me on my journey'; ll.1-2). The "me", of course, is the object to be ultimately guessed,
but the "who" is the Prime Mover behind this terribly forceful and vari-
able creature. Similarly, riddle 38 [40] starts out with the formulaic
phrase "*Ece is se scyppend*" ('Eternal is the Creator'), and the creature
Water of riddle 80 [84] refers to the Trinity ("*fæder*", l.9b, "*sunu, / ...
meotudes bearn*", ll.10b-11a, and what is likely to be correctly recon-
structed as "*[halg]es [g]æ[stes]*", l.12b). These three long riddles, accounting for 268 out of the extant 1345 lines, are riddled with allusions to the
Creator. The Storm refers to Him as its "*latteow*" ('leader'; l.12b) and its

---

[4] For the text of Aldhelm's riddles, with Introduction and Notes, see Pitman (1925).

"*frea*" ('Lord'; ll.31b, 96b). In 38 [40] the appellations found are "*rec-cend*" ('ruler', 'caretaker'; l.3a) and "*cyning*" ('king'; l.3b), "*anwalda*" ('monarch'; l.4a), "*dryhten*" ('warlord'; l.12b), "*waldend*" ('ruler'; ll.14a, 89b), "*leof fæder*" ('dear Father'; l.34a) and "*heahcyning*" ('high king'; l.38b).

Besides these three, eleven more riddles contain references to the power that created their subjects. They are well-spread over the collection, and the objects to be guessed are usually particularly revered ones, such as the sun (4 [6]), a Bible (24 [26] and 65 [67]), a paten or chalice (46 [48] and 57 [59]), a crucifix or cross-shaped sword-box (53 [55]), but also more humble creations such as the ten chickens of riddle 11 [13], which are said to be roused by the powers of "*rodra weardes*" ('the guardian of the skies'; l.7b), a fish in a river (81 [85]) and an inkhorn (84 [88]). To the mysterious creature of riddle 37 [39], which is reported as being obliged to live in accordance with "*wuldorcyninges / larum*" ('the doctrines of the king of glory'; ll.21b-22a), I will return later on. The point to be stressed here is that apparently on average once in every six or seven items the reader is explicitly referred to the Maker of all those "*wundorlice wiht*" ('wondrous creatures'). It is, if the comparison may be permitted, as if we are here holding on to the bottom of a ladder on God's game-board.

Of those riddles exceeding twenty lines, and which do not unambiguously deal with Christian topics, the most notable are 13 [15], 18 [20], 20 [22] and 37 [39]. These frequently remind us of the snakes along whose backs we find ourselves sliding down time and again to square one. As with the longer religious riddles, the scope of these items allows for the appreciation of such characteristic Old English poetic elements as variation, the kenning, and elegiac musings. Irrespective of whether one interprets riddle 13 [15] as the description of a fox or of a badger, one is struck by the prevalence of kennings, metaphorical coinages mostly derived here from the heroic register. Thus, the animal's claws are referred to as "*beadowæpen*" ('weapons of battle'; l.3a); its opponent is a "*wælgrim wiga*" ('bloodthirsty warrior'; l.8a), a "*niðsceapa*" ('malicious harmer'; l.24a) that forces it to a "*guþgemot*" ('battle-meeting'; l.26b) in which the "*laðgewinna*" ('loathed adversary'; l.29a) suffers from the creature's "*hildepilum*" ('war-darts'; l.28b). Although none of these compounds occur in *Beowulf*, they are worthy of its spirit.

The elegiac note in this poem is struck in particular in ll.6b-23, where the creature describes how it is often forced by misfortune ("*M e bið gyrn witod*"; l.6b) to abandon its dwelling with its youthful family ("*geoguðcnosle*"; l.10a) when a "guest" comes to its doors ("*Hwonne gæst cume / to durum minum*"; ll.10b-11a). In what follows one is presented with a pitiful picture of timid ("*forhtmod*"; l.13a) flight with its offspring, pursuit by the enemy, the burrowing of a new hiding-place "*þurh steapne beorg"* ('through a high hill'; l.18a) full of secret tunnels. The safe retreat can then be defended in what appears to be a successful "last stand", unless we assume that the concluding lines of the poem are a *"beot"*, i.e. a warrior's boasting utterance, which would all the same befit one of Reynard's Anglo-Saxon ancestors.

The references to the heroic code of behaviour are by no means peculiar to this riddle. In the next item, almost certainly describing an anchor, the object states of itself that it battles the waves and fights the winds, and in 15 [17] the bees protecting the contents of their hive are so bristling with *"sperebrogan"* ('spear-terrors'; l.4a), *"hyldepilas"* ('wardarts'; l.6b), *"beadowæpnum"* ('battle-weapons'; l.8a) and *"attorsperum"* ('poisonous spears'; l.9a), that their abode has for more than a century been mistaken for a besieged fortress or a ballista—both of which, in a metaphorical sense, of course, it can be said to be.[5] As in the Fox (or Badger) riddle, the references to war and weapons are to be regarded as clues rather than as literal descriptions in terms of the riddle-nature of the poems, and in a broader sense they present precisely that "environment of images" that is part of Alvin Lee's argument about the coherence of Old English poetry (1972:156).

On similar grounds I am tempted to agree to a reading of riddle 3 [5] as describing a chopping-block, prosaic as this may seem, rather than a shield, which is the solution accepted by most early commentators (see Williamson, 1977:146). The creature begins by labelling itself an *"anhaga"* ('solitary one'; 'recluse'), which as Pinsker & Ziegler (1985:155) argue is more appropriate to an object of which there is only one in a household (*"in burgum"*; l.9a) than to a common wooden shield. That it is *"bille gebennad, beadoweorca sæd, / ecgum werig"* ('wounded by a sword, sated with the works of battle, weary of blades'; ll.2-3a) works more potently as a riddle clue to a chopping-block being hacked in metaphorical battles, in other words, as an image, than when it serves as a giveaway to what literally happens to a shield being "wounded" by sword-blows. The compounds, as well as the true kennings *"homera lafe"* (literally: 'remnants of hammers', i.e. the result of hammering; l.7b) and *"hondweorc smiþa"* ('smiths' handiwork'; l.8b) create a sense of irony when applied to homely kitchen knives or hatchets rather than to the more heroic swords they usually paraphrase, as in *Beowulf*, l.2829b, or *The Battle of Brunanburh*, l.6b. The medicinal herbs mentioned in l.12a (*"mid wyrtum"*), which cannot heal its wounds, obtain a humorous ambiguity if they can also refer to the very vegetables that are chopped on the block. But even if both

---

[5] For arguments in favour of the solution Beehive for riddle 15 [17], see Bierbaumer & Wannagat (1981) and Tigges (1991:70-76). This solution has also been adopted by Pinsker & Ziegler (1985:178).

solutions are equally viable, the point is that the images or descriptive elements would be recognized by a contemporary audience as deriving from the heroic register, which would lead the recipient to the notion of a warrior serving the lord of his comitatus up to the very "*deaðslege*" ('deadly blow'; l.14a) that will be finally suffered.

This view has been aptly expressed by Nigel Barley, who discusses the poem in his article from a structuralist point of view (1974:152-5): "The vocabulary and style allocate this piece to the heroic sphere of battle poetry", and moreover "the passage CAN be read as a perfectly straight piece of elegiac verse" (153), i.e. dealing with the motif of the lordless retainer. Quite correct in his general conclusion that many of the EBR "involve the moral values of the heroic system" (171), Barley is less convincing in his earlier suggestion that a scanning (i.e. application of a clue-by-clue analysis) of this particular riddle will enable us to disambiguate it, precisely because he fails to recognize a distinction between description and imagery. It should also be noted that he bases his ultimate solution (Shield) on the runic sign for S in the lower margin of the manuscript. The significance of these marginal annotations is by no means clear, and I refer the reader to Williamson's discussion of this problem in this particular instance (1977:147-8).

About one third of the EBR, spread over the whole collection, contain references to weapons, battle, fighting, contests or struggles, but only some eight to ten of the riddles are actually to be clearly solved as weapons, including the famous "Lorica" or Mailcoat riddle 33 [35], which also occurs in the Leiden University MS. Voss. Q. 106, where it follows the collections of Symphosius and Aldhelm. Another of these is 18 [20], which a majority of commentators solve as Sword, but for which birds of prey, such as a hawk or a falcon have been suggested as well (e.g. by Pinsker & Ziegler, 1985:184). Unfortunately, the riddle is incomplete, breaking off in the middle of l.36a at one of the manuscript lacunae, but it is a fine example of what Pinsker & Ziegler (1985:184) describe as "*elegische Selbstdarstellung*" ('elegiac self-presentation'). In the opening lines, the theme of the loyal retainer ("*frean minum leof*"; l.2a) and that of dependence on an even more powerful lord ("*waldend*"; l.4b) who has given "it" the bright death-gem and points out its way to battle, are combined. After a description of its extraordinary ornamentation, and a remark about its lack of offspring, it deplores its state of bachelorhood:

> Ic wiþ bryde ne mot
> hæmed habban,   ac me þæs hyhtplegan
> geno wyrneð   se mec geara on
> bende legde;   forþon ic brucan sceal
> on hagostealde   hæleþa gestreona.   (27b-31)

> (I may not have intercourse with a bride, but to me this joyous play is as yet refused by him who formerly placed me under a bond; therefore I must enjoy the treasures of men in celibacy.)

Does this refer to a sword which will not be sheathed but must "enjoy" military service, or to a falcon that must serve its master rather than enjoy a mate? It is easy to comment favourably on the poetic qualities of a passage such as this, but not so easy to determine precisely what it refers to. Our conclusion might well be that we can only enjoy these lines as an image, provided we are willing to forego "disambiguation". What remains then is an empathic recognition of the elegiac state of a warrior or warrior-like creature (a sword, a hawk, a falcon) whose "enjoyment" of certain honourable "treasures" entails at the same time the sacrifice of another important human fulfilment. It has been argued that certain riddles can be read allegorically. Thus, for instance, Marie Nelson (1974: 423) suggests the implement described in riddle 32 [34], a rake, can be read anagogically as a spiritual "harrowing". In a more recent article (1991:448-50) she cogently interprets the Ice and Fire riddles 31 [33] and 48 [50] in terms of a warning about the vices of Hatred and Anger. Perhaps riddle 18 [20] allows for a similar interpretation, addressing the predicament of the rich Christian, bound by his sins. Initially this poem, with its emphasis on the Lord as Prime Mover of its subject's activities, even seems to describe, in the imagery of heroic tasks and trappings, the ideal and practice of a medieval monk, shaped for a battle which is dear to his Lord ("*on gewin sceapen, / frean minum leof*"; ll.1b-2a).

I do not, of course, suggest that we should primarily "solve" this riddle as either Soul or Monk. Indeed, the latter reading in particular puts something of a strain on certain of the other clues provided later on. What, for instance, are we to make of the king who occasionally allows the travel-weary subject to move ("*sceacan*"; l.14b) at large in the mead-hall (ll.9-15)? Also, its confession that it is widely outlawed or hostile ("*fah*") and hated among weapons (ll.16b-17a) can hardly point to anything but a very aggressive personality. The basic imagery remains that of the warrior, bound by the laws and restraints of the comitatus. If he serves his master well he shall lack procreation (ll.24-27a)—a victorious sword need not be reforged. And finally, the subject wanders off the manuscript giving a scolding woman tit for tat or at least shrugging off her usual complaints. One momentarily envisages the Anglo-Saxon warrior coming home to a nagging wife, but the fact that the speaker attributes his behaviour to being stupefied or maddened by ornamental wires ("*wirum dol*"; l.32a) must be picked up as a central clue, of the kind that I have elsewhere called a "particularisation" of an anomaly (Tigges, 1991: 69). Whatever the "correct" solution, the subject is apparently constricted in a golden cage, a fact that is stressed from the start. It is the voicing of the combination of being beautiful, brave and circumscribed by the will of others that establishes the elegiac note of this fine sample of the medieval Snakes and Ladders game. That our lack of familiarity with Anglo-Saxon riddling conventions prevents us from ever knowing with certainty whether we were intended to guess a sword or a falcon, or yet something else, becomes less material, and in this sense we must agree with Barley (1974:151-2) when he states that "even if the riddle-giver demands a unique solution, we do not have to believe that there is one and one only formally correct solution for each riddle", and that our judgment must be based on such questions as: "Does this solution fit the facts? Is this the simplest most elegant solution?"

As regards the riddle just discussed I have no preference for one solution as being more appropriate, simple and elegant than another. The case is somewhat different for riddle 20 [22], for which three viable solutions have been mainly defended: a month (December), a bridge, and the circling northern stars. For economy's sake I have so far forborne quoting riddles in their entirety, but as I wish to look at this poem in some detail, and it is not a commonly anthologized piece, I will first quote it in full:

> Ætsomne cwom   sixtig monna
> to wægstæþe   wicgum ridan;
> hæfdon endleofan   eoredmæcgas
> fridhengestas,   feower sceamas.
> 5 Ne meahton magorincas   ofer mere feolan
> swa hi fundedon,   ac wæs flod to deop,
> atol yþa geþræc,   ofras hea,
> streamas stronge.   Ongunnon stigan þa
> on wægn weras   ond hyra wicg somod
> 10 hlodan under hrunge;   þa þa hors oðbær
> eh ond eorlas,   æscum dealle,
> ofer wætres byht   wægn to lande—
> swa hine oxa ne teah,   ne esna mægen,
> ne fæthengest,   ne on flode swom,
> 15 ne be grunde wod   gestum under,
> ne lagu drefde,   ne of lyfte fleag,
> ne under bæc cyrde;   brohte hwæþre
> beornas ofer burnan   ond hyra bloncan mid
> from stæðe heaum   þæt hy stopan up
> 20 on oþerne   ellenrofe
> weras of wæge   ond hyra wicg gesund.

(Sixty men came together to the shore, riding horses; eleven horsemen had stately steeds, four had bright creatures. The warriors could not pass the sea, much as they tried to, the water was too deep, the awful tumult of the waves, the banks too high, the streams too strong. Then the men ascended a wain and stowed their stallions under a pole; then it carried those horses, steeds and warriors proud of their ashen spears, over the bay of water, this wain, to land—so that it was neither drawn by an ox, nor by a troop of servants or by a draught-horse, neither did it stir the waters, covered with guests, nor fly from the air, and it did not turn back either; all the same, it brought the men across the stream, together with their shining horses, from the elevation where they stepped on to the other side, the brave men and their steeds safely from the sea.)

The solution Month, first proposed by the pioneering Dietrich in 1859, and hinging on a rather forced explanation of the numbers mentioned in ll.1-4 (sixty half-days, eleven feast-days and four Sundays) has been satisfactorily enervated by more recent scholars (see Blakeley, 1958:242; Williamson, 1977:201; Pinsker & Ziegler, 1985:193). Pinsker & Ziegler's most recent adaptation of Trautmann's solution Bridge, namely as a bridge of ice, cannot be considered much of an improvement. Their argument runs to the other extreme of not so much ignoring the numbers as "amending" them so that the horsemen become a "*handsceolu*" or expedition unit of sixteen (rather than the usual fifteen) men. They propose that "sixty" be read as "sixteen", and "four" as "five", which keeps the alliteration unaffected, but entirely overlooks the fact that this involves amending the manuscript readings of "*.lx.*" to "*.xvi.*" and "*.iiii.*" to "*.v.*", which I think is unacceptable. Moreover, their reading of this riddle concentrates on the "*wægn*" or waggon, which they read as an image for a bridge, which then in its turn represents a frozen water-plane. In Anglo-Saxon riddling convention, a bridge would be more likely to be circumlocutionarily described as a creature with (two or more) legs (the heads and/or piers), which does not move about, yet carries people across the water, or something to that effect. The element of ice is indeed occasionally referred to as forming a bridge (in *Maxims* I B, 1.2b), but one can safely trust almost any Anglo-Saxon *scop* to have brought in the motif of water turning into bone, or being bound with fetters, as in riddle 66 [68-9], 1.3b, *The Wanderer*, 1.24b, *Beowulf*, ll.1132b-33a, or *Maxims* I B, ll.3-5.

The subject-carrier of riddle 20 [22], i.e. the element in the text representing the object to be guessed, is more likely to be the "horses" and their riders; the horsemen are mentioned eight times, the riders seven. The only other concept that is greatly expatiated on is the water, deep, fiercely pressing, not to be waded or swum. There are, including its shores or banks, no fewer than thirteen references to it. The topic of this riddle, therefore, must be the crossing of these numerous horsemen over an unrestrained water-plane, without touching it by wading or swimming, without turning back and without leaving the air. Most of these allusions would not have any value as a clue if the answer was a frozen lake or river, but they make very good sense if, taking Blakeley's argument as a starting-point, we are meant to guess the circumpolar stars which never set. The sea or water to be traversed could indeed be the night-sky, as Blakeley suggests (1958:243), but also the actual sea-horizon as observed from a coastal position. The "*wægn*" I would interpret with Blakeley as the constellation of Ursa Major, familiarly known in Britain as Charles' Wain or the Plough, in the United States as the Big Dipper and in the domestic Netherlands as the Saucepan. I do not think, however, that the eleven "*fridhengestas*" (stately horses; l.4a) are the eleven visible stars of Canes Venatici, a very undistinguished constellation, even on very dark nights and with the free horizons which must have been more prevalent in pre-electricity rural times. I agree that the number 60 can refer to any "multitude" of stars, but I think it even more probable that the eleven and the four are not so much part of this number as to be added to them. Even on quite dark nights, the circumpolar stars at a latitude of about 52° N. amount to just about 75, which is to say, all stars of the fourth magnitude or brighter. The "Wain", which is lowest in the northern sky in the period October to December after sunset, in August and September around mid-night, and in June and July before sunrise, could (and can) be observed on a clear September night to move from the north-west to the north-east, skimming the horizon and seemingly carrying with it the rest of the northern stars, bordered by the Milky Way, which crosses the zenith, i.e. is "steep", when the stars "ascend" the waggon. The four "shiners" ("*sceamas*"; l.4b, etymologically related to the Dutch word *schimmel* for a pale horse) could be the four brightest stars overhead in this position, and setting off the Galaxy in the north. These in their turn will skim the horizon, namely when the Wain is highest: Vega in Lyra, Deneb in Cygnus (the Swan), Mirphak in Perseus and Capella in Auriga (the Driver!). The other numbers represent the less bright and the weaker stars, and the "*hrunge*" or pole in l.10a could be the pole or shaft of the Wain, which "covers" all these "horses" at some stage of their journey, but also the polar axis.[6] By using the word "pole" in my translation, as well as more

---

6 To ascertain on a star-chart which stars fail to set at any given latitude on earth, one must draw a circle around the pole including just as many degrees. Thus, Vega, which is about 51° from the North Pole, would skim the horizon at the latitude of say Jarrow and Wearmouth (55° N.), but would briefly "dip" at Exeter (50°45' N.). The eleven "stately horses" could be the stars of about second magnitude: Alkaid, Mizar, Alioth and Dubhe in Ursa Major (the Wain); Polaris and Korhab in Ursa Minor; Menkalinan in Auriga; Caph and Alpha Cassiopeiae; Delta Cygni; and Altanin in Draco; all of these are clearly visible and well within 52° from the North Pole. To arrive at a total of about 75 circumpolar stars one would have to include the stars of third and fourth magnitudes, of which in the same area there are 13 in Ursa Major, 1 in Ursa Minor, 10 in Draco, 8 in Cepheus, 5 in Cassiopeia, 6 in Perseus, 6 in Auriga, 3 in Cygnus, 2 in Hercules, 2 in Boötes, 2 in Lacerta, 2 in Andromeda and 1 in Canes Venatici. Stars of magnitude 5 and 6, of which there are several hundred, can be seen with the naked eye, but only on absolutely clear and pitch-

frequent alliteration on <st-> than the original allows for, I realize I am "loading" my interpretation, but then so do practically all modern renderings, as it is in the very nature of a modern translation to disambiguate what is less obviously monovalent in the source text.

The last long riddle I will consider in some detail is 37 [39]. Whatever the solution of this riddle is (suggestions include Day, Moon, Time, Creature Death, Cloud, Revenant, Speech and Dream), the text offers few problems to the translator. The riddler begins by informing us that this "*wiht*" or creature[7] has been described in "*gewritu*", but refuses (of course) to enlighten us as to the identity of these written sources. The creature is seen by men on many (or grave?) occasions ("*miclum tidum*"; l.2b), has an unsuspected special virtue, visits each of us separately, never to return a second night, but as to its appearance and abode it is described almost entirely in negatives: it has no human (or animal) features of any kind except its mobility, but it touches neither heaven, hell, nor earth— and yet it lives ("*leofað*"; l.27b). "*Gif þu mæge reselan   recene gesecgan / soþum wordum, saga hwæt hio hatte*" ('If you can tell the answer straightaway, with truthful words, say what it is called'; ll.28-9), the riddler concludes teasingly.

Erika von Erhardt-Siebold (1946) first proposed "Hypostasis Death" or "Creature Death", i.e. death as a "real" persona in the Platonic sense). Weighing all the evidence, this is the solution I prefer to others, although I find it rather misleading to predicate of death that it "lives", even if in accordance with the teachings of the King of Glory (ll.21b-22a). This solution is also defended by Nelson (1974:428-30), on the very sensible basis that death is "the ultimate negative", as well as by Barley (1974:170). More recently Kennedy (1975) and Meyvaert (1976) independently argued the solution Cloud, which is adopted by Pinsker & Ziegler (1985:242-4), together with Dream, which was proposed by Greenfield (1980), who rejects Williamson's suggestion Speech (1977:258-61). Greenfield's solution is supported by Stanley (1991).

However, Kennedy's succinct argument in favour of Cloud is not very convincing, being based on a romantic notion of "lying on the grass and being soothed and comforted by watching clouds form and reform" (1975:84). Paul Meyvaert, who confesses in a footnote not to be an Old English scholar (1976:197), all the same pretends to "settle once for all the

---

dark nights, and well above a flat horizon. The notion of magnitude would have been known from Ptolemy's *Almagest*. My source is "A Map of the Heavens", *National Geographic Magazine*, Washington, Dec. 1957.

[7] Barley (1974:148, n.3) prefers the translation "wight" so as not to prejudice the issue of whether the subject to be guessed is animate or inanimate. The word "*wiht*" to indicate the riddle topic is used in about one third of the EBR.

problem of what the Anglo-Saxon poet had in mind" (196) when he wrote riddle 37 [39], founding his argument on a very lame comparison with Aldhelm's third *ænigma* (for adverse criticism, see for instance Pinsker & Ziegler, 1985:242-3, and Greenfield, 1980:97-8). Stanley Greenfield (1980:96-7) at least makes an effort to scan the text, adducing fifteen features, but his explanation seems to fall short on feature 6 ("it departs and does not come a second *night*"—surely there are recurrent dreams, perceived as such in the Middle Ages) and on an aspect of feature 9 ("it has no … mental senses …"), which he slurs over, namely that "it" does not speak ("*ne muð hafað, ne wiþ monnum spræc*"; 1.12),[8] and it is rather weak on feature 7 ("it wanders as an exile").

The problem with this riddle is that it is one extended paradox, so that no solution is likely to be entirely satisfactory. Once again, we are dealing with a text that is experienced as "ingenious and fascinating poetry" (Von Erhardt-Siebold, 1946:915), even if we have no clear notion as to what we are to make of its subject-matter. The main idea that appears to be conveyed is that of the eternal exile: "*… hio sceal wideferh wreccan laste / hamleas hweorfan*" ('always it must roam the track of a homeless exile'; ll.8-9a) and "*hio siþas sceal / geond þas wundorworuld wide dreogan*" ('it must perform journeys far and wide through this world of wonders'; ll.16b-17). "She" or "it" is a shapeless outlaw in a labyrinth of wonders, yet by no means despicable, and with a redeeming universal power of bringing comfort or joy. To see in this a universal human predicament is perhaps too (post-)modern a thought—but what else are we to do with it? I find few of the riddles more truly puzzling or intriguing.[9]

From the foregoing discussion it might appear that the "*wundorworuld*" of these Anglo-Saxon riddlers offers more ambiguity than coherence, more confusion than enlightenment, more snakes than ladders, at least to a modern reader entering a 1250-year time-gap. But if we momentarily forget the frustration of inscrutable conundrums, we do see that a coherent "environment of images" is certainly present, and that these poems are indeed "heroic, Germanic, didactic, *and* Christian". And then, of course, we have not yet trod the more familiar ground of brief and pithy riddles, often anthologized, that offer us a glimpse of the Anglo-Saxons' daily concerns and earthy humour.

---

[8] Stanley's single point is to get rid of this objection by amending the second "*ne*" in this line to "*se*"—a dangerous procedure (1991:148).

[9] After completion of this paper I came across John Wilson's "Old English Riddle No. 39: 'Comet'" (1991:442-3). The solution here proposed is fairly plausibly argued, but is subject to the same objections as are solutions such as Cloud and Moon. Does a comet really "come with a message for each individual" (442)?

In some ten riddles (10 [12], 23 [25], 35 [37], 42 [44], 43 [45], 52 [54], 59 [61], 60 [62], 61 [63] and 87 [91]) the ambiguity is clear-cut, of the *double entendre* kind that makes us realize that even in the time of SS. Boniface and Lul a dirty mind was a joy for ever: "A wondrous thing hangs near a man's thigh, under the apron of a lord of creation (*"frean"*; 1.2a); it has a hole in the front. It is stiff and hard, has a good standing. When its 'servant' lifts up his own garment above his knees, it wishes to greet with the head of his hanging thing the familiar hole which, of equal length with itself, it has often filled (and felt) before." Thus riddle 42 [44], which the reader will have no trouble at all disambiguating as a Key, in those days carried on a cord around the waist.

Nor must we omit that old favourite, the Bookworm of riddle 45 [47]: "A moth crammed words—to me that seemed a splendid fate when I heard of that wonder, that the worm devoured what some man uttered, the thief in darkness a speech fixed in glory, together with its firm foundation [the parchment]. The stealing guest was not a whit the wiser for swallowing those words."

The marvellous riddle 24 [26], which instructively describes, with a plethora of well-wrought kennings, how books are made, is too long to quote, but here is riddle 49 [51], attending upon four "travellers", the pen and writing fingers: "I saw four splendid creatures travelling in company; swarthy were their tracks, very black prints. Swift on its course was the more active of birds; it flew in the air, then dived under the billow. Far from silently did the labouring warrior perform who marks out the pathways across the plated gold to all four of them." The scribe surely must have recognized himself in this soldier of the pen. To no fewer than sixteen riddles have solutions related to the scriptorium been proposed (see Shook, 1974, and the monograph by Göbel, 1980).

Finally, the famous "neck-riddle" which only the poser himself can solve, 82 [86]: "A creature came where many men were sitting in assembly, discerning of mind; it had one eye, and two ears, and two feet, twelve hundred heads, a back and a belly and a couple of hands, arms and shoulders, one neck and two sides. Say what I'm called." A one-eyed garlic-seller, of course—you cannot fool a man who knows his Symphosius! At last there is something we can share with our remote ancestors, the benefit of intertextuality.

Although present-day keys are less phallic, our books are devoured by acid rather than the bookworm, our fingers travel the keys of a word-processor, and the garlic-seller no longer stalks our meetings, there may be more in the Anglo-Saxon riddles that we can still share than would appear on first consideration. It may indeed be the case, as Williamson states in his Introduction (1977:5), "that the Anglo-Saxon notion of poetic order remains simply too far removed from our modern sensibilities to be comprehended." His conclusion is that what the riddlers meant to convey is "that reality exists and is at the same time a mosaic of man's perception" (25). Kant and Wittgenstein would have nodded their approval. Marie Nelson, too, noted that the riddles illustrate the essential ambiguity of creation (1974:440). In her more recent article, she emphasizes the social purposes riddling may have had in their time: combining competitive exercise of verbal skills, playful aggression, a response to the destructive forces of the natural world, and the provision of an insight into human destructive powers, leading to self-knowledge (1991:445-6). Whitman, whilst denying the riddlers "high artistic purpose" and labelling their efforts as mostly "intellectual and trivial" (1970:177-8), admits that "a more common view was that the ordinary things of the world bore the marks of the creator and deserved studying because therein lay the path to Godhead" (183). Behind the riddles he discerns three major formative forces: the spirit of play, a grammatical tradition, and the encyclopedic-Christian consciousness (185), thus soberly but certainly not without historical foundation stressing the utility of the genre as against its artistic value. It need not be doubted that the EBR confirm the social relationships of their day, as well as their moral implications, by metaphorically applying these to randomly presented phenomena or objects. In this sense, the comparison can be made with the maxims, where the recurrent "*sceal*" links up physical laws, force of habit, social appropriateness and moral truth (cf. Greenfield & Evert, 1975:340).

In allowing for mental density on the part of the aspirant-solver, incidentally, the objects themselves are more optimistic than the riddling observers. About half the topics speak in their own voices, using the well-known rhetorical device of prosopopoeia. These "creatures" announce themselves with phrases usually starting with "*ic eom*" ('I am') or "*mec ...*" ('me ...'), and in fifteen out of 46 possible instances conclude their presentation with a curt "*saga [frige] hwæt ic hatte*" ('say/discover what I'm called'). The other 44 creatures, which are not unseldom "*wrætlic*" ('splendid') or "*wundorlic*" ('wonderful'), are observed by a third person, who in many cases opens his observation with phrases like "*ic (ge)seah*", "*ic wat*" or "*ic gefrægn*" ('I saw, know, have heard'). Again, in fifteen instances the riddle moreover contains a concluding challenge, but these are of a more teasing kind, as in riddle 37 [39] quoted before. In riddle 40 [42], where the solution (cock and hen) has indeed been made very obvious with the assistance of rune-names (more often a hindrance than a help in the other four runic riddles), the concluding phrase takes up fully one third of the whole poem:

> Swa ic þæs hordgates
> cægan cræfte   þa clamme onleac

þe þa rædellan   wið rynemenn
hygefæste heold,   heortan bewrigene
orþoncbendum.   (11b-15a)

(Thus have I unlocked with the power of a key the fastenings of the trea-
sure-door which held the riddle mind-fast against mystery-solvers, con-
cealed in its heart by cunning bonds.)

So the riddler states, almost sorry he has done the job so poorly after all,
and he concludes by saying that "now it is no secret [even?] to men in their
cups ("*æt wine*") what those two low-minded creatures are called" (ll.15b-
17). That the EBR are not presented in a more "orderly" fashion has in
the outcome a very trite explanation: having to be guessed, the topics of
consecutive riddles must not be too closely related or else the game is
spoiled!

II

"*Nelle ic þe min dyrne gesecgan, / gif þu me þinne hygecræft hylest   ond
þine heortan geþohtas*" ('I do not wish to tell you my secrets, if you hide
your mental powers from me and the thoughts of your heart'; ll.2b-3).
The poet stretches his metre in the opening lines of the Exeter Book
Maxims (henceforth EBM) to inform us that there is more to the verses
that are going to follow than just a set of widely accepted rules of conduct
or general truths briefly expressed, as maxims or gnomes are usually defined.[10] What are these "secrets" the poet wishes us to share? And whose
secrets are they? As we will have occasion later on to connect the maxims
with contemporary history, it may be fitting to preface a brief survey of
observations on these poems by a curious comment on the part of a
famous Anglo-Saxonist, Sir Frank Stenton (1971:197-8):

> The only Anglo-Saxon poems for which peasant origin can
> reasonably be claimed are two collections of so-called Gnom-
> ic verses—sententious observations about the properties of

---

[10] All quotations from the EBM and the Cotton Gnomes are from Shippey (1976:64-79),
a convenient collection of Anglo-Saxon wisdom poetry, which includes translations, notes
and an Introduction. Translations following quotations are my own. For a lengthy introduction to gnomic poetry in general and the Anglo-Saxon maxims in particular, see the
early standard edition by Williams (1914). Krapp-Dobbie (1936) also gives the texts of
the EBM, which are often referred to as *Maxims I*, the Cotton Gnomes being *Maxims II*.
The former, on fols. 88b-92b of the Exeter Book, consist of three separate but consecutive sections of some 70 lines each. The latter, preserved in British Library MS. Cotton
Tiberius B i, fol. 115, where it immediately precedes the C version of the *Anglo-Saxon
Chronicle*, is a single poem of 66 lines.

things—which carry a distinctive atmosphere of rustic wisdom. They range from the crudest assertions of simple fact—
"frost must freeze, fire destroy wood"—to somewhat elaborate descriptions of persons, or of common incidents of life.
They often relate to the virtues, the equipment, or the amusements of nobles, and the finest of them all is the description
of a great lady, discreet, generous, and gracious, in her lord's
hall. They clearly arose among men who were keenly interested in the aristocratic life, but they always regard it from
the outside. A series of them gradually produces the impression of a group of farmers capping alliterative sentences with
one another, and occasionally maintaining a sequence of
thought long enough to yield a definite picture—two men
happily playing at dice on a board, or a sailor returning to his
"Frisian wife". They deserve more attention from historians
than they usually receive, for there is nothing in literature
that approaches so nearly to the authentic voice of the Anglo-
Saxon *ceorl*.

The apparent lack of unity of the maxims struck the earliest commentators. Blanche Williams (1914:54) says that "in both the *Edda* and in
Anglo-Saxon, diversity, total absence of unity, mark the collections."
Later on she writes, following still earlier scholarship, that "analysis of
the contents reveals only an embryonic organism, an organic structure
probably more fancied than real, a creation of the reader rather than of
the writer" (85). When such an analysis is finally presented (88ff.), she
implicitly demonstrates some unity in EBM A, but parts B and C, as well
as the Cotton Maxims ("lack of unity characterizes these lines", 108) are
less well organized. Interestingly, she prefaces this discussion by stating
that "the utterance of proverbs or maxims demanded the same brain-play
as did the propounding and solution of riddles" (86-7, and cf. 14-15). The
opening lines of EBM A which I began by commenting on, she here dismisses as a "flyting" or question-and-answer game that may have existed
in an older version, but was in the extant one abandoned as soon as suggested.

Passing over a brief exposé of EBM B by Malone (1943), who analyses this section as a separate poem (illustrating the apparent lack of
organic coherence in the EBM), we may turn to a more important paper
by R. MacGregor Dawson, who qualifies the gnomic poems as mnemonic
arrangements (1962:15). Rejecting a connection between sections A and B
of the EBM (17), Dawson reads each individual poem as a kind of medieval stream-of-consciousness, operative by a "universal principle of association" (20), which he considers to be "in keeping with the digressive

nature of Old English poetry in general" (15), and which leads him to the conclusion that there is no "total absence of form" (22).

Taylor, in a very informative paper to which lack of space prevents me from doing full justice, elaborates on the thesis that there is "a pervading structural principle defined by the poet of the *Exeter Maxims*: *Fela sceop meotud þæs þe fyrn gewearð, het siþþan swa forð wesan* 'God shaped many things which came about long ago, ordered them to be such henceforth'" (1969:387; the reference is to EBM C, ll.27-8). He continues to argue that whereas the "*bið*"-maxims "focus on the immutable conditions of the universe", the "*sceal*"-maxims "comprise a sort of handbook on ritual" (388), ritual, that is to say, of divinely created nature as well as of (heroic) man: "... the order and functioning of the universe explicit in the *Maxims* echo the order and functioning of the heroic universe in the poetry" (393). This dual reading of the maxims as reflecting both the natural rituals as "God's wonders" (391) and the heroic rituals as a school for princes exercising free moral choice enables Taylor to conclude, along lines shared by Alvin Lee (1972), that "most, if not all, the *Maxims* could find a counterpart in the Old English poetic corpus" (401). This begins to throw a somewhat different light on Stenton's notions of "rustic wisdom" and the "authentic voice of the Anglo-Saxon *ceorl*" quoted above. The maxims, indeed, "reflect the world of Macbeth and Lear rather than the world of Page and Ford" (Taylor, 1969:387).

Barley, in what is a counterpart to his article on the riddles, states about the Cotton Gnomes that they form "a splendid example of 'pensée sauvage', the splitting up of the world into its due and proper order, the establishing of relationships in hierarchy and opposition and the mapping of one structure on another" (1972:745-6), but he regards the universality of the texts as basically formal (747). Greenfield & Evert (1975:339) state that "a collocation of gnomes ... can create a meaning which is greater than the sum of individual gnomes ...." They note "a riddling quality" in the poets' omission of a clarifying context (342) and discuss the unity of the Cotton gnomes in terms of a thematic account of the limitedness of human knowledge (354)—which sounds a bit like the non-plussed riddle-solver throwing up the game. Incidentally, these authors open their discussion with the boosting remark that the Cotton gnomes' poetry evokes enthusiastic reactions from beginning students of Old English (337).

Shippey, finally, introduces first of all what may be no more than a definitional red herring by distinguishing maxims, which are "purposive", from gnomes, which are not (1976:12). More importantly, in view of our unifying approach, he suggests we consider "their lurking hints of connectivity" (13), and regards them ultimately, like riddle contests, as "sportive tests, to probe men's capacity for uncovering moral truth" (19)—in fact, as yet another medieval variant of our Snakes and Ladders game.

Actually, it should not take too much effort to uncover a moral truth in the EBM. After the initial challenge, the first gnomon in section A is "*God sceal mon ærest hergan, / fægre, fæder userne*" ('One must first praise God, our father, fairly'; ll.4b-5a). The remainder of this section expands first of all on the nature of God and on the variety of His Creation: "*Feorhcynna fela   fæþmeþ wide / eglond monig*" ('Many types of life are widely embraced by many an island'; ll.14b-15a). To keep these various civilizations in moral order, "*Þing sceal gehegan / frod wiþ frodne*" ('one wise man must hold a meeting with another'; ll.18b-19a). From the very start, the poet contrasts the themes of diversity and unity: "two is company, three a (welcome) crowd, four a disaster" would neatly summarize the *portée* of ll.23b-34. In the second half of this first section, the poet expatiates on wisdom and foolishness, health and disease, and concludes with the proper and improper behaviour of kings, noble warriors, and women. Greed above all must be avoided.

Section B opens with some of those apparent trivialities that I suspect Stenton of holding for endearingly rustic wisdom: frost typically freezes, fire melts wood, the earth flourishes, ice makes a bridge (ll.1-2). A less condescending way of accounting for these trite utterances is to contrast them directly with what is perhaps less evident to the average churls we all sometimes are, such as the remarks that end section A about women avoiding the stigma of the bad reputation of being too "going" ("*widgongel*"; A, l.65a), or the generosity expected from one who has just received a bonus. Taken on its own, the maxim about ice can moreover be seen in terms of the poetic quality of its description: "*is [sceal] brycgian, / wæter helm wegan,   wundrum lucan / eorþan ciþas.   An sceal inbindan / forstes fetre   felameahtig god*" ('ice [will] form a bridge, water carry a helmet, wondrously lock up the germs of the earth. Only a very mighty God shall unlock the fetters of frost'; ll.2b-5). The semantic contents of the remark may be trivial, the images of a bridge, a covering helmet and fetters being fastened and unbound, are striking and indeed emphasize, once again, the wonder of this created middle-earth.

A further stage in our appreciation of the coherence of the section is achieved by linking up the apparent accumulation of loose remarks, provided we do so in a way which is in accordance with what we know about medieval exegetical practice. If we do this for EBM B, we get the following little allegory: the very changes of the seasons demonstrate the heroic power of God; after He has allowed the winter ice to melt, the ocean will become restless and this may lead to death—in that case it is best to have one's executors preserve one's good name, which we must therefore establish. "*Dom biþ selast*" ('Glory is best'; l.10b). One such "seafarer" at risk is the king, when he sets out to provide himself with a spouse—if only because we all know what women are like! They are not all like the

Frisian sailor's wife, who welcomes her husband home after a long journey, washes his dirty clothes and satisfies the debts of love. Moreover, a good name, even if we deserve it, is easily smudged by backbiters, so we must see to it that we return from whatever wanderings we have allowed ourselves or been forced to undertake, like the good merchant, who provides for his sailors while he has his health. For if one becomes sick, physically or spiritually, through lack of proper food, one becomes dependent on the help of others. So we should keep up our strength and consciously bury the evil we are burdened with. And so ultimately we come round again to God, who provides our spiritual sustenance, as well as the spiritual arms to fight evil. "Woden made idols, the Allruling one, however, glory in the shape of the spacious firmament" (ll.63-4a). And good will prevail, because it is congruous with God.

In this circular organization the poet has established a close relationship between everyday truths, homely events, and the conventional behaviour of whatever nature (good as well as evil) on the one hand, and spiritual desirabilities on the other. We can go even one stage further and translate the references to a king seeking a bride and a sailor returning to his wife in terms of Christ wooing the Church or the individual human soul. In any case, we see once more how this wisdom poetry too is simultaneously heroic, Germanic, didactic and Christian. In Shippey's words: "The poets are writing from within a firmly-held cultural ethic, which may be that of their nation [Germanic], or class [heroic rather than churlish] or profession [didactic and Christian]", even if their intentions have to remain unclear to a modern reader (1976:18). After all, we still fail to see what is so "*dyrne*" ('secret') about these wisdoms.

Indeed, the word "*dyrne*" in EBM A, l.2b, may simply reflect the "*secreta sapientiæ*" ("the secrets of wisdom") referred to in Job 11:6, or the "dark saying(s)" of Psalms 49:4 and 78:2 ("*propositionem/-es*", *Vulgate* 48:5 and 77:2) and Proverbs 1:6 (where the *Vulgate* has "*ænigmata*"). But the Anglo-Saxon glossarists do not appear to use the word "*dyrne*" or "*dierne*" here, but something like "*foresetenesse*" (see, for instance, the Vitellian or Vespasian Psalters). I would like to take the phrase as the expression of a not a-typical Anglo-Saxon attitude of irony: about the individual statements as such there is nothing very secret or obscure. An allegorical reading shifts the meaning of the words in the direction of an address to the understander: *sapienti verbum sat*. There is, however, one more option for culling some secret information out of the maxims, which, although admittedly but necessarily speculative, I wish here to propose to the reader by way of conclusion. This entails the hypothesis that the maxims tell a "story". Let us once again scan section B in this light.

Section A had ended on the theme of a king eager for sovereignty, too eager perhaps. Now, winter (ll.1-4a) has been replaced by spring (ll.

4b-7a), when the sea becomes navigable again. Someone, a person of fame (10b), and hence presumably of authority, possibly the king of section A, has died, holly is burnt, and his property is divided (ll.9-10a). The link between the description of nature and climate and the death is provided by the kenning "*deada wæg*" ('road of the dead'; l.8a) for the sea, with a possible reference to the traditional burial ship.[11]

The next passage may refer to matters of succession: a king (the previous king's son or eligible relative, or his prospective—and posthumous?—son-in-law) bargains to marry a queen (ll.11-22). Probably the queen is a foreign element here, in view of the description of her duties, the traditional ones for which Hrothgar's queen Wealhtheow in *Beowulf* was so renowned, especially that of honouring her lord-and-husband (ll. 19-22). The last line of this episode, "*boldagendum   bæm ætsomne*" ('house-owners both together') emphasizes their normative togetherness and the sharing of responsibilities. The reality, of course, may have been quite different from this ideal.

The transition from this passage on royal marriage back to a seascape may refer to a raid made by the husband-king, during whose absence the wife-queen is unfaithful—her behaviour is unfavourably compared to that of the Frisian sailor's wife (ll.24b-29); the theme of unfaithfulness is broached in ll.30-3.

Lines 34ff. are usually taken to be an expatiation on the Frisian sailor's possible fate, but might also allude to the return of another sailor, the raiding king, let us say. This would justify the reading of "*mægðegsan wyn*" (l.37b) as 'the raider's joy', as proposed by most commentators and adopted by Shippey (see Krapp-Dobbie, 1936:306, note to l.106). Ll. 37-8 I read in the sense proposed by Kock (Krapp-Dobbie, 1936:307, note to l.107), namely "a man possessing goods, a prince, will purchase, when he comes sailing, quarters for his men". I assume that the king has stranded on a foreign shore (ll.35b-38) and falls ill (ll.41-3). It is now summer (l.42b).

Someone (the queen's lover?) plots the king's death (ll.44-6), but the king recovers (l.47b) and his senses are restored (ll.51-4); possibly it is he who murders his attacker, or else he decides to fight the lover (ll. 55-8), as is fitting in the nature of things (ll.59-61). By the grace of God, his power is restored (ll.62-8). Section C may continue the account, as it opens with a long paragraph on proper behaviour and the desirability that

---

11 For the burning of holly ("*holen*"; l.9a), see the note in Shippey (1976:132, n.2). G. Grigson (*The Englishman's Flora*, St. Albans: Granada, 1975:127) tells us that the holly used to be taken down on Candlemas Eve, i.e. 1 Feb., close to the spring season. If "*holen*" means 'chief', as proposed by Malone (1943:65), there is no problem in view of my reading here.

"a hall should stand, ageing in its own time" (C, l.20), and ends with a description of the causes and workings of evil, in particular of violence. War cannot be avoided.

Since the Anglo-Saxons were not in the habit of making up "romantic" stories, my reading, which I realize is speculative and which I mainly adduce for the sake of entering into the "sportive" mood invited by the poet's admonition that *"Gleawe men sceolon gieddum wrixlan"* ('Wise men must exchange sayings'; A, l.4a) and that *"a þæs heanan hyge hord unginnost"* ('the abject mind [will] always be least amply rewarded'; C, l.70), may have a political basis, possibly a coded account of contemporary events. If we are allowed to assume an early eighth-century original composition for these maxims, we are led to an era about which Stenton, with a laconic flair worthy of any Anglo-Saxon, has little more to say than: "There was much fighting in this period" (1971:202). The Venerable Bede, who was in his prime during the first third of the eighth century (he died in 735), is remarkably silent about political events in the period following 692, but the various manuscripts of the *Anglo-Saxon Chronicle* record eleven violent deaths of royal and highly-placed ecclesiastical personages between that year and the "saga" of Cynewulf and Cyneheard and the accession of Offa of Mercia in 757 (see Whitelock, 1986:24-31). Could the reference to Woden and his idols in EBM B, l.63a, have had any bearing on the battle of *Wodnesbeorg* (now Adam's Grave at Alton Priors, Wiltshire) between Ine of Wessex and Ceolred of Mercia in 715 (see Stenton, 1971:71, and *Anglo-Saxon Chronicle, sub anno* 715)?

It is perhaps more reasonable to assume that the compilers of the maxims were commenting on catastrophic contemporary events such as internecine strifes and the destruction of whole cities (as of Taunton by Queen Aethelburg in 722 and of Canterbury in 754) in a more general way, cloaking particularities but holding up a moral mirror in which those involved could recognize their own faces, if so inclined. All the same, in view of the connection which has been made between the Cotton gnomes and the text of the Chronicle which it seems to introduce (Bollard, 1973, esp. 179-81; also quoted by Shippey, 1976:13), a relationship between maxims and historical records need not be dismissed out of hand.

It has been my intention in this paper to introduce the reader to the riddles and maxims of the Exeter Book as texts which are not only of interest as literary artefacts in their own right, but which reflect the fascination of Anglo-Saxon scops as well as clerics with the variety of God's wonderful creation, a variety which also transpires in such wisdom poems from the same codex as *The Gifts of Men, The Fortunes of Men* and *The Order of the World*. This diversity, coupled to the unifying realization that "God directs all", obtains a further framework of organization in the shape of the norms, values and conventions of not only the doctrines of

Christian faith, but also of the heroic code centring around the comitatus and the "*dryht-hall*". It is against the backcloth of these two systems of belief and their institutions, which patterned Germanic life for many centuries up to the Norman Conquest, that the Anglo-Saxons saw the world around them as a "*wundorworuld*", which they sometimes treated as God's guessing-game and sometimes, as befits the game of Snakes and Ladders, as a fount of moral wisdom.

REFERENCES

Barley, N. (1972). A Structural Approach to the Proverb and Maxim with Special Reference to the Anglo-Saxon Corpus. *Proverbium* 20. 737-50.
Barley, N. (1974). Structural Aspects of the Anglo-Saxon Riddle. *Semiotica* 10. 143-75.
Bierbaumer, P. and E. Wannagat. (1981). Ein neuer Lösungsvorschlag für ein altenglisches Rätsel (Krapp-Dobbie 17). *Anglia* 99. 379-82.
Blakeley, L. (1958). Riddles 22 and 58 of the Exeter Book. *Review of English Studies* n.s. 9, 241-52.
Bollard, J.K. (1973). The Cotton Maxims. *Neophilologus* 57. 179-87.
Calder, D.G., and M.J.B. Allen (eds.). (1976). *Sources and Analogues of Old English Poetry*. London: D.S. Brewer, and Totowa, NJ: Rowman & Littlefield.
Dawson, R.M. (1962). The Structure of the Old English Gnomic Poems. *Journal of English and Germanic Philology* 61. 14-22.
Erhardt-Siebold, E. von (1946). Old English Riddle No. 39. Creature Death. *PMLA* 61. 910-5.
Fry, D.K. (1981). Exeter Book Riddle Solutions. *Old English Newsletter* 15. 22-33.
Goldsmith, M.E. (1975). The Enigma of *The Husband's Message*. In: Nicholson and Frese, 1975: 242-63.
Göbel, H. (1980). *Studien zu den altenglischen Schriftwesenrätseln*. Würzburg: Königshausen u. Neumann.
Greenfield, S.B. (1980). Old English Riddle 39 Clear and Visible. *Anglia* 98. 95-100.
Greenfield, S.B., and R. Evert. (1975). *Maxims II*: Gnome and Poem. In: Nicholson and Frese, 1975: 337-54.
Hacikyan, A. (1966). *A Linguistic and Literary Analysis of Old English Riddles*. Montreal: Mario Casalini.
Kennedy, C.B. (1975). Old English Riddle No. 39. *English Language Notes* 13. 81-5.
Krapp, G.P., and E.V.K. Dobbie (eds.). (1936). *The Exeter Book*. Anglo-Saxon Poetic Records, Vol. III. New York: Columbia University Press/London: Routledge & Kegan Paul.
Lee, A.A. (1972). *The Guest-Hall of Eden. Four Essays on the Design of Old English Poetry*. New Haven, CT, & London: Yale University Press.
Malone, K. (1943). Notes on Gnomic Poem B of the Exeter Book. *Medium Ævum* 12. 65-7.
Meyvaert, P. (1976). The Solution to Old English Riddle 39. *Speculum* 51. 195-201.
Nelson, M. (1974). The Rhetoric of the Exeter Book Riddles. *Speculum* 49. 421-40.
Nelson, M. (1991). Four Social Functions of the Exeter Book Riddles. *Neophilologus* 75. 445-50.
Nicholson, L.E., and D.W. Frese (eds.). (1975). *Anglo-Saxon Poetry: Essays in Appreciation. For John C. McGalliard*. Notre Dame, IN, & London: University of Notre Dame Press.

Pinsker, H., and W. Ziegler (eds.). (1985). *Die altenglischen Rätsel des Exeterbuchs*. Heidelberg: Carl Winter.

Pitman, J.H. (ed. and transl.). (1925). *The Riddles of Aldhelm*. New Haven, CT: Yale University Press. 1925. (Facs. repr. Archon Books, 1970).

Shippey, T.A. (ed.). (1976). *Poems of Wisdom and Learning in Old English*. London: D.S. Brewer, and Totowa, NJ: Rowman & Littlefield.

Shook, L.K. (1974). Riddles Relating to the Anglo-Saxon Scriptorium. In: *Essays in Honour of Anton Charles Pegis*. Ed. J.R. O'Donnell. Toronto: Pontifical Institute of Mediæval Studies. 215-29.

Stanley, E.G. (1991). Stanley B. Greenfield's Solution of *Riddle* (ASPR) 39: "Dream". *Notes and Queries* 236. 148-9.

Stenton, F.M. (1971). *Anglo-Saxon England*. 3rd ed. Oxford: Clarendon Press. (1st ed. 1943).

- Taylor, P.B. (1969). Heroic Ritual in the Old English Maxims. *Neuphilologische Mitteilungen* 70. 387-407.

Tigges, W. (1991). Signs and Solutions: A Semiotic Approach to the Exeter Book Riddles. In: *This Noble Craft ... Proceedings of the Xth Research Symposium of the Dutch and Belgian University Teachers of Old and Middle English and Historical Linguistics, Utrecht, 19-20 January, 1989*. Ed. E. Kooper. Amsterdam & Atlanta: Rodopi: 59-82.

Trautmann, M. (1914). Die Quellen der altenglischen Rätsel. Sprache und Versbau der altenglischen Rätsel. Zeit, Heimat und Verfasser der altenglischen Rätsel. *Anglia* 38. 349-73.

Whitelock, D., *et al.* (eds.). (1986). *The Anglo-Saxon Chronicle*. Westport, CT: Greenwood Press. 1986. (1st pub. 1961).

Whitman, F.H. (1970). Medieval Riddling. Factors Underlying Its Development. *Neuphilologische Mitteilungen* 71. 177-85.

Williams, B.C. (1914). *Gnomic Poetry in Anglo-Saxon*. New York: Columbia University Press. (Repr. New York: AMS Press, 1966).

Williamson, C. (ed.). (1977). *The Old English Riddles of the* Exeter Book. Chapel Hill, NC: University of North Carolina Press.

Wilson, J. (1991). Old English Riddle No. 39: 'Comet'. *Notes and Queries* N.S. 38. 442-3.

WULF AND EADWACER:
A WOMAN'S *CRI DE COEUR*—FOR WHOM, FOR WHAT?

HENK AERTSEN

Probably no other English poem of just nineteen lines has given rise to more interpretations and critical essays than the poem known as *Wulf and Eadwacer* (henceforth *W&E*), found in the Exeter Book between *Deor* and the first section of the Riddles. The first editor of the Exeter Book, Benjamin Thorpe, wrote in 1842 in a note to what he considered to be the first of the Exeter Book riddles: "Of this I can make no sense, nor am I able to arrange the verses" (1842:527). Thorpe printed the text of the poem as a riddle but suggested no solution and gave no translation either, the only poem in his edition without a translation. A hundred years later Kemp Malone wrote that "*Eadwacer* is one of the most obscure poems in the English language. We make no attempt to interpret it" (1948:90). Yet Malone went on to quote two passages in translation, and in the case of *W&E* a translation, as will be seen shortly, is at the same time an interpretation. A truly enigmatic poem, then, and no wonder that the early critics thought of it as a riddle, the first of the initial series of riddles in the Exeter Book.

The first critic to solve the riddle, or rather to suggest a solution to what he thought was a riddle, was Heinrich Leo (1857). Leo saw in the poem a kind of charade which yielded the name *Cynewulf*, when the various clues provided by the poem were solved correctly and put in the right order. And since Cynewulf signed his name in runes in some of the poems attributed to him (*Juliana, Elene, Christ II* and *The Fates of the Apostles*), he was for a long time held to be the poet who wrote not only *W&E*, or "The First Riddle" as it was called by Leo, but also, on the basis of supplementary evidence, the other Riddles in the Exeter Book. Richard Wülcker (1878:493-4) came up with the same solution, adding that "die situation ist hier offenbar, dass eine frau ihren geliebten mann, Wulf, anredet" ('the situation here is evidently that a woman is addressing her beloved man [or, husband], Wulf'), which made Wülcker the first to mention the love element in the poem; unfortunately he saw in the occurrence of the name *Wulf* a clue for solving the riddle as Cyne-*wulf*. Moritz Trautmann also looked upon the poem as a riddle, and his solution was 'riddle' (1884: 158ff; see note 6 below).

Before proceeding to a discussion of the poem and its many interpretations, I will first present the text of the poem as found in the Exeter

Book volume of *The Anglo-Saxon Poetic Records*, edited by Krapp and
Dobbie (1936:179-80):

> Leodum is minum   swylce him mon lac gife;
> willað hy hine aþecgan,   gif he on þreat cymeð.
>   Ungelic is us.
> Wulf is on iege,   ic on oþerre.
> Fæst is þæt eglond,   fenne biworpen.   5
> Sindon wælreowe   weras þær on ige;
> willað hy hine aþecgan,   gif he on þreat cymeð.
>   Ungelice is us.
> Wulfes ic mines widlastum   wenum dogode;
> þonne hit wæs renig weder   ond ic reotogu sæt,   10
> þonne mec se beaducafa   bogum bilegde,
> wæs me wyn to þon,   wæs me hwæþre eac lað.
> Wulf, min Wulf,   wena me þine
> seoce gedydon,   þine seldcymas,
> murnende mod, nales meteliste.   15
> Gehyrest þu, Eadwacer?   Uncerne earne hwelp
> bireð wulf to wuda.
> Þæt mon eaþe tosliteð   þætte næfre gesomnad wæs,
> uncer giedd geador.

(It is to my people as if they have been given a present: they will receive
him if he comes to their troop. It is different with us. Wulf is on one
island, I on another. Fortified is that island, surrounded by a fen. There are
cruel men there on that island; they will receive him if he comes to their
troop. It is different with us. I thought with hope of my Wulf's long
journey, when it was rainy weather and I sat weeping, when the one brave
in battle laid his arms around me, it was a joy to me to a degree, however it
was also hateful. Wulf, my Wulf, hopes of you have made me sick, your
rare visits, a sorrowing heart, not at all lack of food. Do you hear, Eadwacer? Our wretched whelp Wulf will carry off to the wood. One easily
tears apart that which was never joined, our song together.)

This translation should be seen as a first attempt at making the poem come
to life through a simple rendering; when the complexities and ambiguities
of the text are discussed below, alternative renderings will be presented
without a suggestion that any particular rendering is *the* correct reading of
the poem: it may well be possible that the poet himself (or herself)
allowed such multiple readings on purpose and that the poem's obscurity
and ambiguity only adds to its appeal, even to modern readers.

That *W&E* was a riddle was the prevailing view until 1888, when
Henry Bradley demonstrated that "the so-called riddle is not a riddle at all,
but a fragment of a dramatic soliloquy," and offered (1888:198) what was
for a long time the most widely accepted interpretation:

The speaker, it should be premised, is shown by the grammar
to be a woman. Apparently she is a captive in a foreign land.
Wulf is her lover and an outlaw, and Eadwacer (I suspect,
though it is not certain) her tyrant husband.

One of the very few things about the poem that seem certain is that the
speaker is a woman: as Bradley says, it is the grammar that tells us so,
because the adjectives *reotugu* (1.10) and *seoce* (1.16) have feminine inflec-
tional endings. But even such an unambiguous reference to a female
speaker has been called into question: in what Marilynn Desmond (1990:
575, n.5) calls "a perverse and willful misreading of the poem in order to
make the speaker male," Norman Eliason (1974:228) has argued that

the poem is a private communication addressed to a colleague,
ruefully but playfully protesting the mishandling of their
poetry, which ... has been separated, some of it being copied
in one place of a manuscript and the rest in another, less
favourable place.

Eliason wisely refrains from explaining the feminine case endings in the
two adjectives mentioned and from giving a complete textual commentary,
and his interpretation drew the following comment from Emily Jensen:
"Obviously critics will go to any length to silence a woman's voice" (1979:
382, n.3).

Since Bradley's highly romantic view, numerous alternative interpretations have been suggested, which, roughly speaking, come in two categories. There are, on the one hand, interpretations that are based on
internal evidence provided by the poem itself (which John Fanagan [1976:
130] has called 'internal interpretations') and on the other those that seek
to place the situation described in the poem in a historical or mythological
context (Fanagan's 'external interpretations'). If we concentrate on the
internal interpretations first and ignore for the time being the attempts
made since 1888 to see in the poem some kind of riddle (in the technical
sense of a poetic genre), we may note the following alterations of Bradley's hypothesis:

- a reversal of the roles played by Wulf and Eadwacer, Wulf becoming
  the husband, first formulated by Sir Israel Gollancz (1902:552)[1]:
  "Wolf, the exiled prince, living the life of an outlaw; his wife kept

---

[1] The same role patterning is implicitly present in Gollancz's earlier contribution to *The
Athenaeum* (1893:883), in which he gives the text of the poem and a translation in the
form of a five-act dramatic monologue ("monodrama"), with headings describing the
action in each of the five acts.

from him by the mighty foe, Odoacer [= Eadwacer], to whose embraces she at last yields herself." Peter Baker (1981:50) makes a similar suggestion:

> It is more likely that Wulf is her husband. He has been out-
> lawed by her people; she, perhaps because she is the wife of
> an outlaw, has been sent to live on an island, where she is
> watched over by Eadwacer, who has made love to her.

- a different role for Eadwacer: P.J. Frankis makes him the speaker's
  father (1962:173, n.34): "Bradley's suggestion that Eadwacer is the
  woman's husband is less satisfactory: exile to a remote island suggests
  rather the action of an outraged father than of a deceived husband."

  For suggestions that Eadwacer is not a separate character but rather
  a characterization, whether ironic or not, of one of the other characters, see below.

- different roles for Wulf: Frankis, discussing the close resemblance
  between *W&E* and *Deor*, thinks of him, like Deor, as a *scop*, which
  would, he claims, make the *uncer giedd geador* of the final line of
  W&E "gain in significance" (1962:174). Dolores Frese makes him the
  speaker's son, the *hwelp*, whose death she laments (1983:16):

> the lyric speaks the particular, personal anguish of a woman
> whose son has lost his life, and consequently cannot fulfill the
> personal, cultural, and religious history of mother and son
> (*uncer giedd geador*, 19a).[2]

Marijane Osborn (1983:184, 186, 188) sees a mother and son relation
as well, but in her view Wulf is an older brother whose absence the
mother laments and whose sudden return poses a threat to her other
son, the *hwelp*. Likewise, Carol Jamison (1987) sees a mother and son
relation in the poem which she too interprets as a mother's lament for
her son.[3] Seiichi Suzuki (1987:175) argues that

> Wulf is the son of the speaker, and ... the poem is the latter's
> expression of grief for her separation from her dear son, who
> is away from home in military service.

---

[2] Frese relates the poem to Scandinavian funerary inscriptions and Norse mythology, and
believes that underlying the poem is the "tension between the heroic pagan past and the
tenuous Christian present" (1983:12).

[3] This is at any rate what the title of her paper suggests. Unfortunately I can give no more
details as her paper is one of two that I have not been able to consult (cf. note 5 below).

• a reduction in the number of characters in the poem—from Bradley's four (the lady, Wulf, Eadwacer, the child) to three (Adams, Keough, Giles and Frese) to two (Greenfield): John Adams (1958:1, 2) turns the proper name Eadwacer into an epithet *ead-wacer*, meaning 'property watcher', which he says the lady ironically applies to Wulf.[4] Terrence Keough (1976:556-7, 558) adopts the same meaning for the epithet but applies it differently:

> If instead of considering *Eadwacer* as a proper noun epithet for an individual, one looks upon it as a collective noun referring to the society as a whole, to the *Leodum minum* of line one, then the need to speculate fruitlessly on a supposed love-triangle for which there is only the barest evidence and precious few parallels in other early literature, is obviated. For if Wulf is in trouble with the society, and the great anxiety of the narrator would indicate that he is, then as a *wulf*, an "out-law," he is a symbol of the antithesis of those who form the society, each of whom, as an *eadwacer*, is a "property-watcher." ... [T]his poem is ... a *giedd* on the personal and social effects of the separation of the outlaw from the society as a whole.

Likewise, Richard Giles accepts Adams' reading of *eadwacer* as an epithet but applies it in still another way: he argues that the "property-watcher" is the woman herself (1981:470-71):

> She speaks to herself when she asks, "Hearest thou, Property-Watcher?" She, ironically, has been given, unwillingly, the task of protecting their "wretched whelp" while Wulf continues his far-wanderings. The answer to her question, "Our wretched whelp / The wolf bears to the woods," is a figurative way of saying, "While I have been daydreaming hope-

---

[4] Although Adams says at the beginning of his article that he reduces the number of characters "from three—the speaker, her lover Wulf, and her husband Eadwacer— to two: speaker and lover" (1958:1), it is clear from the rest of his article that the child is also mentioned in the poem: "... Wulf, who is the woman's lover and the father of her child but who is not her husband" and his rendering of lines 16 and 17 of the poem: "Do you hear, 'home-protector?' The wolf carries our child to the woods" (1958:2, 4).

The first, as far as I could establish, to suggest that Eadwacer is not a proper name but an epithet was W.H. Schofield, who as early as 1902 interpreted it "as a translation of an Old Norse epithet *Auðvakr*, i.e., 'The Easily (or, Very) Vigilant One'." In Schofield's view *W&E* is part of the story of Sigmund and Signy as told in the *Vǫlsunga Saga*, and he says "the epithet 'Very Vigilant One' is especially applicable to Siggeir" (1902:267, n.1); Siggeir was Signy's husband. For further details of Schofield's interpretation, see below.

lessly I have been neglecting the duties of a parent; our child
has gotten into some sort of mischief." The masculine gender
of Eadwacer may be the poet's way of furthering the irony of
the situation the speaker finds herself in. The male should be
the one to protect the young; here a female refers to herself
as one who has assumed the male role.

Dolores Frese (1983:14, 17) sees in *eadwacer* a guardian spirit and
calls him "Heaven-watcher". Stanley Greenfield (1986:10) recognizes
only "the speaker and Wulf":

> Not only are the *beaducafa* who enfolds the speaker in his
> 'boughs' or arms in rainy weather and the *Eadwacer* she ad-
> dresses at the end one and the same with *Wulf*, but in my
> reading the 'whelp' does not exist. Rather, I see it as a
> metaphor for Wulf's and the speaker's joy in love, which is
> metaphorically also 'our *giedd* together'.

It looks as though the interpretation by F. Jones (1985) is an attempt at
a synthesis of several of the interpretations listed above. In his view,
Eadwacer is, as the speaker's husband, the same man as *uncerne earne
hwelp* of line 16: Wulf will eliminate Eadwacer by carrying him, 'our
cowardly whelp', off to the woods, and in doing so Wulf will implement the lady's threat that 'what was never joined is easily parted.' But
Jones sees in Eadwacer also the property watcher, and the poem creates
a powerful tension by contrasting in Eadwacer the *beaducafa* ('the one
brave in battle', l.11), with power over *wælreowe weras* ('cruel men',
l.6) and the *earne hwelp* ('cowardly whelp'), while the juxtaposition of
'property watcher' and 'cowardly whelp' in the same line suggests "a
play on 'guard dog' and 'cur', appearance and reality" (1985:326).

All these interpretations have in common that they take the poem to be
about human beings who have some sort of love relationship with one
another. Completely different are the interpretations put forward by W.J.
Sedgefield (1931), Donald K. Fry (1971), Norman Eliason (1974; mentioned above) and Peter Orton (1985). Sedgefield explains the poem as a
canine love story (1931:74-5):

> A female dog of a romantic temperament is dreaming, day-
> dreaming perhaps, of a wolf with whom she has actually had,
> or dreams she had, a love-affair in the course of her rambles
> in the forest. She dreams that her masters are hot on the trail
> of the wolf, the felon beast, on a neighbouring island in the
> fen. At this juncture she is awakened from her dream by the

terrified yelping of her puppy. Instantly she turns to her law-
ful mate, slumbering by her side, with the cry, 'Wake up,
Eadwacer, a wolf is carrying off our puppy to the forest.' ...
The name of the watch-dog, Eadwacer, is an apt one, as it
means 'guardian of wealth'.

Sedgefield's view was never taken very seriously, but not so long ago
Orton proposed that the poem is literally about wolves.[5] Different, too, is
Fry's reading of the poem as a charm against warts or wens, which is
largely based on a reinterpretation of two words in the poem, *lac* (line 1)
and *wenum/wena* (ll.9, 13), both of which Fry claims may have medical
meanings, 'remedy' and 'wen, wart, tumour' respectively. In an elaborate
reanalysis of the poem as a whole Fry argues, splendidly at times, it is
true, that its female narrator herself is the victim of the disease which the
poem as a charm is directed at, that Wulf is a kind of disease spirit, who
engenders the wen or wart as a child (*hwelp*) on the narrator-victim, and
that Eadwacer is most likely an epithet, "easily-weaker", directed at the
disease as part of a diminishing formula. And Fry concludes (1971:263)

> *Wulf and Eadwacer*, although a medical charm, remains a
> brilliant poetic achievement. The *scop*-doctor (or -patient)
> combines the Anglo-Saxon themes of separation and exile, a
> daring sexual metaphor, ritualistic curing techniques, image
> patterns of water and division, puns, ironic twists, and dra-
> matic address into an amalgam entirely in the spirit of ancient
> medicine, and yet exploiting the evocative potential of the Old
> English wordhoard.

In spite of such an eloquent conclusion, which could be applied to almost
any interpretation of the poem (except for the reference to "ritualistic
curing techniques"), Fry's interpretation somehow fails to convince, either
because we are too romantically inclined or have been preconditioned too
much by Bradley's view.

*

Before turning to a survey of the external interpretations of *W&E*, let me
briefly review the attempts to interpret it as a riddle in spite of its identification as a dramatic monologue by Bradley. To illustrate the way in
which the riddle theory was applied to *W&E*, I will examine some of these

---

[5] Quoted by Marilynn Desmond (1990:589, n.36). Orton (1985) is the second paper that
I have not been able to consult (cf. note 3 above).

riddle interpretations in more detail. It is with Moritz Trautmann that I
would like to start this sketch. We have seen above that Trautmann in
1884 deviated from what was then the traditional view, by suggesting that
the solution to the so-called 'first riddle' was 'riddle' and not Cynewulf.[6]
His solution was almost immediately severely criticized by R. Nuck (1888)
and Fritz Hicketier (1888), both of whom defended the Cynewulf solution.[7] Perhaps as a result of this kind of criticism Trautmann became more
cautious in his comments on the Exeter Book Riddles: when he publishes
in 1894 a list of solutions to the riddles, he still proposes the 'riddle'
solution for the so-called First Riddle but now appends a question mark
("das rätsel?") as a sign of his own uncertainty ("Eine fragezeichen steht
hinten den auflösung, wenn mir ein zweifel an ihrer richtigkeit geblieben
ist" [1894:46]). In 1905 he abandons the idea of W&E being a riddle altogether: he says that the solution he gave in 1894 can be deleted from the
list, "da das "erste rätsel", wie ich mich je länger je mehr überzeugt habe,
überhaupt kein rätsel ist" (1905:167; 'because the "first riddle" is not a
riddle at all, as I have become more and more convinced'). He mentions
the views put forward by Bradley (1888; see above), Lawrence (1902; he
claims that the poem is a translation from Old Norse, see below) and
Schofield (1902; he identifies the Vǫlsunga Saga as the context for W&E,
see below), but he refrains from taking sides with any one of them or
from saying what the poem is about and what kind of poem it is if it is not

---

[6] Cf. Bradley, 1888:198: "Trautmann's opinion is that the speaker is "a riddle" personi-
fied, and that Wulf is *the guesser*, who is compared to a wolf, and who finally seizes and
"carries to the wood" *the answer*, which is the "whelp" or offspring jointly of himself and
of the riddle" (Bradley's italics).

[7] In the same article Hicketier came up with three noteworthy suggestions. Two of them
have gained general acceptance, while the third was soon forgotten. He was the first to
suggest (1888:580) that *Eadwacer* in line 16 may be a vocative, referring back to the subject *þu*, which is still the standard reading of the line. (Up to then *Eadwacer* was taken to
be the object of *gehyrest*, with the line punctuated thus: "*Gehyrest þu Eadwacer, uncerne
earne hwelp?*" 'Do you hear Eadwacer, our [whatever *earne* means] whelp?'—*uncerne
earne hwelp* was an apposition to *Eadwacer*, identifying Eadwacer as the whelp.) He was
also the first to suggest (1888:579) the emendation of *dogode* of line 9 to *hogode* (past
tense of *hogian*, a variant of *hycgan* 'to think about'), which makes good sense and which
is still the most widely accepted solution (cf. below). Finally, he suggested (1888:580)
that instead of the then current reading that *Eadwacer* is the whelp (cf. above) *Eadwacer*
may be the name of a dog and would create a contrast with the wolf. Although hardly any
attention was ever paid to this last suggestion, it is perhaps not so strange as it might seem
at first sight: in this dog/wolf opposition the wolf would have the part of the attacker, the
robber, while the dog would be the defender of the home against the attacker; remember,
too, that Sedgefield saw in Eadwacer a kind of watchdog (1931:75; quoted above), and in
all the interpretations of the name as an epithet it is taken to mean something like 'property
watcher' (cf. Adams, 1958:1, Keough, 1976:557, Giles, 1981:470-71, all of which were
quoted above).

a riddle. Yet this was not the end of the riddle tradition.

In 1910 Frederick Tupper published a monograph on the Exeter Book Riddles which includes a discussion of *W&E*, which he says, after Bradley, is "unquestionably a lyrical monologue" (1910a:liv); yet in an article published later that same year he comes to the conclusion that this lyrical monologue is at the same time both a charade and an acrosticon,[8] and when solved correctly each would yield the name Cynwulf (1910b: 235-8). This time it was Trautmann's turn to be critical. He points out (1912:136) that Tupper's analysis of the poem as a charade is highly dubious since one syllable of his solution occurs as such a number of times in the poem (Wulf), while the other syllable only appears in disguise (Cyn). Furthermore, it is just as dubious that the poem is an acrostic, since Tupper's identification of the runes in the poem often involves the kind of interpretation and guesswork, for which Leo had been condemned: for instance, Tupper claims (1910b:240) that *bogum* (l.11; 'shoulders, arms', lit. boughs) is intended to suggest *boga* 'bow', which is synonymous with *yr* 'bow', the name of the runic letter Y, and that therefore *bogum* of l.11 is a clue for the letter Y. At the end of his review of Tupper's analysis Trautmann (1912:138) answers his own question as to what he thinks the poem really is: "I don't know ... But one thing is certain, ..., the little piece is not a riddle that asks for the name Cynewulf." As Anne Klinck has observed (1987:11, n.39), "the riddle interpretations ... trivialize the poem," and she applies this in particular to the solution suggested by H. Patzig (1923:204-7), who solves the riddle as 'the two stones of a mill', and here is part of his interpretation (in translation):

> The two islands are the two stones of a mill. The woman is the upper part of the lower millstone, ... Wulf the lower part of the upper stone, the turning or 'running' stone. ... — By *leodum minum* is meant the unevenness of the grinding surface of the bottom stone, which was carved in a

---

[8] The distinction between a charade and an acrostic is best illustrated by examples from Tupper's own analysis. In the charade the various clues in the poem yield the syllables of the solution, in this case either *cyn* or *wulf*. For instance, in line 1 *leodum* is dat.pl. of *leod* meaning 'people', and is therefore more or less synonymous with the *cyn(n)* 'nation, race, people': hence *leodum* in line 1 is a clue for *cyn*. The poem thus provides a number of clues for *cyn* and a number of clues for *wulf*, and the solution to the charade is therefore *Cyn-wulf* (or *Wulf-cyn*, which is in theory also possible). In the acrostic the clues are provided by words which are synonymous with words that are also the names of certain letters in the runic alphabet, and these clues yield the letters making up the word of the solution. For instance, in line 1 *lac* meaning 'gift' is more or less synonymous with, or points to, *feoh* 'property', which in the runic alphabet is the name of the letter F. The poem thus provides a number of clues, usually one for each of the letters of the word of the solution, though not usually in the order in which they appear in the solution. Tupper's solution CYNWULF, he suggests, is based on clues in the poem that are given in the order F-N-L-C-N-Y-W-U.

special way... With my people, the woman says, it is like when a man
gives them gifts: they are accustomed to take hold of him, when he comes
on the heap (of corn), i.e. they crush his hand; with the turning ('running')
stone it is similar: when it comes on to the grain that is poured out, the
elevations of the grooves, the *wælreowe weras*, will take hold of it. — ...
Eadwacer is the *hwelp* itself, the little donkey turning the mill. ... the
conversation of the stones suddenly comes to an end, as the mill has come
to a standstill: 'That one easily tears apart which was never joined together,
our conversation with each other.'

Such a highly improbable interpretation illustrates how much one can read
into a poem like *W&E*.

With Patzig the riddle interpretation of *W&E* seems to have died,
for no further attempts to interpret the poem as a riddle have been made
since Patzig, with one notable exception: in 1983 James Anderson "resur-
rects" the riddle theory, to use Greenfield and Calder's description (1986:
300, n.43). Anderson elaborates a point made earlier by P.J. Frankis, who
had noted the close resemblance between *W&E* and the poem immediately
preceding in the Exeter Book, *Deor*. Earlier we saw that Frankis thinks of
Wulf as a *scop*, which is what Deor was.[9] Both poems have purely literary
refrains, which makes them unique in Old English literature, and he conjectures that the two poems were deliberately placed together in the Exeter
Book, and finds support for that conjecture in a kind of cross-textual
wordplay on *deor* 'beast' and *wulf*. And then Frankis reconstructs from
both poems a hypothetical narrative, "the story of a king's daughter who
takes a lover against her father's will, and the lover is forced to flee"
(1962:174), one poem telling the story from the man's point of view
(*Deor*) and the other from the woman's (*W&E*). Anderson thinks that
Frankis's "conjectures were ... very nearly right" (1983:205), but he takes
the wordplay that Frankis detects in *W&E* and *Deor* beyond these poems
into the preceding poem in the Exeter Book, *The Soul's Address to the
Body*: "from their many plays on words and themes, these three texts appear to be a long triple riddle that equates heroic abduction with spiritual
death and exposes pagan heroism as bitterly unheroic in the end" (1983:
205). A long and detailed exposition of the various relations between the
three poems follows. With Frankis, Anderson believes (1983:212) that

---

[9] Frankis even suggests (1962:173-4) that the *scop*'s name in *Deor* is not really Deor but
rather "a riddling reference to the hero's true name: *me wæs deor noma*, 'my name was an
animal'—that is, of course, Wulf." The key to this interpretation is the use of the past
tense in this half line: why should he say that his name *was* Deor? To conceal his real
name and identity from his enemies who have exiled him? But why should he in that case
give away what his name had previously been? This line of reasoning makes Frankis read
deor instead of *Deor*, and as the use of the capital is no more than a modern typographical
device at the disposal of the modern editor, it may well be that the poet allowed an ambiguity of this kind here on purpose.

[*W&E*] takes up the abducted bride's part of the story. From a love turned to bitterness or even hatred, she looks back to proclaim her unlikeness to Deor, whom she calls Wulf either in truth or in riddlic wordplay.

The difference in tone between *Deor* and *W&E*, a "dramatic disparity between Deor's and the woman's tone", he explains (1983:212) as having a technical cause, which the poet has hidden in the ambiguous word *giedd*:

Besides "vow, formal speech," *giedd* also means "song, poem," and thus carries the innuendo of two songs—that is, *Deor* and *Wulf and Eadwacer*—whose marriage has been an uneasy one at best. By inference the two poems themselves make a strange and unlikely pair, perhaps a union of heroic and elegiac song. No one, it seems, had ever joined them, until their tenuous partnership was made with a riddler's wit. Thus, I think, the woman's last lines twist the meaning of the unlikeness which she has already twice asserted in her refrain.

Anderson's claim for a tripartite riddle involving besides *Deor* and *W&E* a poem that seems to have little in common with the other two is in itself ingenious, yet it fails to convince because thematically the poems are miles apart: in spite of certain lexical correspondences *W&E* and *The Soul's Address* belong to different worlds, the latter is a didactic and moralistic poem, and whatever *W&E* may be it is neither didactic nor moralistic. The fact that in l.22 (*Hwæt, wite þu me, werga!* 'How you do worry me, you blasted wolf!') the soul addresses the body with the word *wearg*, which means both 'outlaw' and 'wolf', as Anderson points out (1983:221), can establish no more than a superficial relation between the two poems.

   Anderson's solution (1983:226) to his tripartite riddle follows naturally from the arguments with which he supports his claim for the riddle:

The Soul's Address, Deor, and *Wulf and Eadwacer* seem to make up a riddlic pilgrimage of their own, through the *visibilia* of wasted lives in this world to the *invisibilia* of eternal grief in the next.

What Anderson suggests here is hardly, it seems to me, a solution to a riddle but rather some common element that these three poems share, and which a great many other poems share, for that matter. With regard to *W&E* there may be a level of interpretation at which one might speak of "wasted lives in this world" and "eternal grief in the next", but even so the poem allows other interpretations as well, some of which may seem more probable than what Anderson suggests, as I will show below.

*

Henry Bradley's suggestion that "the so-called riddle is not a riddle at all, but a fragment of a dramatic soliloquy" (1888:198) sparked off a new kind of scholarly activity: the quest for the ultimate source and context of the fragment. If it is a fragment, what is it a fragment of? Who are the people in this "dramatic soliloquy" and what are their respective roles in the larger story? Several attempts have been made over the years to answer these and related questions. A brief review of these theories (which were grouped together by Fanagan as 'external interpretations', 1976:130) is in order here.

W.W. Lawrence believes that *W&E* was originally written in Old Norse and was later translated literally into Anglo-Saxon, because it shows Old Norse influence in strophic structure, refrain and language (cf. 1902: 258-9). In a companion article in the same issue of *PMLA*, W.H. Schofield takes up Lawrence's suggestion and identifies what he believes to be the Old Norse narrative context for the poem: the story of Sigmund and Signy in the *Vǫlsunga Saga*. He suggests that *W&E* is a lament by Signy, who addresses Sigmund as Wolf, because he is an outlaw, since he had, as the saga tells us, committed a murder and could therefore not remain at home with his father. And "the words *ulfr* and *vargr*,[10] meaning wolf, were both used in Old Norse as the designation of an outlaw," Schofield points out (1902:265); he places "Signy's Lament" at the moment in the story when Signy learns that her brother Sigmund and her son Sinfjǫtli whom she bore to this brother, are prepared to undertake the task of avenging her father Vǫlsung on her husband Siggeir (1902:270-71). At the end of that same year, Bradley comments on the findings of Lawrence and Schofield with these words: "while the writers have made a contribution of considerable value to the elucidation of the poem, their main contentions are either erroneous or unproved" (1902:758).

Gollancz (1902:551-2) was also very critical of Lawrence and, especially, Schofield: "it becomes one's duty to express one's doubts as to the correctness of Prof. Schofield's contention. ... I make bold to say that the conclusions will not be accepted." Like Bradley, he rejects Schofield's interpretation of the name Eadwacer as an epithet (cf. note 4 above), and calls the occurrence of this name in the poem "the strongest internal evidence against his [i.e. Schofield's] theory". Consequently, Gollancz's own interpretation is based on this name: "if, as seems probable, the subject of the poem was drawn from Teutonic legend, surely Eadwacer—*i.e.*, Odoacer—points to the cycle of Theodoric; and a stronger case can be

---

[10] This word *vargr* is the ON cognate of OE *werga/wearg*, which is, as we have seen, the term used by the soul in addressing the body in *The Soul's Address*.

made for "Wulf" as applied to Theodoric (Dietrich) than "as suitable to Sigmund"." The episodes in *W&E*, as Gollancz reads the poem, "strikingly recall the statement in the 'Hildebrandslied' that Dietrich fled into exile owing to Odoacer's enmity, and the statement in that poem and in the Anglo-Saxon lyric 'Deor's Lament' that it took him thirty years to regain his kingdoms." Gollancz admits that there is not any particular incident in the Dietrich cycle that is directly treated in *W&E*, but reiterates that "if the Anglo-Saxon hearers readily understood the subject-matter as drawn from legend or history, internal evidence would seem to connect the poem with the glorious story of Theodoric the Great, whose ultimate triumph over Odoacer made him conqueror of Italy."

Gollancz's suggestion of a context for the story told in *W&E* fails to convince because it starts from too many assumptions that cannot be proved. This is also true of Rudolf Imelmann's claim (1907, 1920) for a cycle in Old English literature dealing with Odoaker, not the Odoacer proposed by Gollancz but a Saxon chief named Eadwacer (or Adovacrius in Gregory of Tours) who invaded Gaul in 463, an identification of which Henry Bradley is very skeptical: "Nothing more is known of this Eadwacer; but Dr Imelmann is confident that his deeds must have been extensively celebrated in heroic poetry" (1907:368). Starting from the hypothesis that Eadwacer and Wulf are the same person (which, according to Bradley [1907:366], stands "in such violent contradiction to any natural interpretation of the poem that I do not think it could be arrived at by any scholar merely by way of inference from the text"), Imelmann originally envisaged a cycle consisting of just three poems in a kind of trilogy, *W&E* (on the basis of the occurrence of the name Eadwacer in l.16), *The Wife's Lament* (on the basis of its thematic affinity to *W&E*) and *The Husband's Message* (on the basis of his reading of the runes at the end of this poem as spelling the name of Eadwacer). The credibility of Imelmann's claim suffered greatly as a result of his subsequent claim (1920) that even *The Wanderer* and *The Seafarer* were part of this Odoaker cycle and that an extensive Odoaker cycle must have existed in Old English literature, "for which no evidence is known except Imelmann's hypothesis" (Krapp and Dobbie, 1936:lvi). Just as critical, as we have seen, is Bradley's review of Imelmann's original proposal: with regard to Imelmann's interpretation of *W&E* and *The Wife's Lament*, Bradley notes that "Dr Imelmann reads into the text a good deal that is not there ... there is not enough definite likeness to create even a faint presumption of the identity of ths speaker in the two poems. With the *Husband's Message* the case is still worse ... There is nothing to make it likely that the sender of the message is the Wulf of the lyric" (1907:366). Bradley even speaks of "manipulation" of runes and "curious jugglery" with regard to Imelmann's interpretation of the runes of this poem, S. R. EA. W. M. (or D.): reading the C rune for the S rune (which are, however, quite distinct in shape) and assigning an unprecedented triple value to the EA rune, as *ea*, as *e* and as *a*, he concludes that the runes spell the name of Eadwacer.

Other attempts have been made at identifying the context of *W&E*: the Wolfdietrich B story (Schücking, 1919; perhaps also Frankis, 1962, although he is not very explicit on this point), the Old Norse *Volundar-kviða* (Bouman, 1949), and the Frankish Dietrich legend (Lehmann, 1969). It is probably best to leave this question of the context unsettled and accept Alain Renoir's approach which abandons the idea of some kind of larger plot as a framework for the story of *W&E* (since this would be conjectural anyway and could never be proved or disproved) but which concentrates on the "themes that permeate the entire poem" (1965:152): the themes of separation and union, of hostility and of suffering. Renoir called his approach "a non-interpretation", because his analysis does not follow the traditional pattern of trying to identify a context for the poem and as a result his analysis "might suit most of the usual interpretations" (1965:159). By breaking with that tradition, Renoir's approach marks the beginning of a new type of *W&E* criticism in which the poem as we have it, with all its imagery, emotions, obscurities, ambiguities, is at the centre. In fact, Renoir must have taken his cue from Kemp Malone, whom he quotes and who showed in a couple of sentences the fallacy of the contextual approach (1962:108):

> The poem is based on a tale familiar to the poet's audience but unknown to us. We can reconstruct it only in part, since the poet gives us not a narrative of events but a lyric monologue, put in the mouth of a woman, who tells us how she feels rather than what has happened.

Hence the only valid interpretation of the poem, it would seem, is an interpretation of the poem as poem, i.e. of the feelings and emotions it conveys. In the last part of this chapter I will do just that: examine the poem line by line, explain its many textual difficulties and its syntactic and lexical ambiguities, and suggest alternative translations to the one given at the beginning of this chapter wherever this seems necessary.

*

Bradley's view that *W&E* is a fragment, together with the poem's obscure beginning, has led some critics to postulate the loss of one or two lines at the beginning of the poem. Bradley himself must have felt that the poem lacks its beginning, since his translation of it starts with a line of asterisks between brackets (1888:198). Lawrence (1902:250) prints the text of the poem with a two-line lacuna between lines 1 and 2: it is not necessary, he

says, "to supply anything to complete the sense of the first line. It is perfect in itself. ... 'It is to my people as if one give to them a gift (*or*, gifts).'
For the *hine* and *he* of line 2 an antecedent is necessary, and this is not
found in the first line." Believing that this antecedent must have occurred
in a line now lost, Lawrence assumes the loss of 2 lines after line 1, which
would make a group of four lines followed by the short line *Ungelic is us*,
and this five-line stanza would be a "perfect counterpart" to the second
group which begins at line 4 (of the poem as we have it) and ends with the
second occurrence of the short line *Ungelice is us*. In his translation of the
poem Schofield (1902: 266) follows the text as given by Lawrence and
consequently has the same gap after line 1.

In more recent years similar assumptions about missing lines have
been proposed. Ruth Lehmann (1969:163-5) divides the poem into five
sections or stanzas, assumes the loss of two lines at the beginning of the
poem, assumes furthermore that this first line now lost must have started
with the word Wulf, since this would make the first four of her five
stanzas start with a reference to Wulf (her new line 1, and lines 4, 9, 13 in
the traditional numbering), while in the final stanza Wulf occurs in the
second line (1.17 of the poem) having yielded to Eadwacer in the opening
line of this stanza. Lehmann sees in the formal stanzaic pattern suggested
by the repetitions of Wulf a carefully structured narrative: "the second
stanza deals with present physical circumstances, the third with past emotions, the fourth with present emotions, and the last with the future." On
the basis of this pattern she assumes that the first stanza must have dealt
with "past emotional circumstances", her separation from Wulf (which
would supply an antecedent for *hine*), and may have been addressed to
Eadwacer directly (to clarify *us*). Lehmann's assumption of two lines
missing at the beginning of the poem was accepted by Janemarie Luecke
(1983:200), and Richard Giles believes that "*at least* two lines are missing
before the poem begins where it does. These lines would ... clarify the
difficult first stanza" (1981:472, n.18).

The line-by-line discussion of the poem that follows below takes the
poem in the form that has come down to us; whether any number of lines
are missing anywhere in the poem is an issue that I will not comment on.

Line 1:   Leodum is minum   swylce him mon lac gife;
            (It is to my people as if they have been given a present:)

According to Lawrence (1902:250; just quoted), the first line makes perfect sense as it stands and does not present any difficulty, as his translation
indicates. But, as Ruth Lehmann says, the real problem with line 1 lies
outside the line: "The first line of [*W&E*] gives little difficulty in translation; its problem lies in the ... application of the line to the story" (1969:

158). The problem is caused in part by the noun *lac*, the precise meaning of which is not absolutely clear, and it is because of this problem that Ann Klinck calls the opening line of the poem "puzzling" (1987:4). Most commentators concentrate on this word *lac*, which in Arnold Davidson's view is "a most ambiguous word" (1975:27). His translation of the poem, which gives multiple renderings whenever a word had more than one meaning, reads in the second half of line 1 "as if one might give them (a battle/sacrifice/gift/message/game)" (1975:25). The words in parentheses all translate *lac*, and Davidson dryly observes that "There is a great difference between being given a battle and being given a game, between a gift and a sacrifice" (1975:27). However, Peter Baker (1981:40-41) shows that it is wrong to assign most of these meanings to *lac* in this particular context,[11] and as a result this multiple rendering of *lac* is reduced to a simple, straightforward translation, 'gift'. But for Baker, as for Lehmann, the real difficulty of the first line is not its literal meaning, but its interpretation: "Someone or something is being compared to a gift; some action or situation is being compared to the giving of a gift to the speaker's people. If we assume, in the absence of manuscript evidence to the contrary, that the poem is complete, our first impulse will be to look for the explanation in line 2" (1981:41-2). But line 2, it turns out, is much more problematic.

Lines 2-3: willað hy hine aþecgan,   gif he on þreat cymeð.
            Ungelic is us.
            (they will receive him if he comes to their troop. It is different with us.)

Lines 2 and 3 are usually taken together as a kind of refrain, since they occur in practically the same form again as lines 7 and 8, the only difference being in the first word of the second verse of this refrain: *ungelic* in line 3 and *ungelice* in line 8 (this difference is discussed below). Terrence Keough, however, argues that the repetition is due to the narrator's state of mind, her great concern for Wulf's safety, and "is hardly a 'refrain,' ..., at least not in the sense that *Þæs ofereode, þisses swa mæg* is a refrain in *Deor*" (1976:559, n.1). Similarly, F. Jones suggests that in view of the poem's "mimetic quality" we ought to "refrain from calling 2-3 and 7-8 what it has been called" (1985:327, n.14). Whether one looks upon these

---

[11] Baker (1981:40-41) argues that the 'battle' sense of *lac* "results from a misinterpretation by Bosworth-Toller of a passage in *Guthlac B*" (as shown by Cameron and diPaulo Healey in 1979 and quoted by Klinck, 1987:4, n.6), that the 'message' sense is "a metaphorical extension of the meaning 'gift', conditioned by the context in which it occurs", that the 'game' sense, "imported from Old Icelandic by modern scholars, is not attested in Old English", and finally that 'gift, offering, sacrifice' "are well-attested definitions, but when *lac* means 'offering, sacrifice,' it usually takes a more ceremonious verb (e.g., *offrian, bringan*, ...) than *gifan*."

lines as a refrain or not is obviously determined by one's definition of a refrain, though in the present case not even the simplest definition can remove all doubt as to the refrain status of the repeated lines: if a refrain is simply the recurrence of a line or lines at regular intervals in a poem, is a repetition occurring just once often enough for it to qualify as a refrain? Keough is right to some extent when he says that the refrain in *Deor* is different: there the poet uses the refrain for a kind of personal comment on the events described or alluded to in each of the stanzas. Yet I will not rule out the possibility that in *W&E* the repeated lines have a similar function: although this is difficult to argue for lines 2-3 due to a lack of context, it may very well be true of lines 7-8, where after describing her separation from Wulf and the latter's difficult circumstances the narrator reaffirms to herself her belief that Wulf will be received by her people which is at the same time a reaffirmation of their separation. Seen in this light, the refrain is indeed filled with emotion and as such it comes as a natural climax in lines 7-8, but that does not necessarily imply that we should call it by another name, as Jones urges us to do. Moreover, the refrain here serves to punctuate the narrative: it marks the transition between the narrator's description of Wulf's circumstances in lines 4-6 and of hers in lines 9-12. Harry Kavros (1977:84) sums up this function of the refrain in these terms: "the refrain ... is the poetic correlative to the emotional attitude of the speaker. It expresses her inner tensions and her increasing sense of imposed suffering." Defining a refrain as "the repetition of a group of words [that] is sufficiently regular and conspicuous," Anne Klinck notes that "in *W&E*, the theme of the speaker's separation from and anxiety for her lover, an enemy of her tribe, is emphasized by the repetition of two consecutive lines: 'willað ...' " (1984:134-5).

Line 2, the first line of the refrain, is highly problematic both in syntax and in vocabulary. Syntactically because it is not clear whether it is a statement or a question. Bradley takes the line to be a question, but it is just as possible that it is a statement. Peter Baker (1981:44) maintains that the word order of *willan*-subject-infinitive is rarely found in poetry without an introductory interrogative word like *hu* or *hwæt*, while the same word order occurs in statements but then of course without an interrogative word, as here in line 2. Ruth Lehmann (1969:158) likewise takes the line as statement but on different grounds: "the short line of the refrain *Ungelic is us* makes a better opposition to the first line [of the refrain] if that is taken as a statement, rather than as a question"; she adds, however, that the word order, especially in poetry, allows either reading. Most critics now read the line as a statement, though Keough (1976:554) and Klinck (1984:140, n.20) favour the question in their respective interpretations.

Lexically line 2 is a puzzle, because the meanings of "the two allit-
erating words—hence the most emphatic and most important to the meaning—are in dispute" (Lehmann, 1969:158). The first of these is the verb
apecgan, which Bradley notes "occurs only in this passage" and which he
interprets "as the causative of *picgan*, and as meaning 'to give food to, to
entertain'" (1888:198). Kemp Malone (1962:108-9) lists the various meanings suggested and combines the Bradley gloss and the Bosworth-Toller
gloss 'receive' into his own rendering 'take in', with the implication of
destruction as the result of being literally taken in, i.e. consumed. According to Peter Baker (1983:5), the literal meaning of *apecgan* is 'to serve,
feed' while figuratively it means 'to kill', and he adds that it is very likely
that "our poet had both meanings in mind for this line." A similar less
hospitable meaning 'oppress', derived from Old Norse *áþjá*, is given by
Schofield (1902:266), Imelmann (1907:16) and Tupper (1910b:238). What
seems certain about this verb is that it refers to the kind of reception that
Wulf will be given by the speaker's people; and if its meaning ranges from
'take in; entertain; give food to' to 'oppress; destroy; kill', the verb explains why the lady should be concerned about Wulf's safety. I come back
to this in the discussion of the second occurrence of the refrain.

The second lexical puzzle in line 2 is the meaning of the noun *preat*.
Basically there are three possibilities. Usually it is taken to mean 'troop,
band, crowd, body of people', the meaning given for *preat* in Bosworth-
Toller. Bradley (1888:198) cites the Old Norse phrase *at protum koma* as
the basis for *on preat cuman* and translates 'to come to want', which makes
good sense in combination with his rendering of *apecgan* (see above).
Malone (1963:109) turns to Old Norse as well but cites another phrase, *í
praut* 'in a desperate struggle', which is related to the second meaning of
preat in Bosworth-Toller 'violence, compulsion, force', and he translates
'comes into peril', and this translation too fits in well with Malone's rendering of *apecgan*.

Any rendering of the difficult words of line 2 should take into
account the meaning of the first line and of the word *lac* in particular, and
this I believe rules out any hostile intepretation of *preat*: if a person's
coming is compared to being a gift to someone, this person cannot come
with force or violence at the same time (cf. Baker, 1983:5).

Lines 4-6: Wulf is on iege,   ic on oþerre.
            Fæst is þæt eglond,   fenne biworpen.
            Sindon wælreowe   weras þær on ige;
            (Wulf is on one island, I on another. Fortified is that island,
             surrounded by a fen. There are cruel men there on that island.)

These lines present little difficulty, as the situation described is clear.

Lines 7-8: willað hy hine aþecgan,   gif he on þreat cymeð.
          Ungelice is us.
          (they will receive him if he comes to their troop. It is different with us.)

After all that has been said already about the refrain, two remarks will suffice. First, the adjective *ungelic* of line 3 is now replaced with the adverb *ungelice*, but Baker (1983:5) finds there to be little practical difference between the two usages. Kavros, on the other hand, translates line 3 as 'we are different' and line 8 as 'things go differently with respect to us', which is meant to illustrate a change in tone, from the descriptive tone of line 3 to a tone in line 8 which "suggests a lack of control over the action" (1977:84). The change is meant to emphasize the increased suffering of the speaker. Yet in a footnote Kavros admits that the final *-e* of *ungelice* "may ... be a mere scribal error". I agree with Baker and look upon the *ungelic/ungelice* distinction as having no special significance. The second remark concerns line 7 and the question whether it is a statement or a question. I would suggest that line 2 is to be read as a statement because of the link with line 1—the speaker is sure that Wulf will be received favourably by her people since his coming is to them like a gift; but in line 7 the speaker is full of doubt about Wulf's reception, and therefore full of anxiety for his safety, since in the line immediately preceding she says there are cruel and bloodthirsty men on Wulf's island: in other words, she is no longer confident about the way in which Wulf will be received but wonders how that will be, and so she actually asks herself a question in line 7: will they receive him (i.e. in a friendly manner) ...? The possibility of reading the line in different ways was suggested earlier, though without comment or explanation, by Neil Isaacs (1968:116): "it could be declarative once, interrogative another time."

Line 9:   Wulfes ic mines widlastum   wenum dogode;
          (I thought with hope of my Wulf's long journey,)

With this line the poem begins to move to its emotional climax, and Alain Renoir discusses this gradual buildup in detail (1965:155-9). The interpretation of line 9 is, however, not altogether clear, and the last word in particular is problematic: *dogode* is attested nowhere else in Old English, and there have been several attempts to explain its etymology and meaning (Lehmann, 1969:160-61, cites Scots *dow* 'fade', and Mattox, 1975:34, Middle Dutch *duwen* 'squeeze'), but none of these explanations is entirely satisfactory, so that the best solution still seems to be an emendation of the manuscript reading to *hogode*, which was first suggested by Hicketier in 1888 (cf. above, note 7) and which has even found its way into the new *Dictionary of Old English* (Fascicle D, p.441, s.v. **dogian*).

Lines 10-12: þonne hit wæs renig weder   ond ic reotogu sæt,
              þonne mec se beaducafa   bogum bilegde,
              wæs me wyn to þon,   wæs me hwæþre eac laõ.
              (when it was rainy weather and I sat weeping,
              when the one brave in battle laid his arms around me,
              it was a joy to me to a degree, however it was also hateful.)

The problem here is one of syntax: how are the two *þonne* clauses related
to each other and to the context? Do they make up a correlative pair of the
type 'when ..., then ...', but if so which of the two is the 'when' clause and
which the 'then' clause? Another possibility is to take both of them as
parallel 'when' clauses, as Baker does (1983:5), which are subordinated to
both lines 9 and 12, and although this reading creates an ambiguity, it is an
ambiguity that makes excellent sense in the context: lines 10 and 11
describe the circumstances under which the speaker thinks of her Wulf
(1.9), but at the same time they explain the speaker's opposite emotions of
line 12. In my translation I have chosen for this interpretation, since the
ambiguous reference of the two *þonne* clauses enhances the dramatic effect
of these already highly emotional lines.

Another problem of this passage is line 11: who is *se beaducafa* 'the
one brave in battle', what is the precise meaning of *bilegde*? *Beaducafa* is
usually taken to refer to Eadwacer, who is not mentioned until line 16;
others think it is a reference to Wulf, but this is unlikely, perhaps even
impossible, since line 9 states that Wulf is far away on his long journey
(provided the clause of line 11 is dependent on line 9, as I have assumed;
cf. Klinck, 1987:9, n.29), and why in that case should the speaker dislike
the embraces if it was Wulf who laid his arms around her? Greenfield believes that the embraces are Wulf's all right, and suggests that the reference is either to a "scenario in which Wulf ... once *did* venture from his
island to hers, or [to] an anterior occasion before the lovers were caught"
(1986:12; Greenfield's emphasis). And he explains the speaker's ambi-
valent feelings of line 12 as resulting from "the peril and brevity of their
time together", an explanation that I find improbable in the light of what
follows. *Bogum* seems to mean simply 'arms' (by extension, lit. 'boughs'),
though other meanings have been suggested as well. The unfavourable
connotations of *bilegde* (lit. 'lay around, surround'), resulting from its
subsidiary meanings 'afflict, load, accuse, charge' (cf. Bosworth-Toller),
may be another reason for the speaker to regard the embraces as an un-
pleasant experience.

Lines 13-15: Wulf, min Wulf,   wena me þine
              seoce gedydon,   þine seldcymas,
              murnende mod,   nales meteliste.
              (Wulf my Wulf, hopes of you have made me sick, your rare visits,
              a sorrowing heart, not at all lack of food.)

The speaker is now directly addressing Wulf, her Wulf, *in absentia* of course, and her directness is emphasized by the staccato rhythm of these very short half-lines (which are so short that in the past various additions were proposed to make these lines fit the more usual types of Old English versification): it is almost as if the rhythm is meant to convey the sobbing of her heart. She is blaming Wulf for not coming enough (or for not coming at all, if *seldcymas* is to be taken as a litotes as Baker [1981:48] suggests) and for her illness, which she implies is emotional rather than physical, because she will not attribute it to her lack of food. Frankis rightly observes that this does not mean that she did not experience such a lack of food (1962:172, n.33); it only means that she is not naming it as the cause of her illness.[12]

Lines 16-17:   Gehyrest þu, Eadwacer?   Uncerne earne hwelp
               bireð wulf to wuda.
               (Do you hear, Eadwacer? Our wretched whelp
               Wulf will carry off to the wood.)

With these lines the poem reaches its climax: the speaker is now addressing Eadwacer, and earlier I discussed the various interpretations and implications of the word (or name, for that matter). I take the word as referring to the speaker's husband. She threatens him and makes sure that he will listen, "Do you hear, Eadwacer?" If a further implication of line 4 is that like Wulf she is banished to an island and is therefore not with Eadwacer, she is calling out to him *in absentia*, just as in line 13 when she called out to Wulf. Her threat is full of ambiguities, some of which may be intentional, as *double entendres* designed to conceal the truth from Eadwacer: who are the referents of the possessive *uncerne*? what is the meaning of *earne*? who or what is the *hwelp*? what tense is *bireð*? who or what is the *wulf*?

The dual possessive of the first person refers to the speaker and one other person, usually the person addressed, in this case the woman narrator and Eadwacer, but there can be no absolute certainty that the reference is not to the speaker and a person different from the person addressed: in other words, by using the dual possessive *uncer* the speaker seems to suggest to Eadwacer as the person addressed that the *hwelp* (whatever its meaning) is theirs, but her subsequent use of the word *hwelp* implies that it is not theirs but rather hers and Wulf's.

---

12 It may be that the speaker is suffering from the early morning sickness that often accompanies the first months of pregnancy: if so, the speaker is pregnant of the *hwelp* by Wulf, who will come back to carry off his child to the wood, and *bireð* (1.17) must then be future tense.

The word *earne* has been interpreted in various ways: Bradley first thought it was derived from the adjective *earh* 'cowardly' (1888:198), but later (1893:390) accepted Holthausen's emendation (1893:188-9) of *earne* to *earmne* 'poor, wretched'. This is still the most widely accepted reading, though Baker (1981:50) prefers the original reading by Bradley for his interpretation of the passage. Others derive *earne* from *earn* 'eagle': Fry translates "A wolf, accompanied by an eagle, ..." (1971:261), and Suzuki reads "An eagle will carry our child, Wulf" (1987:179). It seems to me that there is nothing in the poem to justify the sudden appearance on the scene of an eagle.

The key word in the line is, of course, *hwelp*, which many have translated as 'child', a metaphorical sense since literally it means 'cub, pup'. Others suggest it is not a child at all: Fanagan, for instance, reads in it a metaphor for the speaker's link with Eadwacer (1976:135), whereas Greenfield sees it as a "metaphor for Wulf's and the speaker's joy in love" (1986:10). In my view of the line the *hwelp* refers to whatever the speaker and Wulf have or have had together, both literally and figuratively, both to a child and to a happy relationship. In the case of the child it could be that the speaker is still carrying it and that it is as yet unborn: it really makes no difference for the rest of the line—Wulf, she is telling Eadwacer, will come back to carry it off to the wood, i.e. the child and, by implication, herself too, either because she is still pregnant or because she is an integral part of that relationship. The ambiguous reference of *uncerne* also affects the figurative meaning of *hwelp*, as it too can be read as denoting the relationship between the speaker and Eadwacer, a relationship that is truly 'wretched' in the context of the poem.

Three last brief comments on line 17. A minor point first: the verb in the line, *bireð*, can be read as either a present tense or a future. In my interpretation of the line as a threat to Eadwacer that something will take place in time to come, I take it to be a future and translate it as such. Secondly, the word *wulf* may be a common noun or a proper noun; my translation indicates that I think it is the name Wulf; others have suggested that it is literally a wolf, or that it means 'as an outlaw' (Bouman, 1949: 112; he adopts the old punctuation of line 16 and makes Eadwacer the subject of *bireð*; cf. note 7 above). In Old English, as in Old Norse, one of the meanings of the noun *wulf* was 'outlaw', and the identification of Wulf as an outlaw goes back to Bradley. Finally, it has struck me that all critics take it for granted that Wulf should carry the *hwelp* to a forest: why a forest? The answer is perhaps so obvious that no one has thought it worthwhile to comment on it: the forest is of course the natural habitat of the wolf. But there is more to it: the forest is also the place where the outlaw takes refuge and lives. The speaker thus resigns herself to the fact that she, as the mother of Wulf's child as well as being an integral part of the figurative meaning of *hwelp*, will spend the rest of her life in the wilderness away from the civilized world. It is her tragedy that in the poem there can be no reconciliation between that world and the world of outlawry.

Lines 18-19: Þæt mon eaþe tosliteð   þætte næfre gesomnad wæs,
uncer giedd geador.
(One easily tears apart that which was never joined,
our song together.)

The speaker winds up her monologue with a reference to what the Gospel teaches about marriage—What therefore God hath joined together, let not man put asunder (Matthew 19:6)—as many have pointed out (e.g. Frankis, 1962:173; Keough, 1976:558; Spamer, 1978; Baker, 1983:6; Klinck, 1987:12, n.43). But it is an inverted reference, since she says 'what has never been joined is easily put asunder,' by which, I take it, she implies that she was never really married. Therefore the final lines are in my view a reference to the speaker's marriage to Eadwacer: now that in the previous two lines she has revealed to Eadwacer not only that he is not the father of their child but also that her lover Wulf will come back to her and take their child away, she can also tell him that she was never really married to him or in love with him. After the revelations of lines 16 and 17, she deals Eadwacer the final blow: first she denies him the fatherhood of their child, now she takes their love and marriage away from him as well.

In the last line the dual possessive *uncer* occurs again. And here again its reference may be just as ambiguous as in line 16: whereas I take its primary reference in line 16 to be to the speaker and Wulf, in the last line the primary reference is to the speaker and Eadwacer, it is their song or relationship together, with a possible secondary reference to her and Wulf. After all, she and Wulf were never really joined together either, since he was exiled to his island—perhaps as a result of the discovery of their love affair, though this is mere speculation—and the speaker remained behind on hers. That the two *uncer*s of lines 16 and 19 need not necessarily have the same referents in both cases is a possibility suggested by Neil Isaacs (1968:115), again without further comment or explanation.

The exact meaning of *giedd* in the last line has been much discussed. Its basic meaning is 'song', but *giedd* derives a figurative sense from its combination with *geador* 'together': singing together presupposes being together, and in this way *giedd geador* may refer to fellowship together, to time spent together. Or, in a more abstract sense, the combination may denote something like 'sharing something together', e.g. a relationship. Again, the ambiguity of *uncer* extends to this combination as well: primarily it is the *giedd geador* of the speaker and Eadwacer, and on a secondary level of the speaker and Wulf.

The fact that at the climax of her dramatic monologue the lady is speaking in ambiguities is perhaps yet another puzzle of the poem. An explanation could be that even in the anguish of disclosing to Eadwacer the secrets of her heart she is still trying to protect her lover who is held captive by her husband. The poem is a most passionate cry of the heart, a *cri de coeur*, a woman lamenting not only the separation from her lover, but also the uncertainty of what the future will have in store for her child, for her lover Wulf, for her relationship with him, and for herself when she will be reunited with him. It is a poem that has been called "one of the summits of Anglo-Saxon poetry" (Dronke, 1969:91), and rightly so. For all the ambiguity in the poem, it is an ambiguity that "is more artistic than puzzling, and [that] justifies the reputation of *Wulf and Eadwacer* as a little masterpiece of Old English literature" (Baker, 1981:51).

REFERENCES

Adams, John F. (1958). 'Wulf and Eadwacer': An Interpretation. *Modern Language Notes* 73. 1-5.
Anderson, James E. (1983). *Deor, Wulf and Eadwacer, The Soul's Address*: How and Where the Exeter Book Riddles Begin. In: Green, 1983:204-30.
Baker, Peter S. (1981). The Ambiguity of *Wulf and Eadwacer*. In: *Eight Anglo-Saxon Studies*. Ed. by Joseph S. Wittig. *Studies in Philology* 78, no.5. 39-51.
Baker, Peter S. (1983). *Wulf and Eadwacer*: A Classroom Edition. *Old English Newsletter* 16.2, Appendix, 1-8.
Bouman, A.C. (1949). *Leodum is Minum*: Beadohild's Complaint. *Neophilologus* 33. 103-13.
Bradley, Henry (1888). [Review of Henry Morley's *English Writers*, Vol. II, 2nd ed.] *Academy* 33 [March 24, 1888]. 197-8.
Bradley, Henry (1893). [Letter to the Editor.] *Anglia* 15. 390.
Bradley, Henry (1902). The Sigurd Cycle and Britain. *Athenaeum* [Dec. 6]. 758.
Bradley, Henry (1907). [Review of Imelmann, *Die altenglische Odoaker-Dichtung*]. *Modern Language Review* 2. 365-8.
Davidson, Arnold E. (1975). Interpreting *Wulf and Eadwacer*. *Annuale Mediaevale* 16. 23-32.
Desmond, Marilynn (1990). The Voice of Exile: Feminist Literary History and the Anonymous Anglo-Saxon Elegy. *Critical Inquiry* 16. 572-90.
Dronke, Peter (1969). *The Medieval Lyric*. New York: Harper and Row.
Eliason, Norman E. (1974). On *Wulf and Eadwacer*. In: *Old English Studies in Honour of John C. Pope*. Ed. by Robert B. Burlin and Edward B. Irving, Jr. Toronto and Buffalo: University of Toronto Press. 225-34.
Fanagan, John M. (1976). *Wulf and Eadwacer*: A Solution to the Critics' Riddle. *Neophilologus* 60. 130-37.
Frankis, P.J. (1962). *Deor* and *Wulf and Eadwacer*: Some Conjectures. *Medium Ævum* 31. 161-175.
Frese, Dolores W. (1983). *Wulf and Eadwacer*: The Adulterous Woman Reconsidered. *Notre Dame English Journal* 15. 1-22.
Fry, Donald K. (1971). *Wulf and Eadwacer*: A Wen Charm. *Chaucer Review* 5. 247-63.

Giles, Richard F. (1981). 'Wulf and Eadwacer': A New Reading. *Neophilologus* 65. 468-72.
Gollancz, Israel (1893). Wulf and Eadwacer: An Anglo-Saxon Monodrama in Five Acts. *Athenaeum* [Dec. 23, 1893]. 883.
Gollancz, Israel (1902). The Sigurd Cycle and Britain. *Athenaeum* [Oct. 25]. 551-2.
Green, Martin (ed.) (1983). *The Old English Elegies: New Essays in Criticism and Research*. Rutherford, NJ: Farleigh Dickenson University Press, and London and Toronto: Associated University Presses.
Greenfield, Stanley B. (1986). *Wulf and Eadwacer*: All Passion Pent. *Anglo-Saxon England* 15. 5-14.
Greenfield, Stanley B., and Daniel G. Calder (1986). *A New Critical History of Old English Literature. With a survey of the Anglo-Latin background by Michael Lapidge*. New York and London: New York University Press.
Hicketier, Fritz (1888). Fünf Rätsel des Exeterbuches. *Anglia* 10. 564-600.
Holthausen, Ferdinand (1893). Zu alt- und mittelenglischen Denkmälern, 34: Klage um Wulf. *Anglia* 15. 188-9.
Imelmann, Rudolf (1907). *Die altenglische Odoaker-Dichtung*. Berlin: Springer.
Imelmann, Rudolf (1920). *Forschungen zur altenglischen Poesie*. Berlin: Weidmann.
Isaacs, Neil D. (1968). *Structural Principles in Old English Poetry*. Knoxville, TN: University of Tennessee Press.
Jamison, Carol Parrish (1987). *Wulf and Eadwacer*: A Mother's Lament for her Son. *Publications of the Mississippi Philological Association* [1987]. 88-95.
Jensen, Emily (1979). Narrative Voice in the Old English *Wulf*. *Chaucer Review* 13. 373-83.
Jones, F. (1985). A Note on the Interpretation of *Wulf and Eadwacer*. *Neuphilologische Mitteilungen* 86. 323-7.
Kavros, Harry E. (1977). A Note on *Wulf and Eadwacer*. *English Language Notes* 15. 83-4.
Keough, Terrence (1976). The Tension of Separation in *Wulf and Eadwacer*. *Neuphilologische Mitteilungen* 77. 552-60.
Klinck, Anne L. (1984). The Old English Elegy as a Genre. *English Studies in Canada* 10. 129-40.
Klinck, Anne L. (1987). Animal Imagery in *Wulf and Eadwacer* and the Possibilities of Interpretation. *Papers on Language and Literature* 23. 3-13
Krapp, George P. and Elliott Van Kirk Dobbie (eds.) (1936). *The Exeter Book*. The Anglo-Saxon Poetic Records 3. New York: Columbia University Press.
Lawrence, William W. (1902). The First Riddle of Cynewulf. *PMLA* 17. 247-61.
Lehmann, Ruth P.M. (1969). The Metrics and Structure of *Wulf and Eadwacer*. *Philological Quarterly* 48. 151-65.
Leo, Heinrich (1857). *Quae de se ipso Cynewulfus, sive Cenevulfus, sive Coenevulfus, poeta Anglo-Saxonicus tradiderit*. Halle.
Luecke, Janemarie (1983). *Wulf and Eadwacer*: Hints for Reading from *Beowulf* and Anthropology. In: Green, 1983:190-203.
Malone, Kemp (1948). The Old English Period (to 1100). In: *A Literary History of England*. Ed. Albert C. Baugh. New York and London: Appleton-Century-Crofts. 3-105.
Malone, Kemp (1963). Two English *Frauenlieder*. In: *Studies in Old English Literature in Honor of Arthur G. Brodeur*. Ed. Stanley B. Greenfield. Eugene, OR: University of Oregon Books. 106-117.
Mattox, Wesley S. (1975). Encirclement and Sacrifice in *Wulf and Eadwacer*. *Annuale Mediaevale* 16. 33-40.
Nuck, R. (1888). Zu Trautmanns Deutung des ersten und neunundachtzigsten Rätsels. *Anglia* 10. 390-94.
Orton, Peter (1985). An Approach to *Wulf and Eadwacer*. *Proceedings of the Royal Irish*

Academy [1985]. 223-58.

Osborn, Marijane (1983). The Text and Context of *Wulf and Eadwacer*. In: Green, 1983: 174-89.

Patzig, H. (1923). Zum ersten Rätsel des Exeterbuchs. *Archiv für das Studium der neueren Sprachen und Literaturen* 145. 204-7.

Renoir, Alain (1965). *Wulf and Eadwacer*: A Noninterpretation. In: *Franciplegius: Medieval and Linguistic Studies in Honor of Francis Peabody Magoun, Jr.* Ed. Jess B. Bessinger, Jr., and Robert P. Creed. New York: New York University Press. 147-163.

Schofield, William Henry (1902). Signy's Lament. *PMLA* 17. 262-95.

Schücking, L.L. (1919). *Kleines angelsächsisches Dichterbuch*. Cöthen.

Sedgefield, W.J. (1931). Old English Notes. 1. *Wulf and Eadwacer*. *Modern Language Review* 26. 74-5.

Spamer, James B. (1975). The Marriage Concept in *Wulf and Eadwacer*. *Neuphilologus* 62. 143-4.

Suzuki, Seiichi (1987). *Wulf and Eadwacer*: A Reinterpretation and Some Conjectures. *Neuphilologische Mitteilungen* 88. 175-85.

Thorpe, Benjamin (ed.) (1842). *Codex Exoniensis. A Collection of Anglo-Saxon Poetry from a Manuscript in the Library of the Dean and Chapter of Exeter, with an English Translation, Notes and Indexes*. London: W. Pickering (for the Society of Antiquaries of London).

Trautmann, Moritz (1884). Cynewulf und die Rätsel. *Anglia* 6. Anzeiger, 158-69.

Trautmann, Moritz (1894). Die auflösungen der altenglischen rätsel. *Anglia, Beiblatt* 5. 46-51.

Trautmann, Moritz (1905). Alte und neue Antworte auf altenglische Rätsel. *Bonner Beiträge zur Anglistik* 19. 167-215.

Trautmann, Moritz (1912). Das sogenannte erste Rätsel. *Anglia* 36. 133-8.

Tupper, Jr., Frederick (1910a). *The Riddles of the Exeter Book*. Boston: Ginn.

Tupper, Jr., Frederick (1910b). The Cynewulfian Runes of the First Riddle. *Modern Language Notes* 25. 235-241.

Wülcker, Richard P. (1878). Über den Dichter Cynewulf. *Anglia* 1. 483-507.

THE WANDERER AND THE SEAFARER
AS WISDOM POETRY

T.A. SHIPPEY

It is, a little surprisingly, impossible to say how many Old English poems have survived. If one simply counts the entries on the Contents Pages of the six volumes of *The Anglo-Saxon Poetic Records*, accepting the scattered riddles of the *Exeter Book* as one collection, then the answer is eighty-three: but that figure includes besides a number of collections (riddles, psalms, metrical charms etc.), several poems which are known with some certainty to be composites, like *Genesis A* and *B*, or *Christ I, II* and *III*. These eighty-three entries add up to a total of rather over 30,000 lines of verse, but over half of that total comes from only sixteen entries, all narrative poems like *Beowulf*, or narrative composites united by their subject, like *Guthlac A* and *Guthlac B*.

Put these poems aside. Put aside also the collections mentioned above, the historical poems, the liturgical poems, the poems associated with king Alfred's translations, the items attached to Bede, Cædmon or Aldhelm, miscellaneous items like the poem on *Durham*: and what is left is a body of surprisingly homogeneous poetry, appearing in a number of manuscripts, and so not just a personal taste, but nevertheless a body without accepted label or definition. At its core, one might say, is the image of the Ancient Sage, the fiction of an old, wise man talking. Often the wise man is clearly indicated or quoted in the poem: he is *se witiga, frod wita, frod fæder, wis(ne) woðbora(n), snottor on mode, foreþances gleaw* ('the wise man', 'old wise man', 'old father', 'wise prophet', 'wise in mind', 'perceptive in forethought').[1] Often he gives his opinions in direct speech, and the hearer or recipient of his opinions may also be drawn into the poem, to be addressed indeed with direct imperatives in *The Order of the World* or *Judgement Day I*, from the *Exeter Book*, or in the *Exhortation to Christian Living* from MS 201 of Corpus Christi College, Cambridge. Such poems tend also to end with a prayer or exhortation (like *The Seafarer*) or with lines of gnomic conclusion (like *The Wanderer*). But no single generalisation will cover all the poems in this homogeneous but undefinable group. The wise man may be a woman, as in *The Wife's Lament* and *Wulf and Eadwacer*. Direct speech may be absent, as in the

---

[1] All citations from Old English poems are from *The Anglo-Saxon Poetic Records*, ed. Krapp and Dobbie (1931-53).

poems on *The Gifts* and *The Fortunes of Men*, or not directly indicated, as
in *The Seafarer*. While the poems are mostly meditative or philosophical,
this concern shades off in one direction towards personal experience, as in
Deor or the women's songs mentioned above, and in the other direction
towards the delivery of useful information, as in their quite different ways
with the *Rune Poem*, the *Menologium*, or the *Solomon and Saturn* poems.
Symptomatically, attempts to draw neater classifications out of this body
of poems have produced rather, but not completely different sets. A set of
seven "elegies" is by now traditional (*Wanderer, Seafarer, Deor, Wulf and
Eadwacer, Wife's Lament, Husband's Message* and *Ruin*); to it some have
felt inclined to add *Resignation*. The present author translated nine less
well-known poems from the central group (plus a more narrative tenth)
under the heading *Poems of Wisdom and Learning* in 1976. Nicholas
Howe considered four of the latter, plus one of the "elegies" plus four further items as "catalogue poems" (Howe, 1985). Similarly different-but-
overlapping sets have been considered recently by Elaine Tuttle Hansen
(1988) and Marie Nelson (1989). Many critics, in short, now feel that a
definite corpus exists within the larger corpus of Old English verse as a
whole, for which no better title has been found than "wisdom poetry". But
no two critics agree on exactly how that corpus or genre should be defined. Nor is this a result of critical indecision or *Oppositionslust*. As will
be seen the sense of blurred edges, imprecise definitions, continuous rehandling within a perceived continuity, is inherent in and perhaps part of
the circumstances of production for the whole genre of "wisdom poetry".

  The Wanderer and *The Seafarer* are by any definition close to the
core of this group. Most "wisdom poems" come from the *Exeter Book*,
and there is a particularly clear sequence of ten of them running from folios 76b to 95b of that manuscript. Of these *The Wanderer* is first, starting
a fresh page immediately after the manuscript's first sequence of five narrative poems. *The Seafarer* does not follow it directly in the list, coming
fourth instead: nevertheless it and *The Wanderer* have long been seen, and
with reason, as similar or even companion pieces. More subjectively, one
may say that these two and only these two poems occupy as it were a
"hinge" position between the long-accepted set of "elegies" and the more
recently seen and larger category of "wisdom poems" or "Ancient Sage"
poems. What marked the "elegies" out for scholars of the last century was
their autobiographical, or apparently autobiographical quality. While
direct speech is common in "wisdom poems", only in the "elegies" does it
appear to tell a story, of deserted or unhappy wives, of a discarded poet or
an abandoned retainer.[2] Making sense of the stories told or hinted at in

---

[2] *The Ruin* contains neither direct speech nor autobiography. It seems to have been in-

Deor, The Wife's Lament, and the others, has in fact proved obdurately difficult, so difficult as to make one think that perhaps no story was ever intended. But in any case, as has become clearer and clearer during the last few decades, *The Wanderer* and *The Seafarer* conform to this "auto-biographical" model only in part. Thus *The Wanderer* begins a speech at line 8 with the words *Oft ic* ... ('Often I ...'), and then goes on to use the words *ic, mec, min* ('I', 'me', 'my') twelve times between lines 8 and 28, and three more times again in lines 58-60. But from lines 61-115, the end of the poem, no first-person pronoun is used. In almost exactly the same pattern, *The Seafarer* uses *ic, me, mec, min* twelve times between lines 1 and 37, five times again between lines 58 and 66, and then as with *The Wanderer* never uses the first-person singular again—though the words 'we' and 'us' are used six times in *The Seafarer*'s concluding eight-line exhortation. Could one, as it were, read the "autobiography" on from the first half of each poem into the second half, as the "elegiac" label suggests? Or should one not recognise that the second half of each poem is much more similar to the general, impersonal, story-less advice so often found in the "wisdom poems"? The doubt is what makes *The Wanderer* and *The Seafarer* uniquely central: half of each resembles *Deor* and the "elegies", half of each looks towards *Precepts,* the *Maxims* poems, even the "cata-logues".

A natural reaction to this fact might be to see the poems as broken-backed, or at least as less than convincing unities. There has indeed been a long and ultimately inconclusive debate about how many voices, speeches or speakers there are in the two poems, as also where modern editors should put inverted commas: is the *eardstapa* or "wanderer" of line 6 of *The Wanderer* the same as the *snottor on mode,* the man "wise in mind" of line 111? Is either responsible for lines 1-5 and 112-5, or should these be given to the voice of the poet? If they are not the same person, where do they change over? Meanwhile, in *The Seafarer,* why does strong aware-ness of the miseries of seafaring change to eager desire for it in line 33, and what is the force of the stressed word *sylf* ('self'), two lines later? What kind of person is speaking, is it the same person all the way through, and why does the poem reach a conclusion rather like that of *The Wan-derer* at line 108, only to pick itself up again and continue to a different conclusion sixteen lines later?[3] Both poems in their internal structure create very much the sense of "blurred edges" and "imprecise definitions" identified above as characterising their whole external genre. With both

cluded in this set largely because of its similarity to sections of *The Wanderer.*
[3] The arguments may be sampled in Greenfield (1951), Rumble (1958), Pope (1966) and Greenfield (1969).

the structures and the genre, the long-standing inability of modern critics to persuade each other where to put their boundary-lines may well indicate that the whole effort is a mistake, like imposing printers' conventions (inverted commas especially) on a culture used to oral delivery. Can these two poems be held together *without* recourse to "dramatic voices" or "moments of perception", essentially attempts to provide these poems with a plausible, even "true to life", but individual context?[4] One way of doing so may be by considering the structures which make these poems look so much like companion pieces.

As has been seen, *The Wanderer* is unlike *The Seafarer* in that it has clear indications of voices speaking, with the verbs *cwæð, acwið, cwæð* ('spoke', 'speaks', 'spoke') in lines 6, 91 and 111. Yet *The Seafarer* too looks like direct speech. The difference is only that it starts straight away with a voice speaking, without any contrasting introduction: its lines 1-2, "I can make a true song about my self, tell my journeys" are parallel to *The Wanderer*'s lines 8-9, "I have often had to say my care alone, every dawn". Thereafter the two poems resemble each other closely, at least in superficial structure. *The Seafarer*'s opening first-person account runs from lines 1-38, *The Wanderer*'s from 8-29. Both then revert to generalised third-person figures, *mon ... he ... sume* ('man ... he ... some people') in *The Seafarer, se ... he ... wineleas guma* ('the one ... he ... the friendless man') in *The Wanderer*, between respectively lines 39-57 and 29-57. In both cases the first person then returns for some six to ten lines, only to be dropped for extensive third-person passages from respectively lines 68 and 64 on. One clear point is that the status of the generalised "man" in the medial passages, the passages sandwiched *between* first-person accounts, is in both poems much the same: he is (or they are) not exactly the same as the speaker, the "I" who has been talking. But he has had very much *the same experience* as that speaker, either suffering at sea (*The Seafarer*) or loneliness and painful memory (*The Wanderer*). Does it make any difference, then, whether we have first-person speech or third-person narration? Most readers have surely tacitly accepted that the speakers of both poems are doing what speakers of North European cultures still feel obliged to: namely, not talk too much about themselves, and if impelled to, to disguise this impolite self-centredness by extending it to general experience. They are saying, in effect, "I feel this. But my feelings may be interesting to others because other people in these circumstances do feel, would feel, would understand the same. So (returning to me), that is why ..." And the poems, both at line 58 precisely, return for a few lines

---

4 "Dramatic voices" is the phrase used by Pope (1965). For "moments of perception" and "true to life", see Greenfield, 1980:207.

to "I" and "me". The "polite generalisation" theory is perhaps strengthened by one of the more striking indications of these two poems' parallel or companionate nature. On four occasions the "wanderer" or *eardstapa* picks out by means of a relative clause, in lines 29, 31, 37, 56, the "person like himself", and makes him the possessor of special knowledge: *Wat se þe cunnað ... þam þe him lyt hafað ... , wat se þe sceal ..., cearo bið geniwad þam þe sendan sceal ...* ('He knows who experiences it ... for him who has few [protectors] ... , he knows who has to ..., care is renewed for him who has to send ...'). This relative-clause survivor of bitter experience, the man who *knows*, is matched by the "seafarer's" creation of an opposite figure in lines 12-13, 27 and 55, the man who does *not* know: *Þæt se mon ne wat, þe him ..., him gelyfeð lyt, se þe ..., Þæt se beorn ne wat ... hwæt þa* ('The man does not know that, who ..., he little believes, he who ..., That the man does not know, what those ...'). The opposition between the two poems—as usual—is not perfectly symmetrical, for the "seafarer" extends his relative clauses to take in people like himself (lines 47, 51, 57), as well as those not like himself. But both poems make the same distinction, implied or overt, between those who share their narrators' knowledge and those who don't; both freely create imaginary but typical figures at once to personalise and to generalise their arguments. These third-person figures (bearers or flouters of the "wisdom" tradition) are creations of the first-person speakers (aspects of the "autobiographical" or "elegiac" tradition).

Yet one could go on from there to make that statement the other way round! In the contexts of the poems as a whole, and of their surrounding generic corpus, the first-person speakers are evidently there largely as vivid illustrations of conclusions already reached. This is, if not proved, then very strongly suggested by two related features of both poems, both of them exhibiting once again that sense of non-definability, of "blurred edges", already mentioned twice above. The two features are: (1) these poems' relation, not only to each other, but to other poems of the "wisdom" group, and beyond, and (2) these poems' high degree of proverbiality or gnomic expression. Neither feature is well demonstrated by selective quotation, but one may begin by pointing out that both poems say things which are exactly paralleled elsewhere in Old English. *The Seafarer*'s line 106 is:

Dol biþ se þe him his dryhten ne ondrædeþ; cymeð him se
    deað unþinged.

(He is a fool who does not fear his Lord; death comes to him unexpected.)

Further on in the *Exeter Book*, in *Maxims I* line 35, we find an almost identical line, except that *nat* ('does not know') has replaced *ne ondrædeþ* ('does not fear'). Line 109 of *The Seafarer* begins *Stieran mon sceal strongum mode* ('One must restrain the strong mind'), and line 50a of *Maxims I*, again, is virtually identical, *Styran sceal mon strongum mode*. Meanwhile lines 65-8 of *The Wanderer* read *Wita sceal ... ne to forht ne to fægen*, meaning according to the 1969 edition of Dunning and Bliss, "a wise man must not be too timid or too servile". A similar, but not quite identical saying is found in the collection *The Durham Proverbs* (ed. Arngart, 1956), where it reads *Ne sceal no to ærforht ne to ærfægen*; here the addition of the prefix *ær-* and the accompanying Latin gloss make it clear that the meaning is, "One must not be afraid-too-soon (i.e. pessimistic) nor glad-too-soon (i.e. optimistic)".

Which has priority, *The Durham Proverbs* or *The Wanderer*, *Maxims I* or *The Seafarer*? It must already be clear that there is no way to tell, and that such questions are hardly sensible. In all probability *all* these authors are repeating ideas already generally known and already with a traditional—if not absolutely fixed—form of expression. This opinion can only be confirmed by the repeated parallels visible between these poems and the surrounding corpus. The *eardstapa* declares that he knows it is a good custom (lines 13-14) "that one should bind his breast firmly, hold back his heart, think as he will". But so does the author of the otherwise unmemorable *Homiletic Fragment II*, lines 3-4, *heald hordlocan, hyge fæste bind / mid modsefan*: one should note that while the sense is virtually identical with *The Wanderer*, the words have as it were shuffled into different positions, not quite definably once more. *The Seafarer* says, in separate places, that (lines 39-43) no-one is so gifted as to be without care at sea "as to what fate the Lord will assign him", *to hwon hine dryhten gedon wille*; that (line 47) he who sets out to sea always has anxiety; that (lines 97-102) *post mortem* gifts do nothing for the soul. The last thought is found—one has to say more cogently expressed—in the *Exhortation to Christian Living* in ASPR VI, lines 22-26. That might be mere similarity of thought, but the same poem declares that it is in death, not on the sea, that one does not know *tohwan þe þin drihten gedon wille* ('what fate your Lord will assign you', line 61). Meanwhile the *longung/lagu* connection is made, with further echoing of *The Seafarer*, in the poem *Resignation*, line 98. Mere lists do not make the point adequately. One can say only (a) that these two poems show at the very least a dozen major or minor similarities to their related texts, (b) that there is no sign that any of these poems has priority over or was the original for any of the others, and (c) that these are not mere parallels of vocabulary, idea or metre, but parallels approaching verbal and semantic identity—if always with the now-familiar sense of slight blurring.

The reason for this situation is furthermore quite easy to understand, namely that all these poems and poets are simultaneously using and reinforcing, aiming to reach and exploiting, an established tradition of proverbial expression. The point about proverbs is that they are common property, commonly recognised. However, how is one to recognise a commonly-used proverb if one is not a member of the culture that uses it? Is there anything in the nature, the grammar or vocabulary, of proverbs which marks them out? Marie Nelson (1989:72-3) remarks of the *Wanderer* passage already partly cited, lines 65b-72, that these lines "have the ring of maxims", and the parallel between one half-line and the *Durham Proverbs* tends to confirm the supposition. But does that mean that all the *other* half-lines in the passage were in general circulation as well? Evidently, we cannot be sure. What we can say is that both poems repeatedly and extensively aim for a verbal quality which one might call (inventing a new word) not "proverbiality" but "proverbiousness": one becomes "proverbious" not necessarily by repeating well-known sayings, but by repeating some, rehandling others, and on other occasions producing sayings which sound as if they might be (ought to be, perhaps one day will become) acceptedly proverbial. No non-native speaker of Old English can be a secure judge of this, but one could point out that in several cases already cited—and one might add *Wanderer* 108-9, *Seafarer* 68-71—resemblance to other surviving texts makes it look as if the poems are using items from a common tradition. In other places, one might think that the poems are drawing on an established tradition but not necessarily agreeing with it. *The Seafarer*'s lines on *lof*, 72-80a, are close in phrasing and in sense to *Beowulf*'s lines on *dom*, 1386-9: but while both *lof* and *dom* can mean "praise, glory", with special importance as "reputation after death", it is nevertheless clear that the "seafarer" is considering *heavenly* glory as *Beowulf* is not. Meaning can be substantially altered by slight shifts within a proverbial tradition. Such shifts might be accidental, but it is worth noting that the *Wanderer*-poet, at least, creates ambiguous or ironic effects by putting apparently proverbial statement—i.e. statement we find elsewhere—within what may be an entirely personal frame. "I know as truth", he says in lines 11b-14, "that it is a noble custom in a warrior that he should bind his breast firmly, hold back his heart, think as he will". But to say that one knows for sure that something is *customary* is not the same as saying one believes it to be *true*; the next four lines of the poem, though still insistently generalising, looking very much as if they might also be or become accepted maxims, nevertheless in context create a doubtful impression. Is the *eardstapa* recommending silence as a virtue (as "wise men" often do)? Is he complaining about the social pressure that enforces it? Is he (as seems most likely) reluctantly conceding that social pressure and conformity are, if not correct, then irresistible? Silence is not as easy as the wise men say, but grumbling will do no good, certainly not for the *domgeorne* (those eager for reputation). "Proverbiousness", one may say,

gives a writer or speaker resources which would not be reached by "proverbiality" alone. It allows one to say the common/recognised/accepted/
socially-valued thing, but at the same time, by alteration, framing or
juxtaposition, indicate an attitude towards the socially acceptable which is
quite different from mere parrot-repetition.

In brief, I would suggest that a high proportion of both *The Wanderer* and *The Seafarer* consists of items related to what have been called
the "core-clichés" of their society, see Bloomfield and Dunn (1989:24);
but that their society was significantly more sophisticated than our own in
handling and rehandling formalised gnomic expression. Our modern proverbial corpus is largely closed, and its forms of words are fixed, stable,
even fossilised.[5] By contrast these poems seem capable of inventive variation. *The Wanderer*'s sententious *wyrd bið ful aræd* ('fate is fully determined') is not found anywhere else in Old English; but in sense it is similar to Beowulf's own *Gæð a wyrd swa hio scel* ('Fate always goes as it
must', line 455), while the word *aræd* appears only once elsewhere in Old
English poetry, predictably in *Maxims I*, line 191, where it forms part of
another half-line with the "ring" of a maxim, *geara is hwær aræd*, "ready
is always resolute", or, perhaps, "forewarned is forearmed". Without the
intimate knowledge of a native speaker one can never be sure. But I would
suggest again that just as the invented first-person speakers of these poems
invent third-person characters on to whom they project their own experiences, so the first-person speakers themselves are not—as used to be
thought in the days of "self-expression"—the voices of autobiographical
poets, but rather reflections, projections, or mouthpieces of an established
"Ancient Sage" tradition. *The Wanderer* and *The Seafarer*, in short, are
set in the imaginative space between individual "elegy" and traditional
saying or cliché.

* * *

Having discussed the manner of these poems, what can be said of their
matter? Have the poems anything to express beyond those staples of traditional wisdom—caution, scepticism and forethought? Here one can make
some relatively clear and definite statements. A major feature of *The
Wanderer* is its repeated use of the word "all" (seven times) and, in its
varying grammatical forms, "this" (ten times). The two words are divergent though not opposite in meaning: obviously, the one implies universality, total coverage, the other immediacy, concentration on something at
hand, close by, actually present. Yet in this poem the two words reinforce

---

[5] See further Shippey (1977), for examples of culturally different ways of using proverbs.

each other. On one occasion out of ten, "this" modifies "words", in line 91, *ond þas word acwið* ('and says these words'). On each of the other nine occasions it modifies *either* a word for "world", *þas woruld, þes middangeard, þisse worulde, þisne middangeard, þisne wealsteal, þis eorþan gesteal*, in lines 58, 62, 74, 75, 88 and 110 respectively; *or else* it modifies "life", *þis deorce lif* ('this dark life', line 8a); *or else* it modifies the words *eardgeard, stanhleoþu*, in lines 85 and 101. These latter two words could very plausibly have particular meaning. *Eardgeard* almost certainly means "city", with clear reference to the departed "citizens" or *burgwara* and the still-standing ruins of the two lines that follow it. *Stanhleoþu* meanwhile could easily refer to the "stone walls" of the same ruins, which the speaker has been contemplating since line 76.[6] Yet while both these words have particular, here-by-me meaning, one cannot help noticing how close they are to the other words preceded by "this"—the words for "world-in-general". *Eard-geard* = "city" is similar to *middan-geard* = "middle-earth". The *stanhleoþu* or "stone walls" are similar to the *wealsteal* or "walled foundation" of line 88; but that word in its context—"he who has then thought wisely over this walled foundation, and thinks deeply over every part of this dark life"—clearly has the general meaning of "the world as a whole", as is further corroborated by *þis eorþan gesteal*, "this earth's foundation" at line 110. Briefly, one can say that the words introduced by "this" show the speaker's determination to generalise about every part of life in the world—as is also the force of his repeated preposition or prefix *geond*, used seven times in the poem—while at the same time drawing his generalisations from things which are resolutely particular, present and visible.

Meanwhile the word "all" is used with similar generalising force, but again a force which is multiplied by use of repeated grammatical pattern. There are several lines in *The Wanderer* (62b-63, 95b-96, 106-7, 110) which look as if they might serve as the poem's "moral". That incipient repetition is picked out, however, by the parallels in lines 36 and 79, *wyn eal gedreas / duguð eal gecrong* ('all (that) joy has failed', 'all (that) company has fallen'), or in lines 74 and 110, *eal þisse worulde wela weste stondeð / eall þis eorþan gesteal idel weorþeð* ('all this world's wealth stands waste', 'all this earth's foundation grows useless'). Given these many tightly-patterned associations and repetitions round the words "all" and "this", it is hard to miss the poem's meaning, whether it is said by *eardstapa* or *snottor on mode* or whether (as seems intended) they are the same man: what he wants to say is that everything in this world, life,

---

[6] See further the extremely useful notes on individual words provided by Dunning and Bliss in their edition of *The Wanderer* (1969).

wealth and people, will turn into ruin! And that is what the wise man must understand, *Ongietan sceal gleaw hæle*, line 73.

What is the obstacle to understanding it? In a sense that is brought before us—it cannot be put before us—in the poem's first half, and especially in the moving sequence from lines 34 to 52, which the *eardstapa* tactfully (?) ascribes to his invented *wineleas guma*, "friendless man". In this sequence (much easier to understand since the discussion of its grammar by Bruce Mitchell, 1968), "When sorrow and sleep bind the wretched survivor *(anhagan)* ..., it seems to him in his mind" (i.e. in dream) that he is greeting his lord as he used to do. "Then the friendless man wakes up again, sees before him" not his dream-vision but depressing reality; "then the wounds of the heart are heavier ..., sorrow is renewed, when the mind revisits every part of *(geondhweorfeð)* its memories ..." To answer the question posed just above, what keeps people from understanding the harsh truth about this world is immediate and temporary happiness: happiness which is so strong that the unwary or sleeping mind will invent it even after it has *vanished*. The stages on *The Wanderer*'s journey from ignorance to wisdom are perhaps: first, the thoughtlessly happy man in hall with his friend and patron; then the man who wakes from dream to realise how he has cheated himself; then the man who sees in every happiness a potential loss, in every city a ruin-to-be; then the man who can view every part of existence, both present and future, the "all" and the "this"; finally, at the very end, the man who looks beyond endurance to a better world, not this world, *þær us eal seo fæstnung stondeð* ('where the *feste Burg* stands for us all').[7]

In this progression, as in the poem as a whole, very striking effect is created by the opposition of tangibles and intangibles. Which are more powerful: the stone walls, the massive ruins, the cold waves and "this middle-earth" itself; or the dreams, the memories, the songs and sayings which (not being written down) vanish like past time, *swa heo no wære*, "as if it had never been"?[8] The answer ought to be an easy one, but the poem makes clear that it is not. Wisdom demands self-mastery, not just knowing things. In that respect *The Wanderer* is a demonstration of the very difficulties involved in reaching wisdom: one of which, and not the least, is a sense that the wise man (or woman here, for the theme recurs in the two female-centred "elegies" also) cannot even trust himself, is prey to the rebellions of his own psyche. This theme becomes even more promi-

---

[7] Dunning and Bliss (1969:50) make the point that *fæstnung* can mean both "stability" in the abstract and "a fortification"; they also draw the apt parallel with Martin Luther's hymn.

[8] William Alfred (1982) suggests that the poem itself includes references to maxims as supportive forces: see his translations on pp. 37-8.

nent in *The Seafarer*.

This poem resembles *The Wanderer* not merely in its overall structure, but also in its imagined environment (the cold sea, the indifferent or mocking sea-birds), and in its vocabulary. Especially in its first half, *The Wanderer* deploys a variety of words for "mind, thoughts, heart, spirit", which modern commentators often find hard to translate. The phrase *modsefa(n) min(ne)* is for instance used three times, at lines 10, 19, and 59, and each time there is a sense that "the mind", although "mine", is getting more and more out of the speaker's control. He does not dare to speak "my mind" at line 10, at line 19 he has had to "bind my mind with fetters", at line 59 he cannot understand "why my mind does not (?)/ should not (?) grow dark"—it is as if the mind is refusing the evidence of its senses (as it did, in a way, during the dream). In *The Seafarer* we have again a string of words and phrases for "mind" or "spirit": but the tension or contrast of *The Wanderer* has become almost a dissociation. Where in *The Wanderer* the speaker seemed to view his mind as shut up inside himself, operating on its own, in *The Seafarer* the speaker from lines 33 on talks as if he were a split personality, with a part of himself outside himself urging a stay-at-home part to act, to move. So (lines 33-5) *cnyssað me heortan geþohtas*, "thoughts beat my heart" for me to make trial of the sea for myself; (lines 36-8) "desire of the mind urges (*monað*) my spirit to fare ...", (lines 50-1) "all these urge (*gemoniað*) the one eager in spirit, the heart ..."; in line 53 it is the cuckoo which urges (*monað*), though it does so only by offering "sorrow in the heart". Many readers have been puzzled by the way in which the speaker feels urged towards known hardship; but much of the puzzle comes from the varying status in the poem of words like *mod, ferð, sefa* and *hyge*, sometimes active urgers, sometimes passive non-responders. In a famous passage the speaker seems finally to imagine his mind leaving its body and flying off, like the birds he has mentioned repeatedly, only to come back *gifre and grædig*, "eager and greedy" like a famished bird of prey, once more to "urge the heart irresistibly" across the ocean.[9]

Has this speaker then *no control at all* over his mind? One of the points which have made critics likely to see *The Wanderer* and *The Seafarer* as companion pieces rather than works by the same poet is a sense that while we repeatedly find the same situation in both poems, the attitude to it may be almost 180 degrees different. So, in *The Wanderer* one gets the impression that the speaker is right, his mind wrong—disobedient, undisciplined, unguarded. In *The Seafarer* it seems to be the mind that is

---

[9] See further Godden (1985) for commentary both on these poems and on Anglo-Saxon images of the mind.

right, the speaker wrong—inert, sluggish, timid. As one moves on also into the second, reflective half of *The Seafarer*, one finds again that the "moral landscape" of both poems remains similar—one might compare *The Seafarer*'s lines 66b-67 with *The Wanderer*'s lines 73-4 for passages which are verbally close to each other while still throwing up the sharp contrast *ece/weste* ('eternal'/'desolate')—but the uses made of it point in different directions. Briefly, one might say that *The Wanderer* can function perfectly well as a secular prudential poem about how things are in this world: it mentions God only three times, at beginning and end (lines 2, 115), and rather paradoxically in the middle where the "Creator of men" lays their city waste. By contrast *The Seafarer* contains "the Lord" (*Dryhten*) as a continuous presence, in lines 43, 65 and 106, with God, *Meotod* ('the Ruler') and *Dryhten* again appearing repeatedly from line 101, and the devil, angels and life after death dominating the quasi-Beowulfian gnomic section of lines 72-80. Where *The Wanderer* in effect says that all life is a ruin and one must brace oneself to endure it (though, at the very end, there may be a *feste Burg* elsewhere), *The Seafarer* agrees that visible happiness is deceptive, but urges the wise spirit to withdraw from it even while its happiness is still present. The one poem sees transience, the other temptation; the one recommends prudent restraint, the other passionate self-denial; while one is stubbornly literal, concentrating on "this world" and the evidence in it, the other—as many critics have thought—reaches out towards metaphor or even allegory with suggestions of the land as life, "this dead life" in line 65, and seafaring then conceivably as the road to a better life through a kind of death.[10]

A final point to consider is this. We are often told nowadays that "Every literary text is built out of a sense of its potential audience" (Eagleton, quoted in Horgan, 1987:40), or that "an interpreter's preliminary generic conception of a text is constitutive of everything that he subsequently understands" (Hansen, 1988:44). *The Wanderer* and *The Seafarer* offer serious challenge to these assertions. We have no idea at all of their (original) potential audience: the noblemen and retainers whom the poems mention, the monks and canons who appear to have passed the poems on? We have no very good idea of what they were for: to be read aloud as entertainment, to be circulated in manuscript for a coterie? As for one's "generic conception", it is suggested that they do relate to a genre of wisdom poetry: but that genre has been created in our minds only by a process of elimination and the recognition of a certain blurred homogeneity. And yet these poems have attracted readers, imitators and trans-

[10] The "allegorical" view of *The Seafarer* was put forward forcibly in Smithers (1957). The best attempt to give the poem a literal context remains Whitelock (1950).

lators in modern times, regardless of our total ignorance of what their authors thought they were doing. They are in a modern sense pure "texts", uncluttered by presupposition. Though this essay has suggested that they do spring from the "core-clichés" of a vanished culture, that their mode of thought is analogous to the skilful "proverbious" reworkings of formal expression found in pre-literate societies, and that they belong in a wider Anglo-Saxon genre, nevertheless both poems have most often been read in modern times by people with no knowledge of the vanished culture, the pre-literate society, or the associated genre. For all that, few have found *The Wanderer* and *The Seafarer* unreadable or unapproachable.

REFERENCES

Alfred, William (1982). The Drama of *The Wanderer*. In: *The Wisdom of Poetry: Essays in Early English Literature in Honor of Morton W. Bloomfield*. Ed. Larry D. Benson and Siegfried Wenzel. Kalamazoo, MI: Medieval Institute Publications. 31-44.

Arngart, O.S. (ed.) (1956). *The Durham Proverbs*. Lund: Lunds Universitets Årsskrift 52:2.

Bloomfield, Morton W., and Charles W. Dunn (1989). *The Role of the Poet in Early Societies*. Cambridge: D.S. Brewer.

Dunning, T.P., and A.J. Bliss (eds.) (1969). *The Wanderer*. Methuen's Old English Library. London: Methuen.

Godden, M.R. (1985). Anglo-Saxons on the Mind. In: *Learning and Literature in Anglo-Saxon England: Studies Presented to Peter Clemoes*. Ed. Michael Lapidge and Helmut Gneuss. Cambridge: Cambridge University Press. 271-98.

Greenfield, S.B. (1951). *The Wanderer*: A Reconsideration of Theme and Structure. *Journal of English and Germanic Philology* 50. 451-65. [Repr. in Greenfield, 1989: 133-47.]

Greenfield, S.B. (1969). *Min, Sylf* and "Dramatic Voices in *The Wanderer* and *The Seafarer*". *Journal of English and Germanic Philology* 68. 212-20. [Repr. in Greenfield, 1989:161-9.]

Greenfield, S.B. (1980). *Sylf*, Seasons, Structure and Genre in *The Seafarer*. *Anglo-Saxon England* 9. 199-211. [Repr. in Greenfield, 1989:171-83.]

Greenfield, S.B. (1989). *Hero and Exile: The Art of Old English Poetry*. Ed. George H. Brown. London and Ronceverte, WV: Hambledon Press.

Hansen, Elaine Tuttle (1988). *The Solomon Complex: Reading Wisdom in Old English Poetry*. Toronto: University of Toronto Press.

Horgan, A.D. (1987). *The Wanderer*—a Boethian Poem? *Review of English Studies* 38. 40-46.

Howe, Nicholas (1985). *The Old English Catalogue Poems*. Anglistica 23. Copenhagen: Rosenkilde and Bagger.

Krapp, G.E., and E. Van K. Dobbie (eds.) (1931-53). *The Anglo-Saxon Poetic Records*. 6 Vols. New York: Columbia University Press.

Mitchell, B. (1968). Some Syntactical Problems in *The Wanderer*. *Neuphilologische Mitteilungen* 69. 172-98.

Nelson, Marie (1989). *Structures of Opposition in Old English Poems*. Amsterdam and Atlanta, GA: Rodopi.

Pope, J.C. (1965). Dramatic Voices in *The Wanderer* and *The Seafarer*. In: *Franciplegius: Medieval and Linguistic Studies in Honor of Francis P. Magoun, Jr.* Ed. Jess B. Bessinger Jr. and Robert P. Creed. New York: New York University Press. 164-93.

Rumble, T.C. (1958). From *Eardstapa* to *Snottor on Mode*: The Structural Principle of *The Wanderer*. *Modern Language Quarterly* 19. 225-30.

Shippey, T.A. (ed.) (1976). *Poems of Wisdom and Learning in Old English*. Cambridge: D.S. Brewer, and Totowa, NJ: Rowman and Littlefield.

Shippey, T.A. (1977). Maxims in Old English Narrative: Literary Art or Traditional Wisdom? In: *Oral Tradition, Literary Tradition: A Symposium*. Ed. H. Bekker-Nielsen *et al*. Odense: Odense University Press. 28-46.

Smithers, G.V. (1957). The Meaning of *The Seafarer* and *The Wanderer*. *Medium Ævum* 26. 137-53.

Whitelock, D. (1950). The Interpretation of *The Seafarer*. In: *Early Cultures of North-West Europe (H.M. Chadwick Memorial Studies)*. Ed. Sir Cyril Fox and B. Dickins. Cambridge: Cambridge University Press. 261-72.

OLD ENGLISH RELIGIOUS POETRY:
CHRIST AND SATAN AND *THE DREAM OF THE ROOD*

DAVID F. JOHNSON

The history of Old English religious poetry begins with Cædmon. Not only is his *Hymn*, made famous by Bede's account in his *Ecclesiastical History,* the oldest extant piece of poetry in Old English (ca. 658 x 680), but it epitomizes the fusion of the native Germanic medium with Christian subject matter so characteristic of much of the Old English poetic corpus. While I will not offer here an analysis of the *Hymn*,[1] it does seem useful to begin this chapter with Bede's often quoted account of Caedmon's miraculous gift of song. Cædmon is a cowherd who had "never learnt anything of versifying". Having left a feast to avoid his turn at the harp, he retires to the stable at which he is to watch, is visited by someone in a dream who asks him to sing and lends him inspiration, and is subsequently brought before the Abbess Hild of Whitby where he is "taught the course of sacred history," upon which subjects he composes suitable songs:

> And remembering all that he could learn by listening, and like, as it were, a clean animal chewing the cud, he turned it into most harmonious song, and, sweetly singing it, he made his teachers in their turn his hearers. He sang of the creation of the world and the origin of mankind, and all the history of Genesis, of the exodus of Israel from Egypt and the entry into the land of promise, of very many other stories of Holy Scripture, of the incarnation of the Lord, his passion, resurrection, and ascension into heaven, of the coming of the Holy Spirit, and of the teaching of the Apostles. Also he made many songs about the terror of the future judgment, and the horror of the pains of hell, and the sweetness of the heavenly kingdom; besides very many others about the divine blessings and judgments, in all of which he endeavoured to draw men away from the love of vice and to incite them to the love and practice of well-doing. [2]

---

[1] For analyses see Wrenn (1968); Huppé (1959:99-130); Schwab (1983) and Orton (1983). Blake (1962) looks to the Psalms, rather than Germanic tradition, for the chief influences on Cædmon; as does Howlett's analysis of the *Hymn*'s theology (1974). On the textual transmission of the *Hymn* and its oral origins, see O'Keeffe (1987).

[2] Bede's *Historia Ecclesiastica* (= *HE*), Book IV, ch. 24 (Whitelock, 1979:723). Bede's

Now, the merits of Cædmon's *Hymn* as poetry have been variously
assessed, and many interpretations seeking to establish a symbolic burden
of meaning for the *Hymn* have been put forward. Most important for the
purpose of this discussion, however, is not how to interpret the poem, but
rather what the circumstances of its composition as reported by Bede can
tell us about the genesis of Old English religious poetry. To modern and
medieval audiences alike the most miraculous aspect of Bede's account is
perhaps Cædmon's sudden transformation, as a result of divine interven-
tion, from a seemingly ignorant and talentless herdsman to an accomplished composer of songs. But it bears pointing out that from a cultural
(and literary) point of view it is only slightly less miraculous that to Cædmon's audience the *Hymn* and his subsequent compositions seemed "most
harmonious song". The songs sung by Cædmon's fellows at the *gebeorscip*
were of the kind inveighed against by Alcuin with his famous rhetorical
question *"Quid Inieldus cum Christo?"*. It is not hard to imagine that, at a
time and place in which a relatively young church had still to compete
with pagan beliefs and habits, men and women like Bede and the Abbess
Hild would have viewed not only the content but also the medium of such
songs with contempt.

Despite this, "a Christian Anglo-Saxon did not cease to be an Anglo-
Saxon" (Opland, 1980:102). Moreover, the kind of accommodation and
assimilation advocated by Pope Gregory I in his letter to Mellitus, Archbishop of Canterbury (*HE* I, 30), was in time extended to the realm of
poetic expression; Cædmon's *Hymn* is, in fact, a testimony to both these
observations. From the inevitable clash between the Anglo-Saxon secular
and Christian poetic tastes and traditions there emerged much that may
rightly be termed "most melodious" verse, even today. Cædmon's vision
and subsequent compositions mark, then, a turning point for the English
poetic tradition. As Wrenn points out, if Cædmon was indeed the first to
apply "pagan traditional poetic discipline to Christian matter", then he "set
the tone and method of subsequent Anglo-Saxon poetry".[3]

While current scholarly consensus recognizes the *Hymn* as Cædmon's only surviving work, all of the subjects upon which he composed
songs are represented in the extant corpus of Old English religious poetry.

---

metaphor to describe the process by which Cædmon internalized what he had heard is a
traditional one in the monastic context. For a description of *ruminatio*, see LeClercq
(1985:72-3); for its significance to Cædmon's *Hymn*, see Wieland (1984).

[3] Wrenn, 1968:417. This is not to disregard Aldhelm (Abbot of Malmesbury and first
Bishop of Sherbourne, ca. 639-709) as an early composer of religious verse in the vernacular, but while claims that he did this survive, no poetry in Old English that can be
positively attributed to him has. See Opland (1980:120ff.) for a convenient overview of
the relevant data from William of Malmesbury's account of Aldhelm in his *Gesta Pon-
tificum Anglorum*.

Cædmon's *Hymn* touches on the "creation of the world", and this, as well as "all the history of Genesis", is also recounted in *Genesis A*. The Old English *Exodus* deals with "the exodus of Israel from Egypt and the entry into the land of promise", while poetic accounts of "the incarnation of the Lord, his passion, and resurrection and ascension into heaven" survive in *Christ I, II*, and *III, The Dream of the Rood*, and *Christ and Satan*. The "coming of the Holy Spirit and the teaching of the Apostles" are moreover related in *Christ II* and *The Fates of the Apostles*. Cædmon's songs "about the terror of future judgment and the horror of the pains of hell, and the sweetness of the heavenly kingdom" did not survive; nonetheless these topics received an almost disproportionate amount of attention in the surviving poetry.

Indeed, Bede's short summary of Cædmon's repertoire only hints at the wide range of genres and subject matter represented in Old English religious poetry, for in addition to Saints' Lives and Biblical narrative, the corpus includes elegy, devotional prayer, liturgical hymns, Psalms, riddles and even Christianized charms.[4] That there should be so much poetry in Old English dealing with Christian topics comes as no surprise when we consider that it was men of the Church who were largely responsible for the preservation and transmission of literature in Anglo-Saxon England. Literacy as we know it came to the British Isles with Christianity, and the bishops, abbots and monks of the period acted as the custodians of that literacy.

Given the predominance of Christian material in the corpus, then, the notion that anything like an apology for Old English religious poetry should be necessary may strike one as odd; and yet in the light of a perceived and long-standing bias against the Christian poetry in some traditions of Old English scholarship, such an apology seems necessary.[5] It is useful in this context to quote from a recent analysis of one of the most clearly Christian works in the Old English poetic corpus. In the opening paragraph of his discussion of *Christ I*, George Brown (1986:15) writes:

> Even today some readers who come to the overtly Christian poems in the Anglo-Saxon Poetic Records typically regard those poems as weakened and diluted mutations of earlier heroic pagan verses. Reacting with the same humanistic distaste that classicists often display for Christian Latin poetry, these readers by deploring the historic evolution of the poetry and fruitlessly searching for an 'urgermanischen Geist' fail to

---

[4] On the charms, see Jolly (1985).
[5] For the roots of the tradition I have in mind, see Stanley (1975).

appreciate the beauty of the actual poetry. Other readers, long
and perhaps overly familiar with the tenets of Christian dog-
ma, simply accept the appearance of Christian doctrine in the
Old English poems as commonplace and conventional, or they
leave the poem and an analysis of its inherent merits too soon
in order to discover its biblical and patristic sources. Some
others, with good will, simply do not see that the Christian
Old English poems are as good as the secular ones. For all
these and others, I would urge that we take a fresh look at the
best Old English Christian poetry with an eye to how the
poets express, incorporate and assimilate the religious matter.
We can then perceive better the qualities of its composite art.

In the following discussion I shall focus on two works. One is perhaps the
best known of the overtly Christian poems and arguably the showpiece of
Old English religious poetry; the other a somewhat lesser literary achievement and certainly less often discussed and read. These poems have in
common a blend of tradition and innovation, and they exhibit what Wrenn
terms the "union of Latin Christendom with ... a Germanic cultural set of
linguistic values" (1968:417). I hope that by approaching the topic in this
way, something of the range of Old English religious poetry will emerge,
at least to the extent that the "qualities of its composite art" may be de-
tected in these two poems.

I

Christ and Satan

The poem now commonly referred to as *Christ and Satan*[6] is in many
ways a difficult and perplexing work. The condition of its transmission
compounds the problems posed by its structure and content, for the text as
we have it is strewn with difficult readings, apparently corrupt passages
and probable lacunae. What is more, in addition to the hands of the three
scribes responsible for transcribing the poem, the hand of a fourth, contemporary scribe (referred to by editors as the Corrector) is very evident.
Christ and Satan is preserved in just one manuscript (Bodleian Library
Oxford, Junius 11) and its 728 lines occupy the final 17 pages of the manuscript.

Two issues which have traditionally presented problems for critics
of *Christ and Satan* are the poem's structure and theme. At the highest

---

[6] There is no authority for this title in the manuscript itself; it was first bestowed upon the
work by Grein (Sleeth, 1982:3).

structural level the poem combines a number of different genres (plaint, exemplum, homily, New Testament and apocryphal narrative, among others). At other levels it has clearly derived details from a variety of sources, while some features have no identifiable source.[7] Because *Christ and Satan* is not the most widely read of Old English poems, it would be well to have some idea of its structure in mind at this juncture. Since the earliest critical studies of the poem it has been divided into three main structural units. Part I (ll.1-364) comprises the plaints of the fallen angels. This is a series of laments by Satan and his followers in which the events of their rebellion and fall are recounted, the pains of hell and joys of heaven are described, and the direness of their condition in hell is emphasized. This section is punctuated by two hortatory addresses to the listener/ reader that he should learn by Satan's example and avoid the fate of the devils.

Part II, encompassing lines 365-622, narrates the salient events in Christ's post-Resurrection life. Following a brief recapitulation of Satan's history, lines 379-513 recount Christ's Harrowing of Hell, incorporating an impassioned address by Eve to the Saviour (408-42), and including His release of the souls of the just from hell and their translation to heaven, where Christ addresses the blessed and provides a synopsis of both the creation and fall of man, and His own career on earth. The poet then treats in rapid succession of the Resurrection, the Ascension, Pentecost, and Christ's enthronement at the right hand of God the Father. The final lines of this section constitute two distinct divisions, the first deals with the Day of Judgement (ll.597-641), while the second forms the final exhortation in the work (ll.642-666).

Part III, the Temptation of Christ (cf. Matth. 4:3-11), is curious in that it is considerably shorter than the other two (a mere 63 lines, 667-729), and its subject matter appears out of chronological order, at least with respect to Part II, where it should logically have preceded the poet's treatment of events in Christ's post-Passion career. This has occasioned no small amount of negative commentary on the part of scholars who have studied the *Christ and Satan*, leading some to posit a theory of fragmentary and almost arbitrary composition to account for the many structural disjunctions in the poem. These structural problems have inevitably rendered speculation on the intended theme of the work extremely difficult, and this difficulty in making sense of the poem's unity and theme[8] are in

---

[7] On the putative sources for *Christ and Satan*, see Finnegan (1977:37-55), Sleeth (1982: 50-67), Clubb (1972:xxiv-xlii), and Calder and Allen (1976:221-2). See also Hill (1981) for a discussion of the most striking detail for which no source has yet been adduced: Satan's measuring of hell (ll. 695-722).

[8] Sleeth (1982:3-26) offers the most convenient and comprehensive discussion of

turn to a degree responsible for the work's relative obscurity. For the present discussion, however, I should like to disregard issues of structure and theme altogether, and focus instead on the poem's language and imagery.

Its many editorial problems notwithstanding, *Christ and Satan* is a fascinating piece of poetry. For many this fascination lies in the opening movement of the poem, i.e. the section traditionally referred to as the "Lament of the Fallen Angels" (Part I: ll.1-364). It will be useful for the discussion that follows to present a more detailed synopsis of Part I, in which I shall draw upon (and augment) Clubb's "Structural Outline" (1925:41-2).

The first 33 lines form an "introduction" of sorts to the laments of Satan and his followers that comprise the bulk of this section. The poem opens with an account of the creation, in which *Meotod* ('the Measurer', i.e. God) is able by his own might to create the earth with its stones and streams, the waters and the heavens; He establishes the sun and the moon in their appointed places; He is the Author of all middle earth. It is at lines 9-13 that we encounter the first indications of the poem's marked Christocentricity:

> He selfa mæg   sæ geondwlitan
> grundas in heofene,   *Godes agen Bearn*;
> and he ariman mæg   rægnas scuran,
> dropena gehwelcne;   daga enderim
> seolua he gesette   þurh his soðan miht

> ('He Himself, God's own Son, can see through the sea to the foundations
> of heaven, and he can reckon the rain-showers, every drop; He Himself
> established the final sum of days by His true power.')[9]

Christ is here (and elsewhere) established as the main protagonist of the narrative. Though there are oblique references to the other members of the Trinity at various points in the poem, special (and at times unusual)

---

scholars' views on unity and theme in *Christ and Satan* (1982: 3-26).

[9] All quotations from *Christ and Satan* are from Finnegan's edition of the poem. I do not reproduce Finnegan's length marks, brackets, etc. The italics in this and any other quotations are, of course, my own. The reader should at least be aware of the discrepancies in the text as presented by the poem's four most recent editors (Clubb, Krapp, Finnegan and Sleeth) and the consequences these differences have for interpretation and translation. In this passage, "Heaven" stands for "Creation", the foundations of which were held to be located there. For a discussion of the less-than-transparent imagery in these lines, see Hill (1969), and Finnegan's notes to lines 4-6, 5b and 10a (1977:91).

emphasis is given to God the Son.[10]

Lines 19-33 recount the creation of men and the angels, and provide an encapsulated description of what will emerge as the main thematic concern of the remaining narrative of Part I: the folly of the apostate angels, their abasement and consequent loss of heavenly bliss. This section is comprised of a series of laments reported by a narrator, expressed in speeches delivered now by Satan himself, now by his followers, and punctuated by a pair of authorial, homiletic exhortations. Satan's first plaint recounts his fall from glory (34-50), to which his followers respond with scorn and regret (51-64). Lines 65-74 constitute a short authorial reflection on the fall. The poem's Christocentric focus is again emphasized—*Crist heo afirde* ('Christ drove them out', 67)—and the cause of the fall is made explicit—*for ðam anmedlan* ('for pride', 74). Next follows Satan's second lament, in which he compares his present condition in hell with his former status in heaven (75-125). Lines 126-89 comprise two further laments, in the first of which Satan dwells on the former bliss of the apostates in heaven (126-59), while in the second he utters a cry (opened by eight exclamations each beginning "*Eala!*") of despair, self-recrimination and recognition of his enduring guilt (160-89). This is followed by the first homiletic exhortation: let each man take care not to anger the Son of God the Creator; let Satan's fall and punishment serve as an example for us all, let us be mindful of the Lord, and seek an eternal abode in glory with the King by bearing in our hearts not pride, but peaceful thoughts, love and discretion (190-224). The narrator next informs us that, *Þa get ic furðor gefregen   feond ondetan* ('then further I heard the fiends confess'), and lines 230-79 are indeed Satan's confession, in which he again describes their former blissful state (225-46), their sin and expulsion from heaven (247-62), and the respective fates of himself and his followers: they all must lead the life of the exile, some to inhabit the air, others to roam throughout middle earth stirring up strife among men, while the Devil himself must suffer in hell, lamenting his loss of the joy and favour he once enjoyed in heaven (163-279). This lament is brought to a close in an extremely affective (and potentially unorthodox) way when Satan wonders,

> Hwæðer us se Eca   æfre wille
> on heofona rice   ham alefan,
> eðel to æhte,   swa he ær dyde?   (277-9)

('Will the Eternal One ever grant us a home in the Kingdom of Heaven, a

---

[10] See especially Finnegan's remarks on the possible significance of this pronounced Christocentricity for dating the poem (1977:60-3).

homeland to possess, as he did in the past?')

This final lament is the poet's cue to include a second exhortation to his listeners: lines 289-315 constitute a call to renounce wickedness, please the Lord and extinguish sin, to "shine forth, steadfast in truth."

Having begun my discussion with the example of Cædmon and his poetry, one might ask at this point how *Christ and Satan* compares with Cædmon's *Hymn*, how it measures up as an example of the fusion of Latin Christianity and Germanic linguistic and cultural values. Despite its homiletic tone and possible homiletic inspiration and its obvious status as a Christian poem, there are features in the work—especially diction and imagery—that derive from the poet's inherited Germanic repertoire.

Such imagery manifests itself early on in the poem. For example, in his account of Creation, the poet first introduces the creation of man and the fall of the rebel angels as follows:

> *Dreamas he gedelde,   duguðe and geoguþe:*
> Adam ærest,   and þæt æðele cyn   20
> engla ordfruman,   þæt þe eft forwarð.
> Ðuhte him on mode   þæt hit mihte swa,
> þæt hie weron seolfe   swegles brytan,
> wuldres waldend.   Him ðær wirse gelamp,
> ða heo in helle   ham staðeledon,   25
> an æfter oðrum,   in þæt atole scref,
> þær heo brynewelme   bidan sceoldon
> saran sorge;   nales swegles leoht
> habban in heofnum,   *heahgetimbra,*
> ac gedufan sceolun   in ðone deopan wælm,   30
> niðær under nessas   in ðone neowlan grund,
> gredige and gifre.

('He distributed joys to old and young: first Adam and that noble race (the princes of angels), which later was degenerated. They thought in their minds that it might be so that they themselves could be Lords of heaven, Rulers of glory. It turned out the worse for them, when they took up an abode in hell, one after the other, in that horrible cavern where they must endure grievous affliction in surges of fire; not at all would they enjoy the ethereal light in heaven, or the high-halls, but they—greedy and rapacious creatures—would plunge into the deep surging flames, down beneath the earth into the deep abyss.') [11]

---

[11] The lines I have marked off with italics are not without problems for the editor, for both the phrase in l.19 and the word in l.29 have been the subject of debate. Editors have interpreted them variously; Clubb, for example, maintains the MS reading of *duguðe and geþeode* which Finnegan rejects, while the opposite is true of *heahgetimbrad* found in the

The first image here bearing clear heroic resonance is that of the lord dealing out "joys", or gifts, to his retainers, an image further specified in this instance in terms of the older, veteran retainers on the one hand, and the younger, untried thanes on the other. Finnegan has argued convincingly for a chiastic structure in these lines, taking *geoguðe* to refer to Adam, and *duguþe* to Lucifer and his fellow angels (1977:92-3). Finnegan bases his emendation of line 19 (MS: *geþeode*) in part on the occurrence of the same collocation of *duguðe and geoguþe* three times in *Beowulf*, where in each case it refers to Hrothgar's retainers in contexts that epitomize the mutual relationship and responsibilities of the Germanic lord and his retainers. That the relationship of God, man and the highest order of angels should be expressed in precisely these terms is extremely apt in view of how the sucessive narrative unfolds, for Lucifer's crime of rebellion and presumptuous pride is rendered all the more perfidious because of his status as the leader of the tried and trusted veteran retainers of the Lord. Likewise, the magnitude of the blessing bestowed by God upon man—the untried *geoguðe*—is increased dramatically by this image, for it constitutes an oblique expression of what we may assume was the ultimate desire of every member of this latter group: to join the ranks of the *dugupe*.[12] This is exactly what the poet exhorts his audience to do: if only they will reject the ways and avoid the crimes of the old *duguþe* , they may earn a place at God's side in the new.

This conceptualization of relationships—Christ and Lucifer, Christ and man, Christ and His apostles—in the heroic terms of a lord and his retainers resonates throughout *Christ and Satan*. Many of the oppositions set up by the poet have clear heroic resonances in addition to their obvious Christian portent. It is the heavenly *dryht* ('warrior-band') that one must aspire to, with its heavenly hall where gifts of joy and grace are dealt out, and the *duguð* and *geoguð* sing praises of their Lord. Angelic, heavenly light takes the place of gold and favours as chief among the joys of dwelling in such an *eðel*. Satan's condition, by contrast, is portrayed in terms of undesirable opposites. The *comitatus* of Satan and his followers constitutes an anti-*dryht*, which has as its dwelling not the high halls of heaven (l.29, above) but a wind-swept and terrifying anti-hall. Instead of praising their Lord as do the members of the heavenly *dryht* (cf. ll.151b-55 and 210-24), Satan's followers scorn him (ll.51-64). Unlike Christ, who deals out gifts of love and salvation (ll.19ff.), Satan has nothing to offer his followers but the trials of exile and the absence of all joy; in fact, torments

---

MS: Finnegan retains this, but Clubb emends to *heahgetimbra*.
[12] The term *duguþ* was also often used to refer specifically to the heavenly host. See the *Dictionary of Old English* s.v. *duguþ*, 4.b.ii.

are their *hyht* ('hope'; e.g. ll.70 and 335).

With regard to the secular heroic imagery used by the *Christ and Satan* poet, the motif of the demons' fate as wandering exiles is a particularly vivid and striking one. Generally speaking, one can discern two distinct attitudes towards exile current throughout Anglo-Saxon England. To the pious monk who has taken his vows and embarked upon a spiritual pilgrimage, the object of which is to be reunited with God, the condition of exile—be it an actual sojourn in a foreign land as missionary, pilgrim or hermit, or figural, as in his rejection of the world and retreat to a monastic cell—is ideally always voluntary and desirable. Germanic exile, on the other hand, is never voluntary, and separation from one's native land and the protection of one's lord is often portrayed in the Old English elegies as the worst fate a warrior could endure. It is for this reason that our poet's use of the motif to describe Satan's fate is especially effective, and whether it is a holdover from heroic diction or an indication of the status and tastes of his own audience, it constitutes an important thematic feature of the work. Beginning at l.119, Satan laments his fate in the following terms:

> Forðon ic sceal hean and earm   hweorfan ðy widor,
> wadan wræclastas,   wuldor benemed,
> duguðum bedeled,   nænigne dream agan
> uppe mid ænglum,   þes ðe ic ær gecwæð
> þæt ic wære seolfa   swægles brytta,
> wihta wealdend.   (119-24a)

('For this reason I, miserable and wretched, must turn further afield and travel the paths of exile, denied heaven and deprived of blessings, not to possess any joy with the angels above, since I lately said that I myself was the lord of heaven and ruler of its creatures.')

Likewise, in lines 187b ff. Satan remarks, *[Ic] sceal nu wræclastas / settan sorhcearig,   siþas wide.* ('Now I, sorrow-bound, must trace the paths of exile, far-flung journeys.') Finally, the active image of wandering the paths of exile is applied to Satan and his followers yet again at 256b ff., *Cuð is wide / þæt wreclastas   wunian moton / grimme grundas.* ('It is widely known that we must inhabit the paths of exile, the cruel abysses.')

Vivid and effective as this imagery is, its use brings to light a potential "vagary" in our poet's composition (cf. Keenan, 1975). One may observe that, prior to the introduction of the exile imagery with its heroic resonances, Satan repeatedly describes his own post-lapsarian condition as one of total and absolute confinement. These references to chains and fetters are slightly ambiguous, seeming now to apply to his prison, now to his own body, but taken together they form an image of restricted mobility:

Þis is ðeostre ham   ðearle gebunden
fæstum fyrclommum;   flor is on welme,
ætre onæled. ...
          ...   And ic in wite sceal
bidan in bendum,   and me bettran ham
for oferhygdum   æfre ne wene.   (38-40a, 48b-50)

('This is a dark home, tightly bound in firm shackles of fire; the floor is
surging, burning with venom. ... And I must remain under torment in
chains, and because of pride never expect for myself a better home.')

Satan's followers describe him further,

          Nu earttu sceaðana sum
in fyrlocan   feste gebunden.   (57-8)

('Now you are one of the criminals, bound fast in a fiery prison.')

Lines 102 ff. reinforce the idea that for Satan at least, hell is inescapable:
is ðis wites clom / feste gebunden ('This chain of punishment is bound
tight.') This same expression finds an echo in a further passage suggesting
Satan's being bound in chains,

          Nu ic eom dædum fah,
gewundod mid wommum;   sceal nu þysne wites clom
beoran beornende   in bæce minum,
hat on helle,   hyhtwillan leas.   (155b-8)

('Now I am stained [guilty] by my deeds, wounded with evils; now I must
bear this chain of punishment on my back, hot in hell, deprived of the hope
of joy.')

Finally, the Prince of Devils (*heora aldor*) is depicted as "bound fast in
fetters of fire and flame" (*fæste gebunden / fyre and lige*, ll.323b-4a).
     To the literal-minded reader these details—the binding of Satan in
hell and his simultaneous "wandering the paths of exile"—would seem to
conflict. One might account for this apparent contradiction by pointing out
that the hell in which Satan and his angels dwell is a vast one (it is a *wide
... winsele*, an expansive wine-hall [1.319], and a paradoxically wind-swept
one, at that [*ðes windiga sele*, 1.135b]), thus any wandering that Satan
might do would have to be within the confines of this "hall". So too, the
chains with which the Old Adversary is bound might be perceived in
terms of those flames of hell which the poet describes as accompanying the
lesser devils wherever they wander (ll. 261b-4). Yet even the notion that
Satan is locked firmly in hell seems to be contradicted in at least three

places. Perhaps foreshadowing the introduction of the imagery of exile introduced at lines 119ff, and seemingly in flat contradiction to all descriptions of his situation up to this point in the poem, Satan remarks:

> Nu ic feran com
> deofla menego   to ðissum dimman ham;
> ac ic sceal on flyge   and on flyhte ðragum
> earda neosan,   and eower ma
> þe ðes oferhydes   ord onstaldon.   (109b-13)

('Now I have come travelling with a multitude of devils to this dim home. But I, and more of you who authored the beginning of this pride, must from time to time take wing in flight to seek out homes.')

Further down the Devil indicates to which souls of men he is allowed to lay claim:

> Ne ic þam sawlum ne mot
> ænigum sceððan
> butan þam anum   þe he agan nyle;
> þa ic mot to hæftum   ham geferian,
> bringan to bolde   in þone biteran grund.   (144b-8)

('None of these souls am I able to harm except those that He does not want; those I may carry home to bondage, bring them to an abode in this dire place.')

In having Satan describe the dwelling places and powers of his fellow fallen angels, the poet again seems to disregard his previous description of the bounds of Satan's mobility, by having Satan say:

> Sceal nu þeos menego her
> licgan on leahtrum;   sume on lyft scacan,
> fleogan ofer foldan,   fyr bið ymbutan
> on æghwylcum,   þæh he uppe seo.
> Ne mot he þam sawlum   þe ðær secað up,   265
> eadige of eorþan   æfre gehrinan.
> Ah ic be hondum mot   hæþenre sceale
> gripan to grunde,   godes andsacan.
> Sume sceolon hweorfan   geond hæleða land
> and unsibbe   oft onstyrian   270
> monna mægðum   geond middaneard.
> Ic her geþolian sceal   þinga æghwylces,
> bitres niðæs   beala gnornian,
> sic and sorhful)   þæs ic seolfa weold,

þonne ic on heofonum   ham staðelode.   275

('Now this multitude must lie here in its sins; some to hurry in the air, to
fly above the earth—fire surrounds each of them, though he be on high.
He may never lay hold of those blessed souls that seek upwards there from
earth. But I, with my hands, may clutch down to the abyss the heathen
throng, the enemies of God. Some shall wander about the land of men and
often stir up strife among the races of man throughout middle earth. I,
here—sick and sorrowful—must bewail the woes of my bitter malice, I
must suffer the loss of each thing over which I myself held power when I
possessed a home in heaven.')

Thus the pattern which emerges concerning Satan's freedom of movement
may be summarized as follows: he is initially described as suffering extreme limitation in his mobility, both in terms of being locked in the
prison of hell, and of being further restricted within those confines (ll.
38ff., 48ff., 57-8 and 102ff.). In apparent contradiction to this, Satan himself remarks that he must from time to time seek out another abode
(109ff.). Next, he describes his fate and that of his followers in terms of
"wandering the paths of exile" (ll.119ff.), and, moreover, seems to indicate that he is capable of personally carrying back down to hell the souls
of sinners, despite his previously detailed confinement to (and apparently
fettered condition within) hell. Shortly hereafter Satan complains of the
"burning fetters" on his back, again suggesting a degree of limited mobility hardly consistent with his movements just described (ll.154ff.). Finally,
in the longer passage cited above, the contradiction we are scrutinizing
here seems most pronounced: Satan describes both the freedom of his
followers to fly above the earth (ll.262-7), and his own restriction to suffering in hell, while sandwiched in the middle of these descriptions is his
claim to be able to snatch down into the abyss errant souls "with his
hands" (ll.268-9).

These two ways of depicting Satan's situation sum up the meeting of
Christian content and Germanic form, for the notion that Satan was
chained in hell has Biblical authority, while, as I have mentioned above,
the condition of exile carried a particularly ominous connotation for the
secular circles of Germanic society.[13] Nor is the use of this pair of images

[13] The chief Biblical witness to Satan's bondage is of course Revelation 20:1-3. The idea
has further New Testament witnesses in Jude 6 and 2 Peter 2:4. Many commentators take
these passages to refer to Christ's actions during his post-Passion descent and the Harrowing of hell, though in *Christ and Satan*, which itself contains an account of the Harrowing (derived from the apocryphal *Gospel of Nicodemus*; see Morey (1990) for a recent
discussion of the relationship of this text to *Christ and Satan*), they are clearly applied to
Satan's condition *before* the Passion of Christ. The clearest and least ambiguous parallel
example of the belief that Satan was bound in hell after his fall from heaven, and prior to
the Harrowing, is found in the same manuscript containing *Christ and Satan*, namely

unique to *Christ and Satan*. It occurs in a number of Old English poems, including *Guthlac A, Andreas,* the poetic *Solomon and Saturn* and *Elene*.[14] All of these have in common with *Christ and Satan* a portrayal of Satan's condition after his fall in terms of confinement. In some (particularly *Andreas* and *Elene*), the suffering of the apostate angels is underlined by the mention of their state of exile. Yet I would suggest that in their expression of this latter image there is a fundamental difference between these poems and *Christ and Satan*. Whereas Satan is portrayed in both *Andreas* and *Elene* as existing in a state of exile, i.e. separation from his native home in heaven, the *Christ and Satan* poet is much more specific in his use of active verbs to describe Satan's condition: not only has he been cast out of his former home, but he "wanders" and "traces" the paths of exile.

Once we recognize that our poet's use of these two seemingly conflicting motifs is potentially bewildering, then the next step is to posit a way of accounting for it. We might attribute it to the poet's "absentmindedness" (Gollancz, 1927:civ-cv), and accept it as a feature akin to, for example, his apparent disregard for chronology in the larger structure of the poem. Alternatively we might simply assume that the poet has employed these two motifs as general expressions of extreme hardship and suffering, juxtaposing the "original" Biblical one alongside of the secular one merely for poetic effect. Yet it seems unlikely that either the poet or his audience would have been unaware of the conflict inherent in the two differing descriptions of Satan's mobility I have cited: they are dramatic and compelling, but taken together literally they seem irreconcilable.

Rather than assume that the poet was confused, lax, or merely using these motifs for poetic effect without regard for the disjunction they create in the narrative logic of this section of the poem, we might instead suppose that he has imposed a different kind of logic on his material. And we find a clear formulation of a means for interpreting precisely this kind of passage in a text that exerted a profound influence on Christian thinking throughout the European Middle Ages: Augustine's *De Doctrina Christiana*. Among the so-called "Tyconian Rules" contained in this treatise are two that are of some relevance to the situation presented in *Christ and*

Genesis B (ASPR I, pp.15ff., ll.371ff.) The force of this imagery in the religious context is reinforced by the fact that fettering was common and hence much used throughout the poetic corpus for describing a state of helplessness. Cf. e.g. *The Seafarer* 9-10: *waeron mine fet, forste gebunden / caldum clommum* ('my feet were bound by frost, with cold fetters'); further *Wanderer* 21. The "Imma and Timma" episode in Bede's *HE*, Bk. 4:22 should also be taken into consideration. I thank Rolf Bremmer for bringing this to my attention.

[14] For *Guthlac A,* see Roberts (1979:101ff., ll.592ff.); *Andreas, ASPR II* (pp. 36ff., ll. 1185ff.); *Solomon and Saturn, ASPR VI* (pp.47ff., ll.451ff.); *Elene ASPR II* (pp. 87ff., ll.759-71).

Satan.[15] These rules, which were meant as keys for unlocking the meaning of difficult passages in Scripture, provided an alternative to the literal reading of the text. Rule number one, "Of the Lord and His Body", is immediately recognizable as an elaboration on Paul's metaphor (in 1 Corinthians 12:12-13) in which he interprets Christ as the "Head" of the Church, whose members are His "limbs." Thus, echoes Tyconius, both the Head and the Body (i.e. Christ and the Church) are represented in one and the same person; nevertheless, it is understood that the actions of that person are to be distinguished as applying now to Christ, now to His Body or the Church. We encounter, in fact, a sure resonance of this way of viewing Christ and the church in *Christ and Satan,* though it need not have derived directly from Tyconius. At lines 151ff., Satan recalls how before his fall he and the heavenly troop had worshipped Christ:

> Ful oft wuldres sweg
> brohton to bearme   bearne hælendes,
> þær we ymb hine utan   ealle hofan,
> *leomu ymb leofne,*   lofsonga word
> drihtne sædon.   (151b-5a)

('Full often we offered praise to the Son of God the Saviour when we, round about him as limbs about the loved one, all raised the words of the songs of praise, addressing them to the Lord.')

At line 381 we find yet another use of this imagery; the souls waiting in hell for Christ's appearance at the Harrowing see him thus: *Blis wearð monnum / þa hi hælendes   heafod gesawon* (ll.380b-81: 'Joy was to the mortals when they saw the Saviour's head.'). This is a clear allusion to the divine aspect of Christ, and one which evokes as well the head and body imagery given expression in the Tyconian Rules.[16]

Not unexpectedly, Tyconius formulates an equal and opposite rule concerning the Devil:

---

[15] Augustine includes the *Liber Regularum* of Tyconius towards the end of Book III of his *De Doctrina Christiana.* The work is comprised of seven rules for the interpretation of Scripture, and their inclusion in *De Doctrina Christiana* accounts for the important role they played in medieval exegesis. That they were known in Anglo-Saxon England is attested by Bede's citation of them in the preface to his *Explanatio Apocalypsis* (Bede, *PL* 93 129 ff.), and we also know that Alcuin made use of them.

[16] For a discussion of this figure in these very lines, see Hill, 1970:5-8. See also Clubb, 1972:74, note to lines 154-6 on *leomu* and head and body imagery. Greenfield (1979:4) detects a figurative hierarchical structure in secular Lord-retainer relationships (in *Beowulf*) that seems relevant. His proposition that "references to the literal physical extremities resonate with the concept of thaneship" might be used in conjunction with Tyconius to account for Satan's use of his "hands" to snatch down souls of sinners.

The seventh rule of Tyconius, and the last, is "Of the Devil
and his Body." For he is the head of the impious, who are in a
way his body, and who will go with him to the tortures of
eternal fire in the same way that Christ is the head of the
Church, which is His body, and will be with Him in His
Kingdom and everlasting glory. Therefore, just as in the first
rule called "Of the Lord and His Body" it is necessary to be
alert in order to understand what pertains to the head and
what pertains to the body when Scripture speaks of one and
the same person, so in this last one, sometimes things are said
concerning the Devil which may be understood not with
reference to himself, but rather to his body ...
                                                        (Robertson, 1984:115-16)

The passages from Tyconius's *Liber Regularum* provide a key of
sorts for reconciling the narrative inconsistencies in the first section of
Christ and Satan. While it is an obvious fact that the Rules were meant as
an aid for the interpretation of Scripture, and that the text we are dealing
with forms no part of that canon, we may with some confidence infer that,
given the influence of Augustine's treatise, the exegetical methods it embodies would have informed the thinking of the *Christ and Satan* poet. I do
not mean to suggest that he would have had the Tyconian Rules in front of
him, or even that he need necessarily ever have seen them. Rather I would
stress that the alternative they offer to the *literal* reading of obscure passages would have been so familiar as to have conditioned his thinking and
poetic composition.

Apparently the presence of the incongruous representation of
Satan's mobile capacities—the result of a mixture of images—was not in
the least disturbing to the poet or his audience. I would, in fact, argue that
it need not have been, but the incongruity—certainly at the literal level—
remains. To argue that these images did not appear problematic to their
medieval audience should not deter us from adducing the perspective by
which they might be reconciled. If we assume that we are dealing merely
with the blending of two distinct genres here—the Christian, in which
Satan is conceived of as bound, and the secular, which allows the introduction of the heroic motif of wandering the paths of exile—then we may
be too willing to leave the poet open to charges of carelessness, or even
incompetence. I would instead suggest that we have here another example
of the fusion of Germanic and Christian modes of thought, for while the
poet seems understandably drawn towards the dramatic, traditional Germanic topos, and while he exploits the image to full effect, it is the Christian, symbolic mode of interpretation that allows him to do so without
violating the internal logic of his narrative.

Viewed in Tyconian terms, the Devil in *Christ and Satan* becomes at once a more wretched and a more fearsome creature. He is wretched, because as the "head of the impious" he is imprisoned, having been defeated by Christ and thrown out of heaven, bound in chains and the sufferer of both physical and psychological torments, the least bearable of the latter being his state of exile from his former joy and glory. He is fearsome, because despite his confinement he is able through the actions of his Body, i.e. his fellow apostate angels, to strike out at and ensnare the souls of men. Thus, one way of reading the passages discussed here is to understand that when Satan speaks of "flying out" (ll.111ff.), of himself carrying back down to hell the souls of men (ll.114ff.), or of snatching them down with his own "hands" (ll.267-8), such actions are to be understood "not with reference to himself, but rather to his body". That the Devil is not, in the end, portrayed as the heroic, tragic figure of *Genesis B* or *Paradise Lost* has been noted by other critics (e.g. Greenfield and Calder, 1986:210; Finnegan, 1977:48). Indeed, the poet's didactic, hortatory tone and his treatment of Satan's situation and plaints leaves little room for any "sympathy for the Devil" on his audience's part. Moreover, the pair of images discussed here helps the poet, within his didactic framework, to illustrate an important Christian paradox: the simultaneous power and impotence of the sin and evil embodied in Satan.

II

The Dream of the Rood

The Dream of the Rood, fifth poem in the Vercelli codex, could not be more different from *Christ and Satan* in its structure, content, tone, and, significantly, in its reception by critics. It is one of the most widely read and frequently anthologized Old English poems in the corpus. Greenfield describes it as "Perhaps the finest Old English religious poem", and he adds that it may owe this distinction to "its lyrical combination of narrative and drama, and, despite its penitential "program", to the absence of homiletic exhortation" (1986:198-9). Unlike *Christ and Satan, The Dream of the Rood* has always garnered praise for its distinctive blending of tradition and originality. The poet's novel use of prosopopoeia (the speech of the Cross), though not without its analogues,[17] has often been singled out as one of the most significant factors contributing to the poem's modern appeal. This central episode of the poem, which takes up some three-fifths of the entire work, has captured the attention of critics in part, no doubt,

---

[17] For these see Schlauch (1968), Woolf (1958:149, note 32) and Braswell (1978).

because it is here that the fusion of Germanic and Christian elements is
most prominent. The relationship between the animate Cross and Christ is
recounted in heroic terms: metaphors of battle abound, and the portrayal
of Christ as warrior-hero, a favourite theme with Anglo-Saxon poets,
achieves its ultimate expression in *The Dream of the Rood*.[18]

The apparently original treatment of Christ's Passion as narrated
from the perspective of the Cross has deservedly received much praise and
critical discussion.[19] There can be little doubt that the centrality of Christ's
Passion in the poem commands the reader's attention. The multiple and
paradoxical roles of the Cross—narrator and subject of its own narration,
simultaneously retainer and *bana* ("slayer") of Christ, his own Lord—as
well as the portrayal in epic terms of Christ embracing and at the same
time defeating Death, constitutes the most striking and compelling treatment of the subject in Old English poetry. Scholars who have approached
The Dream of the Rood as essentially a crucifixion poem, however, have
tended to play down the importance of the poem's dream frame (lines 1-
27 and 122-56). Despite its reputation as the finest religious work in the
corpus, the poem's integrity as it is preserved in the *Vercelli Book* has
received its share of criticism as well. A previous generation of scholars
asserted that lines 122-56 were a later addition, thus calling into question
the poem's unity (Woolf, 1958:153; Dickins and Ross, 1965:17-18). In
fact, critics have met with particular difficulty in interpreting the framing
sections of the poem, and it has been noted that these sections are composed in such an allusive and compacted fashion, with very little elaboration, that the poet appears to be "relying on the reader's recognition of the
details and of the scene that these details comprised in order to complete
the effect" (Payne, 1976:330). Recently, however, the lines comprising the
dream frame have been reassessed, and these discussions have added much
to our understanding of the content, function and thematic relevance of
these sections.[20]

The apparent centrality of the Cross and its account of the Crucifixion notwithstanding, some scholars have recognized that the dominant
themes in *The Dream of the Rood* are eschatological (e.g. Fleming, 1966:
70), and that this eschatological orientation is present from the outset in

---

[18] Studies that deal in whole or part with this aspect of *The Dream of the Rood* include
Wolf (1970), Cherniss (1973), Klinck (1982) and Woolf (1958:144-45), but Fleming
views this imagery in a different light (1966:49-50).

[19] But it should be noted that Payne (1973) has done much to modify and define the
extent of the poet's "originality".

[20] On the eschatological character of the final section, see Brzezinski (1988); N.A. Lee
(1972) is concerned primarily with its unity, and Payne (1976) discusses in detail the
eschatology of the opening scene.

the vision framework.[21] As Burrow concludes, "the Dreamer in the Old English poem moves from fear and sorrow to hope, and it is this simple emotional sequence which links the closing soliloquy with the opening vision and sets the tone of the central Crucifixion scene" (1959:133). The Dreamer's "fear and sorrow" are prompted by his encounter with the unmistakable sign of Judgement as described in the opening scene, and his "hope" is engendered by his newly acquired conviction that his reward at Judgement will be everlasting life (135b-44a). In what follows I shall elaborate on one of the narrative details in this opening section of the vision framework that our poet no doubt felt would be readily recognized by his audience, but which to date has not been noted in discussions of the eschatological allusions in *The Dream of the Rood*.[22] For convenience' sake I quote this opening section in full below (from Swanton's edition):

> Hwæt! Ic swefna cyst   secgan wylle
> h[w]æt me gemætte   to midre nihte,
> syðþan reordberend   reste wunedon.
>   Þuhte me þæt ic gesawe   syllicre treow
> on lyft lædan,   leohte bewunden,   5
> beama beorhtost.   Eall þæt beacen wæs
> begoten mid golde;   gimmas stodon
> fægere æt foldan sceatum,   swylce þær fife wæron
> uppe on þam eaxlegespanne.   Beheoldon þær engel
>   Dryhtnes ealle,
> fægere þurh forðgesceaft.   Ne wæs ðær huru   10
>   fracodes gealga.
> Ac hine þær beheoldon   halige gastas,
> men ofer moldan   ond eall þeos mære gesceaft.
>   Syllic wæs se sigebeam,   ond ic synnum fah,
> forwunded mid wommum.   Geseah ic wuldres treow,
> wædum geweorðode,   wynnum scinan,   15
> gegyred mid golde;   gimmas hæfdon
> bewrigene weorðlice   wealdes treow.
> Hwæðre ic þurh þæt gold   ongytan meahte

---

[21] This is not surprising, for in a way any medieval Christian vision poem is bound to be "eschatological" to some extent, given the emphasis placed upon the fate of the soul in medieval Christianity. When I describe sections or details of the poem as "eschatological" in this discussion, I think of them as alluding to motifs or narrative traditions used to describe the events of the Last Day.

[22] The basis for the argument I develop below has appeared in print once before. See Hill, 1973:242, note 18. I feel justified in developing the notion here, in particular because studies of the eschatology of *The Dream of the Rood* that have appeared subsequent to Professor Hill's article have failed to take note of the suggestion.

earmra ærgwin,   þæt hit ærest ongan
swætan on þa swiðran healfe.   Eall ic wæs mid   20
      s[o]rgum gedrefed.
Forht ic wæs for þære fægran gesyhðe.   Geseah
      ic þæt fuse beacen
wendan wædum ond bleom;   hwilum hit wæs mid
      wætan bestemed,
beswyled mid swates gange,   Hwilum mid since
      gegyrwed.
Hwæðre ic þær licgende   lange hwile
beheold hreowcearig   Hælendes treow,   25
oððæt ic gehyrde   þæt hit hleoðrode.

('Listen! I wish to relate the choicest of visions, what I dreamt at midnight
when speech-bearing men lay in bed. It seemed to me that I saw a most
wonderful tree borne on high, wound about with light, the brightest of
trees. That sign was all covered with gold; beautiful gems shone at the
corners of the earth and there were also five on the crossbeam. All beheld
there, throughout fair creation, the angel of the Lord. Indeed, that was not
the gallows of a criminal. Rather, holy spirits gazed upon it, men throughout the earth and all this glorious creation. Wondrous was the tree of victory, and I was guilty of sins, wounded by evil deeds. *I saw the tree of
glory, adorned with its vestments, decked with gold, shine beautifully;
gems had worthily covered the tree of the Ruler.* However, through that
gold I could discern *the former strife of wretched men, when it first began
to bleed on the right side.* I was entirely oppressed with cares. I was fearful in the presence of that fair [hostile?] sight. *I saw that urgent sign
change its vestments and colour; at times it was soaked with wetness,
drenched with courses of blood, at times adorned with treasure.* Nevertheless, lying there a long time I beheld, troubled, the Saviour's tree, until
I heard that it spoke.')

I am here particularly concerned with accounting for the function and
significance within the vision framework of the passages italicized above.
Hence, a close scrutiny of the lines leading up to these passages is called
for. My aim is to demonstrate that the poet's use of eschatological conventions was even more subtle, and in a sense more original, than has hereto-
fore been supposed.

   Practically every line in this opening scene contains an allusion to
conventions of Christian speculative eschatology. The Dreamer informs us
in line 2 that his vision appears to him *to midre nihte* ('at midnight') while
others are asleep. That the last day should arrive unexpectedly has Biblical
authority in I Thessalonians 5:2-7, but the exact hour of its advent was derived from Matth. 25:6.[23] There is ample evidence to demonstrate that

---

[23] *Media autem nocte clamor factus est ecce sponsus venit exite obviam ei* ('But at mid-

Insular Christians believed that the Day of Judgment would begin at midnight, and one clear instance occurs in the Old English *Christ III* (ll.867-74; see Biggs, 1986:6-7), a work whose theme is irrefutably eschatological.[24]

The appearance of "a most wonderful tree borne on high, wound about with light, the brightest of trees" (ll.4a-6a) is, as scholars have shown, a theme with explicit eschatological associations. It, too, has Biblical origins, (Matth. 24:30),[25] and the shining Cross as a sign of the Second Coming of Christ and impending Judgement was developed by early Christian exegetes, among whom was St. Ephraem of Syria, whose writings on the subject were instrumental in establishing early medieval Judgement Day iconographical conventions (Payne, 1976:331). In Old English texts it appears in Blickling Homily VII[26] and *Christ III* (ll.1064-5), among others.

In the ensuing lines (5b-9a) the poet elaborates on the appearance of the Cross, describing its adornment with gold and jewels. Besides the Constantinian image of the Rood extending to all four corners of the earth (*æt foldum sceatum*; see Swanton 1970:50-1 and 102-3), these lines carry a symbolic burden of meaning that will prove important for my argument. As Rosemary Woolf remarks, "The splendour of gold and jewels symbolized not only the triumph of Christ, but also His divinity" (1958:137, n.3). That we are indeed meant to see the Cross as the Divine manifestation of Christ is strongly suggested by lines 9b-12. In this passage, *Beheoldon þær engel Dryhtnes ealle* has seemed problematic to some editors (e.g. Dickins and Ross, who emend to *engeldryhte*), but if one reads the line from the viewpoint of conventional Christian eschatology, the manuscript reading makes good sense as it stands, though, as Swanton (1970:103) points out, the word order is "awkward, if not impossible." Taking *ealle* as nominative plural subject, and *engel* as accusative singular object renders: "All beheld there the Angel of the Lord".[27] Thus the main elements of the con-

---

night a cry was made: behold, the Bridegroom comes, go forth to meet him').

[24] *Christ III* is invariably cited in connection with discussions of eschatology in *The Dream of the Rood*. Payne (1976:329) begins his study with a relevant passage, and all the passages analysed by Hill (1973) are of general relevance.

[25] *Et tunc parebunt signum Filii hominis in caelo / Et tunc plangent omnes tribus terrae / et videbunt Filium hominis venientum in nubibus caeli cum virtute multa et maiestate* ('And then shall appear the sign of the Son of man in heaven: and then shall all the tribes of the earth mourn: and they shall see the Son of man coming in the clouds of heaven with much power and majesty.')

[26] *Ond seo rod ures Dryhtnes bið arœred on þæt gewrixle þara tungla* ('and the Rood of our Lord shall be raised in the course of the stars'), Morris (1880: 91).

[27] William Helder (1975) argues convincingly for this reading of the line. Moreover, the Angel of the Lord frequently appears in the Old Testament, and was soon interpreted by

ventional Judgement tableau are present: the unmistakable sign (*beacen*, l.6) of Doomsday appears in the sky, and in this visionary version of that event the sign appears in glory, just as Christ will do at the real last Judgement. And just as the angels and all mankind will come together before Christ the Judge on that Final Day, so too the Dreamer sees them (*halige gastas, men ofer moldan*) assembled here before the "angel of the Lord".

By line 12, then, the poet has clearly established the scene of his dream-persona's vision as that of the last Judgement. With lines 13-14a the Dreamer ceases to be a mere witness to a vision unfolding, for by turning his visionary gaze upon himself he enters the narrative as a participant, a move of particular significance for the further development of the poem's theme. *Syllic wæs se sigebeam   ond ic synnum fah* would appear at first sight to effect a visual contrast between the Cross and the Dreamer, especially if one translates the adjective as "stained", for in that sense the *sigebeam* (Victory tree, symbol of Christ's triumph) arrives in resplendent and innocent glory, while the Dreamer looks on, humbled and impure. But *fah* in its most frequent manifestation entails guilt and enmity, and it is to this sense that I think we should give preference (Bosworth and Toller, s.v. *fah*).[28] At the sight of the Cross appearing in the sky before all of creation, the Dreamer (and, we may assume, the poet's audience) recognizes the situation as that of Judgement, and the Cross as Christ the Judge, and he is suddenly acutely aware of his own sins.

Having set the scene and established his own (or his persona's) presence among the *men ofer moldan* at the final reckoning, the Dreamer reports what he sees next, and while lines 14b-17 might be characterized as just another instance of poetic variation, in that they seem merely to repeat the contents of 6b-9a, I would suggest that 14b-20a be taken together as a unit. These lines strengthen the equation of the Cross with Christ, and in so doing they introduce a contrast with important eschatological connotations. This is followed immediately by a coda of sorts (lines 20b-21a), and the sight is subsequently repeated with some urgency in lines 21b-3.

Thus in lines 14b-17b, the Dreamer again sees the Cross in all its bejeweled splendour, but then the vision shifts, and through the gold he watches as the Rood begins to bleed *from its right side*. Swanton notes that there is no biblical authority for the position of the wound inflicted on Christ by the soldier's lance, but he remarks that medieval exegetes had their reasons for deciding on his right side, and it is thus that contemporary Crucifixion scenes depict it (1970:109). These lines constitute the

the early Christians as a manifestation of Jesus Christ.
[28] Compare also *Christ and Satan* 155-6, where Satan laments his guilty state: *Nu ic eom dædum fah, gewundod mid wommum.*

first of two instances of a highly symbolic means of alluding to Christ through the vehicle of the Cross. Thus the golden, shining Cross represents Christ's Divine aspect, while the bleeding one signifies His humanity.[29] This is an essential identification to keep in mind when we turn our attention to the closing lines of this scene.

The "coda" (20b-21a) to this dual description of the Cross/Christ as now bright and glorious, now ominous and wounded, constitutes an even stronger indication of the Dreamer's reaction to what he sees than the concern for his state of sin expressed earlier: now he is consumed with anxiety and fear (*Eall ic wæs mid s[o]rgum gedrefed*) and this fear is prompted by the *fægran gesyhðe*. If one takes the form *"fægran"* to be the weak declension form of the adjective *fæger* ('beautiful', 'fair'), then one might conclude that the Dreamer is merely awed by this apparition which by virtue of its dual aspect could be terrible and yet beautiful. Swanton (1970:103) has suggested, however, that it is possible to interpret this adjective in a way that is more in keeping with the context and contents of these lines: it could well be construed as the comparative of *fæge*, in which case its sense would be "more doomed, more inimical". This same sight, be it beautiful or more exclusively indicative of doom, is repeated in lines 21b-23, for the Cross "urgently" (*fus*) shifts from one state to the other: now it is covered in gore, now adorned with treasure. Recognizing it as the "Saviour's tree" (*Hælendes treow*, line 25) does nothing to relieve the Dreamer's fear; on the contrary, he remains in a state of seemingly heightened anxiety until the Rood speaks. The "urgency" with which the Rood shifts its aspect, coupled with the Dreamer's assertion that he remained "for a long time" gazing at it suggests that the sight held some particularly fearful meaning for him, perhaps going beyond the expected awe and fear all men should have in the presence of the Lord.[30] It is also important to note that we are never told whether the Cross ceases to alternate between these two aspects, and if so, which one finally appears to the Dreamer.

In my analysis so far, I am in agreement with Payne's assertion that "when we turn to a consideration of the Dreamer's reaction to the vision as it is presented in lines 13ff, we arrive at the thematic core of the poem, and we can begin to see the intended effect of the poem's eschatological

---

[29] Êamonn Ó Carragáin elucidates the liturgical background to line 20a in a learned article, and one of his conclusions, that "the poet is concerned not with Christ *on* the Cross, but with Christ *in* the visionary object" (1983:14) is consonant with my own view. He fails, however, to account sufficiently for the use of the image in the opening vision.

[30] The compound *hreowcearig* has connotations that extend, quite possibly, beyond mere "sorrow". The semantic range of *hreow* extends to 'penitence' and 'repentance', an appropriate sense given the Dreamer's admission in line 13.

locus" (1976:334). In fact, both Payne and N.A. Lee touch on many of the points made here thus far, but neither addresses satisfactorily an issue that to my mind so firmly establishes the eschatological context in this opening scene and beyond, namely, what exactly is the significance of the shifting appearance of the Cross as portrayed in 21b-3?

Swanton documents the conventionality of colour variation in medieval Christian cross imagery, citing Hrabanus Maurus and the cross riddle of the eighth century Anglo-Saxon Archbishop Tatwine as possible analogues (1970:111). Swanton would explain the image presented in these lines thus: "The allusion is presumably to the changing colours appropriate to different seasons of the church year. A plain wooden cross, blood-red, the colour of death ... was carried during Lent until Good Friday, while on Easter Sunday a magnificent and richly jewelled cross appeared" (1970:111). Payne (1976:335) recognizes this allusion, but adduces a passage from Revelation 19 (11-13; a white horse clothed with a garment sprinkled with blood, representing Christ) to account for the immediate significance of these lines. He draws the following conclusion:

> Thus I should probably not be far afield in suggesting that the descriptive detail of the dual appearance of the cross in *The Dream of the Rood*, like its counterpart in Revelation, suggests the paradoxical coexistence of Christ in glory and Christ crucified. The only thing that has happened is that the dual appearance has been transferred from the Judge to the cross that heralds His coming.

Payne makes two important points here: first, that the poet equates the sign of His coming in these lines with Christ Himself, and second, that what the Dreamer sees in the changing aspect of the cross is alternatively Christ in glory and Christ suffering. He thus comes tantalizingly close to unravelling the problem presented by these lines.

In order to resolve this issue ourselves we turn to a discussion by Hill of some relevant passages in another poem with a pronounced "eschatological locus". In "Vision and Judgement in the Old English *Christ III*" Hill is concerned, among other things, with the poet's emphasis on vision, in particular what the blessed and the damned will see at the last Judgement. Three times in this poem we are told in no uncertain terms that the damned will see Christ as a suffering man—that they will see his wounds (1101-10 and 1115-7; 1204-18; 1454-61). "That sinners should see the wounds of Christ at the last Judgement is of course a commonplace of the medieval eschatological tradition" (Hill, 1973:235-6). The relevance of this issue for the present discussion will be obvious. Hill formulates the problem, and offers its solution, as follows:

Since both the sinners and Christ are present at Judgement, then the sinners must in some sense behold Him; and yet in Christian tradition the beatific vision, the sight of God, is the ultimate reward of the blessed. For patristic authors the terms of the question were defined by two apparently conflicting Biblical texts. At the last Judgement, how could the sinners "behold him whom they pierced" (Zacharias 12:10; echoed in John 19:36 and Apoc. 1:7) if it is only the blessed, those who are pure in heart, who will behold God (Matthew 5:8)? The traditional answer to this problem is clearly stated by Augustine in his treatise *De Trinitate*:

> And the Jews indeed, who persevere in evil, are to be punished at that judgment—as it is written elsewhere, 'they will look upon the one they pierced' (Zach. 12: 10). For when the good and the evil are going to see the Judge of the living and the dead, without doubt the evil cannot see Him except according to the form in which He is the son of man; but even so in the brightness in which He will judge, not in the humility in which He was judged. That other form of God in which He is equal to the Father, the wicked will doubtless not see. For they are not pure in heart. For "Blessed are the pure in heart for they will see God" (Mt. 5:8). And that vision is face to face (I Cor. 13:12) which supreme reward is promised to the just.

This is a well-established theme in the patristic Latin tradition (Hill, 1973: 236ff. *passim,* and 238, n.9). It was a familiar one to Anglo-Saxons writing in the vernacular as well, for in addition to the allusion in *Christ III*, Alfred incorporates it into his translation of St. Augustine's *Soliloquies*, as does Ælfric in one of his homilies (Wallace, 1990:141-2). One last example (after Wallace, 1990:142), this one from the Vercelli homilies (Homily XV), should suffice to make the point:

> On þæm dægre ure Dryhten in his þam mægen-þrymme, 7 his onsyne ætweð 7 his lichoman, þonne bið seo wund gesewen þam firen-fullum, 7 þam soð-fæstan he bið hal gesewen.

> ('On that day our Lord [will come] in His majesty and show His face and His body; then the wound will be seen by the sinful, and to the trustworthy he will be seen whole.')

Lines 21b-3 in *The Dream of the Rood* may well have been influenced by the liturgical practice cited by Swanton, but that association tells us little about the significance of the allusion in the narrative context of the Dreamer's visionary experience. Payne's suggestion comes closer to the mark, for it seems clear to me that the dual appearance of the Cross does indeed "suggest the paradoxical coexistence of Christ in glory and Christ crucified" (1976:335). Its presence and function is explained by reference to this motif—that the blessed and the damned see Christ in different ways. The Dreamer recognizes in the shifting aspect of the Cross the two possible fates of his soul at Judgement. But the poet has adapted the traditional image to his own purpose by suspending the expected resolution of Judgement inherent in the conventional use of the motif. As may be apparent from the preceding discussion (and as Payne's analysis demonstrates), what earlier critics have taken to be the product of the poet's originality in his construction of the opening scene is in fact a masterful manipulation of existing convention. If we consider the poet's use of the motif discussed above in light of the observation that "the one unconventional (and apparently original) detail in the description of the Last Judgement scene with which *The Dream of the Rood* opens is ... the substitution of the cross for the Judge" (Payne, 1976:341), we may appreciate just how skilfully he has employed convention and innovation in his depiction of the Dreamer's situation. The Cross is recognized by the Dreamer as a symbol for Christ; and yet it is both significant and logical that it is not Christ Himself who appears before him; after all, this is not a vision of the true last Judgment, but one that prefigures that event. The ambivalence of the Cross's aspect serves to heighten the Dreamer's anxiety, for he does not at that moment know which he will see on the real Last Day—Christ's shining face or His wounds. While the Cross is arguably meant to be perceived as the Incarnate Body of Christ in the central Crucifixion narrative (see Woolf, 1958, and Hill, 1993), its intended role in the opening vision scene embodies a symbolic representation of both manifestations of Christ. This use of the Cross serves to drive home to the Dreamer (and to the poet's audience) the uncertainty of the fate of his soul, and this realization is as significant a factor in the Dreamer's cathartic experience—which leads to his conversion in lines 122ff.—as is the account of the Crucifixion in lines 28-121.

The imagery of the Cross employed by the poet throughout *The Dream of the Rood*—as sign of Doom; as animate, speaking messenger; as Christ's heroic retainer and reluctant traitor; and as cult object—is complex and sophisticated. Recognizing the lines discussed here as a clear allusion to a conventional eschatological motif, and one that is perfectly suited to the poem's narrative situation, heightens our awareness of that complexity. Moreover, it also helps us discern more clearly the link between the opening vision and the closing soliloquy, and it contributes to our sense that *The Dream of the Rood* is "a poem of extraordinary thematic unity" (Fleming, 1966:55).

REFRENCES

Amos, Ashley Crandell, *et al.* (eds.) (1986-91) *The Dictionary of Old English*. Four fascicles published to date: D, C, B and Æ. Toronto: Pontifical Institute of Mediaeval Studies.

Bessinger, Jess B. Jr and Stanley J. Kahrl (eds.) (1968). *Essential Articles for the Study of Old English Poetry*. Hamden, CT: Archon.

Biggs, Frederick M. (1986). The Sources of *Christ III*: A Revision of Cook's Notes. *Old English Newsletter Subsidia* 12.

Blake, Norman F. (1962). Cædmon's Hymn. *Notes and Queries* 207. 243-6.

Bosworth, Joseph and T. Northcote Toller (1898). *An Anglo-Saxon Dictionary*. Oxford: Oxford University Press.

Bradley, S.A.J. (trans.) (1982). *Anglo-Saxon Poetry*. London: Dent.

Braswell, Bruce Karl (1978). *The Dream of the Rood* and Aldhelm on Sacred Prosopopoeia. *Mediaeval Studies* 40. 461-7.

Brown, George Hardin (1986). Old English Verse as a Medium for Christian Theology. In: *Modes of Interpretation in Old English Literature*. Ed. Phyllis Rugg Brown, Georgia Ronan Crampton and Fred C. Robinson. Toronto: Toronto University Press. 15-28.

Brzezinski, Monica (1988). The Harrowing of Hell, the Last Judgement, and *The Dream of the Rood. Neuphilologische Mitteilungen* 88. 252-65.

Burrow, J.A. (1959). An Approach to *The Dream of the Rood. Neophilologus* 43. 123-33.

Calder, Daniel G. and M.J.B. Allen (1976). *Sources and Analogues of Old English Poetry: The Major Latin Sources in Translation*. Cambridge: D.S. Brewer.

Canuteson, John (1969). The Crucifixion and the Second Coming in *The Dream of the Rood. Modern Philology* 66. 293-7.

Cherniss, Michael D. (1973). The Cross as Christ's Weapon: The Influence of Heroic Literary Tradition on *The Dream of the Rood. Anglo-Saxon England* 2. 241-52.

Clubb, Merrel Dare (ed.) (1972).*Christ and Satan: An Old English Poem*. Hamden, CT: Archon. (Repr. from: *Yale Studies in English* 70 [1925]).

Colgrave, Bertram, and R.A.B. Mynors (1969). *Bede's Ecclesiastical History of the English People*. Oxford: Oxford University Press.

Dickins, Bruce, and Alan S.C. Ross (eds.) (1965). *The Dream of the Rood*. 4th ed. Methuen's Old English Library. London: Methuen. (1st ed., 1934).

Finnegan, Robert Emmett (ed.) (1977). *Christ and Satan: A Critical Edition*. Waterloo, Ont.: Wilfred Laurier University Press.

Fleming, John V. (1966). *The Dream of the Rood* and Anglo-Saxon Monasticism. *Traditio* 22. 43-72.

Gollancz, Sir Israel (1927). *The Cædmon Manuscript of Anglo-Saxon Biblical Poetry*. Oxford: Oxford University Press.

Greenfield, Stanley B. (1968). The Formulaic Expression of the Theme of "Exile" in Anglo-Saxon Poetry. In: Bessinger and Kahrl, 1968:352-62 (rept. from *Speculum* 30 [1955]. 200-06).

Greenfield, Stanley B. (1979). The Extremities of the *Beowulf*ian Body Politic. In: *Saints, Scholars, and Heroes: Studies in Medieval Culture in Honor of Charles W. Jones*. 2 vols. Ed. Margot H. King and Wesley M. Stevens. Collegeville, MN: Saint John's Abbey and University Press. I:1-14.

Greenfield, Stanley B., and Daniel G. Calder (1986). *A New Critical History of Old English Literature*. New York: New York University Press.

Helder, William (1975). The *Engel Dryhtnes* in *The Dream of the Rood. Modern Philology* 73. 148-51.

Hill, Thomas D. (1969). Apocryphal Cosmography and the "stream uton sæ": A Note on *Christ and Satan*, lines 4-12. *Philological Quarterly* 48. 550-4.

Hill, Thomas D. (1970). "Byrht Word" and "Hælendes Heafod": Christological Allusion in the Old English *Christ and Satan*. *English Language Notes* 8. 5-8.

Hill, Thomas D. (1973). Vision and Judgement in the Old English *Christ III*. *Studies in Philology* 70. 233-42.

Hill, Thomas D. (1977). The Fall of Satan in the Old English *Christ and Satan*. *Journal of English and Germanic Philology* 76. 315-25.

Hill, Thomas D. (1981). The Measure of Hell: *Christ and Satan* 695-722. *Philological Quarterly* 60. 409-14.

Hill, Thomas D. (1993). The Cross as Incarnate Body: An Anglo-Latin Liturgical Analogue to *The Dream of the Rood*. *Neophilologus* 77. 297-301.

Howlett, D. R. (1974) The Theology of Cædmon's Hymn. *Leeds Studies in English* 7. 1-12.

Huppé, Bernard F. (1959). *Doctrine and Poetry: Augustine's Influence on Old English Poetry*. New York: State University of New York.

Jolly, Karen L. (1985). Anglo-Saxon Charms in the Context of a Christian World View. *Journal of Medieval History* 11. 279-93.

Keenan, Hugh T. (1975). *Christ and Satan*: Some Vagaries of Old English Poetic Composition. *Studies in Medieval Culture* 5. 25-32.

Klinck, Anne L. (1982). Christ as Soldier and Servant in *The Dream of the Rood*. *Florilegium* 4. 109-16.

Krapp, George Philip, and Elliot Van Kirk Dobbie (eds.) (1931-53). *The Anglo-Saxon Poetic Records*. 6 vols. New York: Columbia University Press.

Leclercq, Jean (1985). *The Love of Learning and the Desire for God*. 3rd ed. Trans. Catharine Misrahi. New York: Fordham University Press. (1st ed.1961).

Lee, Alvin A. (1972). *The Guest-Hall of Eden: Four Essays on the Design of Old English Poetry*. New Haven, CT: Yale University Press.

Lee, N.A. (1972). The Unity of *The Dream of the Rood*. *Neophilologus* 56. 469-86.

Morey, James H. (1990). Adam and Judas in the Old English *Christ and Satan*. *Studies in Philology* 87. 397-409.

Morris, R. (ed.) (1874-80). *Blickling Homilies*. EETS O.S. 58, 63, and 73. London. (rpt. London: Oxford University Press, 1967.)

Ó Carragáin, Éamonn (1983). *Vidi Aquam*: The Liturgical Background to *The Dream of the Rood* 20a: "Swætan on þa swiðran healfe". *Notes and Queries* N.S. 30. 8-15.

O'Keeffe, Katherine O. (1987). Orality and the Developing Text of Caedmon's *Hymn*. *Speculum* 62. 1-20.

Opland, Jeff (1980). *Anglo-Saxon Oral Poetry: A Study of the Traditions*. New Haven, CT: Yale University Press.

Orton, Peter R. (1983). Cædmon and Christian Poetry. *Neuphilologische Mitteilungen* 84. 163-70.

Payne, Richard C. (1976). Convention and Originality in the Vision Framework of *The Dream of the Rood*. *Modern Philology* 73. 334-41.

Roberts , Jane (ed.) (1979). *The Guthlac Poems of the Exeter Book*. Oxford: Clarendon Press.

Robertson, D.W. Jr. (trans.) (1984). *St. Augustine: On Christian Doctrine*. The Library of Liberal Arts. Indianapolis: Bobbs-Merrill.

Schlauch, Margaret (1968). *The Dream of the Rood* as Prosopopoeia. In: Bessinger and Kahrl, 1968: 428-41. (Repr. from *Essays and Studies in Honor of Carleton Brown*. Ed. P.W. Long [1940] New York. 23-34.).

Schwab, Ute (1983). The Miracles of Caedmon. *English Studies* 64. 1-17.

Sleeth, Charles (1982). *Studies in Christ and Satan*. Toronto: University of Toronto Press.

Stanley, Eric G. (1975). *The Search for Anglo-Saxon Paganism*. Totowa, NJ: Rowan and Littlefield.

Swanton, Michael (1969). Ambiguity and Anticipation in *The Dream of the Rood*. *Neu-*

philologische Mitteilungen 70. 407-25.

Swanton, Michael (1984). *Three Lives of the Last Englishmen.* New York: Garland.

Swanton, Michael (ed.) (1970). *The Dream of the Rood.* Manchester: Manchester University Press. (repr. with minor corrections and supplementary bibliography, 1978).

Szarmach, Paul (1987). Ælfric, the Prose Vision, and *The Dream of the Rood.* In: *Studies in Honour of René Derolez.* Ed. A.M. Simon-Vandenbergen. Gent: Seminarie voor Engelse en Oud-Germaanse Taalkunde R.U.G. 592-602.

Wallace, D. Patricia (1990). King Alfred's Version of St Augustine's *Soliloquies* III, 23-26, *The Vision of the Damned. Notes and Queries* N.S. 37. 141-3.

Whitelock, Dorothy (1979). *English Historical Documents vol. I c. 500-1042.* 2nd ed. London: Methuen.

Wieland, Gernot (1984). Caedmon, the Clean Animal. *American Benedictine Review* 35. 194-203.

Wolf, Carol Jean (1970). Christ as Hero in *The Dream of the Rood. Neuphilologische Mitteilungen* 71. 202-10.

Woolf, Rosemary (1958). Doctrinal Influences on *The Dream of the Rood. Medium Ævum* 27. 137-53.

Wrenn, C.L. (1968). The Poetry of Cædmon. In: Bessinger and Kahrl, 1968: 407-27. (Repr. from: *Proceedings of the British Academy* 22 [1946]. 277-95.).

ABRAHAM AND THE OLD ENGLISH *EXODUS*

WILLIAM HELDER

Compared to the other examples of Old Testament narrative verse in the corpus of Anglo-Saxon poetry, *Exodus* is in some ways notoriously complex and difficult. Students of literature have nevertheless long admired it for its poetic quality, even praising it as "one of the most stirring and exciting of Old English poems" (Greenfield and Calder, 1986:212). At the same time it has remained extremely controversial and has therefore received a considerable amount of critical attention. Commentators continue to disagree particularly on the extent to which it is helpful or permissible to interpret *Exodus* in a manner that may loosely be termed allegorical. For that reason, no consensus has yet been reached on the theme or the unifying literary purpose of the poem. In this paper I propose first to offer an introductory overview of mostly recent publications in which the relevance of Christian allegorical exegesis and biblical typology to the study of *Exodus* has been investigated; then, in an attempt to contribute to a valid and coherent interpretation of the poem, I shall proceed to explore the typological implications of a motif which has apparently not been examined in this connection, the poet's recurring references and allusions to Abraham.

    As our brief introduction implies, the Old English *Exodus* is far more than a re-telling of the biblical story of Israel's departure from Egypt. Its overall structure is, nevertheless, quite perspicuous. After sketching the praiseworthy credentials of a heroic Moses, the poem proceeds with a concise treatment of the tenth plague as the occasion leading to the release of God's people from Egyptian bondage. The account of their journey towards the Red Sea ends with the alarming news that Pharaoh and his host are pursuing them. At this point there is a gap in the manuscript. The narrative resumes with the approach of the warlike Egyptians. Tension is created by the poet's repeated shifting back and forth from the despondent Israelites to the advancing enemy. Summoning his people and exhorting them to show faith and courage, Moses then strikes the sea with his rod and the waves move aside to form ramparts; the ancient sea bottom becomes a dry path. Now changing pace, the poet at length describes the tribes as they begin their crossing and digresses to include stories of Noah and the Flood and of Abraham and the sacrifice of Isaac, identifying the location of the latter event as the place where Solomon would eventually build the temple. After another lacuna, the drowning of the Egyptians is vividly described in dramatic detail. This glorious triumph over those who had warred with God gives rise to a homiletic passage ostensibly representing the preaching of Moses. The poem concludes with the celebration of victory and the distribution of Egyptian treasure on the shore of the Red Sea. All this is presented in an allusive style remarkable for its bold vigour and rich variety.

In the context of our discussion of the poem, a seminal study is James W. Bright's article, "The Relation of the Caedmonian *Exodus* to the Liturgy", published in 1912. Taking his starting point in Israel's exodus from Egypt as a well-known type of baptism, Bright tries to show that the poem derives its structure from the lections of Holy Saturday, the point in the liturgical year at which the rites of the medieval church focused almost exclusively on the baptism of catechumens. Critics may not agree on the exact link between the poem and the symbolism of baptism, but there appears to be widespread recognition that the Old English *Exodus* does have an important allegorical—or, to use a more appropriate term, typological—dimension. Even Edward B. Irving, Jr., who in his 1953 edition of *Exodus* provocatively insists that the poet "is interested primarily in facts, in recreating historical events as accurately as possible" (1953:20), admits a few pages later, "On one level the poem is clearly to be seen as a religious allegory ..." (1953:29). In a frequently cited short article responding to Irving, J.E. Cross and S.I. Tucker, however, judge this approach to be "unmediaeval" and assert that the events described in the poem "are not presented to be recognised as one consistent allegory" but as "symbolic pictures" which "would occur naturally to a learned Christian's mind" (1960:123). Demonstrating that Anglo-Saxon religious poets were shaped by a mental climate in which the Red Sea or the exodus of Israel from Egypt was immediately identified with baptism, Cross and Tucker's significant contribution to the debate is their defence of the principle that "it is reasonable to accept the influence of allegorical tradition particularly to illuminate *unrealistic* collocations in the poem" (1960: 123). They consequently resort to an "allegorical" explanation of the widespread occurrence of martial details in the poem, arguing on the basis of patristic evidence that, since no actual battle seems to take place in the poem, these elements must derive from the warfare waged by Christians against post-baptismal temptations (1960:125-6).

When in 1970 James W. Earl joined the debate about the interpretation of *Exodus*, he was confident that a coherent critical attitude based on Scriptural exegesis in the medieval Christian tradition had begun to emerge (1970:543); however, today it must be observed that the consensus he expected has not come about. What has emerged instead is a new controversy. Although it is generally accepted that the Christian allegorical or typological tradition is indeed available to explain unrealistic collocations, scholars disagree fundamentally about the extent to which this approach is applicable.

The debate on this topic can be traced first of all in further attempts to make sense of the battle imagery in *Exodus*. Earl reminds us that any warfare related to baptism is not confined to the struggle against post-baptismal temptations but that the martial aspect to the baptismal rite is more likely to be derived from the typological analogy between the crossing of the Red Sea and Christ's defeat of Satan in the Harrowing of Hell, the military victory which typologically made baptism possible in the first place. Earl, too, does not think that in the poem a battle occurs; he sees the details of war as anachronistic and conflated references to the later conquest of the Promised Land (1970:566). In his *"Exodus* and the Battle in the Sea"*, John F. Vickrey shows quite persuasively, however, that in a sense a struggle does take place[1] and that the poet sees the chosen people as a treasure plundered from hell. He concludes that, typologically speaking, the role of Israel as the *spolia*, 'spoils', of the devil therefore points to the formation of the church (1972a:140).

In a related study, *"Exodus* and the Treasure of Pharaoh"*, Vickrey corroborates this interpretation by analyzing the function of the much-discussed *"Afrisc meowle"* (1.580b, 'African woman')[2] who, standing *"golde geweorðod"* (1.581b, 'gold-adorned') on the shore of the Red Sea, participates in the celebration of victory. She has been convincingly identified by Fred C. Robinson (1962:373-8) as the *"uxor Aethiopissa"* or Ethiopian wife of Moses (Numbers 12:1), whom the Church Fathers took to be a type of the *ecclesia*. Vickrey's study lends support to the conclusion (also reached by others)[3] that in a typological sense she shares in a baptismal plundering of treasure and thus, adorned with the spoils of the Egyptians, represents the church gathered from among the nations (1972b:160-61). A further refinement of this argument follows in his *"Exodus* and the Robe of Joseph"*, where he suggests the strong possibility that the *"gold and godweb, Iosepes gestreon"* ('gold and splendid fabric, Joseph's treasure') mentioned in 1.588 is Joseph's coat of many colours (Genesis 37:3), another patristic symbol of the varied membership of the church and as such a remarkably suitable form of adornment for the *"Afrisc meowle"* as

---

[1] J.R. Hall rejects Vickrey's solution, arguing that it "lacks a theological basis" since the water of baptism is "sanctified by Christ's sacrifice that destroys sin, not the candidates' own efforts" (1983:32); however, the detailed patristic documentation provided by Jean Daniélou, shows that such objections lack validity (1956:54-61).

[2] All quotations from *Exodus* are taken from G. P. Krapp's standard edition of *The Junius Manuscript* (1931). Although Krapp emends *"afrisc meowle"* as *"afrisc neowle"*, the manuscript reading, now widely accepted, is here retained.

[3] For a discussion of a possible typological link between the *"Afrisc meowle"* and the Ethiopians mentioned in the poem, see Helder, 1975:11-12 and 21-2.

ecclesia. Vickrey thus confidently reiterates his earlier conclusion, stating that the *Exodus* poem "sets forth the perfection of the body of Christ" (1989:17).

The typological interpretation of *Exodus* has, of course, not gone unchallenged. Responding to Vickrey's identification of the "*Afrisc meowle*" as representative of the universal church, J.E. Cross—from whom, ironically enough, Vickrey in "*Exodus* and the Battle in the Sea" first took his cue (1972a:121)—vigorously argues that the relevant details "may be taken historico-realistically without missing anything of the power of the poem" (1974:187). In his fine edition of *Exodus*, Peter J. Lucas here, as elsewhere, shows similar caution. He agrees that the "*Afrisc meowle*" is the Ethiopian wife of Moses and that in allegorical exegesis this wife is a standard type of the church gathered from the gentiles, but he nevertheless comments: "There is ... no evidence that the poem was intended to suggest this allegorical equation here" (1977:147). The basic question arises whether in our interpretation of *Exodus* we may readily make use of an entire tradition underlying Anglo-Saxon religious poetry or whether we should, with the utmost reluctance, refer to it exclusively when the text is totally meaningless in any literal or historical sense.

Scholarly caution should be respected and enthusiastic excesses guarded against, but in view of the standard patristic and mediaeval reading of the exodus of Israel from Egypt, we may well be surprised that so much energy has gone into efforts to resist an allegorical or typological interpretation of the Old English *Exodus* poem. As Lucas also points out, "references to the exodus are to be found almost everywhere in the Church Fathers", so that "the area of search for possible influences on the OE poem is almost immeasurable" (1977:57). Again and again literary commentators remind us that in the Middle Ages the exodus was not only seen universally as a historical event but also interpreted consistently as a type of baptism, that is, of redemption from sin and from the power of the devil. Typology, the allegorical method of scriptural exegesis according to which the historical realities (events, persons, or things) of the Old Testament prefigure those of the New, was the prevailing mode of thought and imagination.[4] The connections between the exodus and baptismal liturgy render it all the more plausible that many elements of the poem, including the role of the above-mentioned "*Afrisc meowle*", can on one level be interpreted in terms of the church, for it is through the binding and plundering of the devil in baptism that the *ecclesia* is formed.

---

[4] A detailed explanation of biblical typology and its application in the liturgy and patristic writings can be found in Daniélou (1956:19-126). For impressive evidence that typology also shaped the Anglo-Saxon imagination, see Burlin (1968).

In accepting the medieval prevalence of typology as a given that is to be taken into account in interpreting *Exodus*, one need not at all feel compelled, as some have feared, to ignore or explain away the wonderfully vivid realism employed in depicting the Israelites of the *Exodus* as a society of Germanic warriors or to conclude that this realism is somehow incompatible with a Christian emphasis, for the typological outlook is firmly rooted in the acknowledged historicity of the events of the poem and in the importance of its concretely historical and realistic details. Neither should one assume that an attempt to view the poem from a typological perspective implies some kind of moralistic obligation to search for consistent and logically developed allegory. But instead of arbitrarily limiting the use of typological criticism to the attempt to explain only the obviously unrealistic collocations in *Exodus*, we should feel free to discover and appreciate the way the poem with unusual effectiveness exploits the typology of baptism in what Alvin A. Lee refers to as an "extraordinary fusion of heroic diction and biblical symbol" (1972:48). If we take such a position, we are likely to be all the better equipped to grasp something of the author's purpose in writing the poem and to discern its essential artistic unity.

The work of Vickrey and others indicates that the unifying principle governing the poem may well be the Anglo-Saxon author's view of Israel as *figura* of the church. A wealth of references to patristic and liturgical sources having a bearing on a typological approach is certainly available in the publications cited above. If, however, our brief and incomplete survey of *Exodus* criticism has inadvertently left the impression that a typological study is rather esoteric and not essential to a basic understanding of the poem, it is worth noting that many of the poet's allusions to the church are really not all that obscure. The description of the encampment of the Israelites at Etham before they reach the Red Sea is a good example:

> hæfde witig god
> sunnan siðfæt   segle ofertolden,
> swa þa mæstrapas   men ne cuðon,
> ne ða seglrode   geseon meahton,
> eorðbuende   ealle cræfte,
> hu afæstnod wæs   feldhusa mæst,
> siððan he mid wuldre   geweorðode
> þeodenholde.   Þa wæs þridda wic
> folce to frofre.   (80b-88a)

(God in his wisdom had covered the course of the sun with a sail, so that men did not have knowledge of the ropes of the mast, and those who dwell on earth could not by any power see the sailyard—how the greatest of tents was made fast—after he had with glory adorned the faithful people. Then was the third camp a joy to the nation.)

We find here an unusual blending of images commonly applied to the *ecclesia*. The Israelites are assumed to be sailors on the ship of the church which, having the cross as its mast, is the church pictured as ark. They prefigure the company of all those owing their deliverance from sin and the devil to the baptismal victory associated with the Flood. As a type of the universal church they are to be linked also to the imagery of the tent of meeting, the tabernacle. As Peter J. Lucas (1970) has suggested, the sails of the vessel are simultaneously the veils of that greatest of tents. This powerful concentration of *ecclesia* symbolism so early in the poem is a veritable key to the interpretation of *Exodus* and serves to justify the impression that the role of Israel as type of the Christian community is never far from the author's mind.

Building further on the foundation laid by scholars already mentioned, I shall now proceed to corroborate the same position in yet another way. The rest of this paper is an attempt to trace a motif found in *Exodus* which has apparently not yet been commented on, the recurrence of allusions and references to Abraham and to the promised land. A glance at the glossary in Lucas's edition of the poem reveals that, except for Moses and Abraham, no Israelite is named more than once in the poem. The name of Moses, the great leader of Israel, occurs ten times. Abraham is referred to by name as often as seven times (*Exodus*, pp.196-7), even though he is not a participant in the exodus at all and his name is not to be found in the chapters of Scripture which form the basis of the poem. Interestingly enough, Irving, too, has noticed that there is something special about the poet's treatment of Abraham; making the observation that "there is little characterization of individuals in the poem", he adds that other than Moses, "only Abraham could be said to be individualized at all, and his actions are almost ritualistic in their symbolic significance" (1953:29-30). As may become evident in the ensuing discussion, the poet makes use of Abraham to point to his central theme.

Historically, Abraham is, of course, the ancestor of the Israelites, but, as Anglo-Saxon Christians would also recognize, in the epistles of Paul his more prominent position is that of father of all believers, of the universal church.[5] The land which was first promised to Abraham, the

---

[5] Especially relevant here is the epistle to the Galatians. In 3:6-7, it is the Christian believers of the new dispensation who are referred to as the sons of Abraham: "*... qui ex fide sunt, ii sunt filii Abrahae. Providens autem Scriptura quia ex fide iustificat gentes Deus, praenuntiavit Abrahae: Quia benedicentur in te omnes gentes* [Genesis 15:6]"). Galatians 3:27-9 even indicates that gentiles become Abraham's offspring through baptism: "*Quicumque enim in Christo baptizati estis, Christum induistis. Non est Iudaeus, neque Graecus ... Si autem vos Christi, ergo semen Abrahae estis, secundum promissionem haeredes.*" Also important is Romans 4:16-18, where Paul, interpreting Genesis 17:5, refers to Abraham as the "*pater multarum gentium*", the father of all believers. (These and

very real destination of the Israelites described in the poem and in the Old Testament, is typologically the home or destination of all Christians. Already in the opening lines of the poem it becomes clear that the poet is not concerned simply with historical facts and that we would not be justified in focusing exclusively on the "historico-realistic". Moses is introduced as the source of wisdom not for Israel, his own nation, but for all humanity:

> Hwæt! We feor ond neah   gefrigen habbað
> ofer middangeard   Moyses domas,
> wræclico wordriht,   wera cneorissum,—
> in uprodor   eadigra gehwam
> æfter bealusiðe   bote lifes,
> lifigendra gehwam   langsumne ræd,—
> hæleðum secgan.   Gehyre se ðe wille! (1-7)

(Lo, we have heard far and near over middle-earth of the judgments of Moses, the wondrous laws for the generations of men—for all the blessed a reward in heaven after the perilous journey, long-enduring counsel for all the living. Let him hear who will!)

When the poet begins to tell the story of the exodus, he is thinking of all mankind, all the blessed, all those travelling towards the heavenly homeland, the church in the anagogical sense. In the words "Let him hear who will" (l.7b), we hear the invitation to the audience to discern the true meaning of the historical account to be presented. The poet addresses the universal *ecclesia* formed by the seed of Abraham.

When he adds that Moses was instrumental in restoring the sons of Abraham to their homeland (*"onwist eðles   Abrahames sunum"*, l.18), the author maintains the typological perspective that he has established (cf. Galatians 3:7, 29). He does the same subsequently whenever he mentions Abraham or alludes to the concept of the homeward journey. When, for example, the Israelites learn that they are being pursued by the Egyptians, their predicament is presented as that of an exile lacking a homeland (ll. 137a-9). In the description of the martial prowess of the Egyptians, the Israelites are again seen as *"nydfara"* ('travellers by necessity', l.208a) despairing of their rightful homeland (*"orwenan   eðelrihtes"*, l.211). When Moses is about to declare that Israel will be provided with a safe route right through the Red Sea and counsels dependence on *"se ecea   Abrahames god, / frumsceafta frea"* ('the everlasting God of Abraham, the Lord of creation', ll.273-4a), the allusion to Abraham is another clear instance of the homeland motif, reminding us that the Israelites are entitled

other Scripture quotations are from the Vulgate.)

to Canaan because Abraham is their ancestor. The symbolic function of
the many references to Abraham and the promised land is further developed when, at the end of the account in which the tribes of Israel are
described as beginning their actual *transitus* through the sea, the poet emphasizes:

>   Him wæs an fæder,
> leof leodfruma,   landriht geþah,
> frod on ferhðe,   freomagum leof.
> Cende cneowsibbe   cenra manna
> heahfædera sum,   halige þeode,
> Israela cyn,   onriht godes[.]   (353a-8)

> (One forefather had they all, dear prince of his people; wise of heart, he
> had received the right to the land [of Canaan], beloved among his kinsmen.
> As patriarch he had begotten a nation, a holy race of valiant men, the
> people of Israel, the lawful possession of God.)

The expression "*Him wæs an fæder*" (1.353a) is evidently an allusion to
Abraham as father of many nations (Genesis 17:4-5 and Romans 4:16-
17)—an obvious reference to Abraham as the father of all believers, the
church gathered from among the nations. The exodus being a commonplace type of baptism, the sacrament by which those of all tribes, tongues,
and nations enter the universal church, the poet appears to take it for
granted that the story he tells has typological implications.

In the much-discussed digression which immediately follows (ll.
362-446), the role of Abraham is even more obviously significant. The
poet rather abruptly introduces seemingly extraneous material dealing
with Noah and Solomon as well as Abraham and Isaac—all of which has
been shown to be connected with the non-literal aspects of the exodus as
type of baptism. It seems not to have been noticed that the entire digression is one long and elaborate occurrence of the Abraham motif. The
apparent interruption that so many have found fault with may interfere
with the progress of the narrative, but symbolically speaking it is not a
digression at all. In fact, it is the poet's means of underlining that the
exodus story is worth telling because of its connection with the body of all
believers, the church. The sudden mention of Noah and the Flood is in
itself appropriate because the latter is another commonly accepted type of
baptism. What we should not overlook is the fact that, very suggestively, it
is Noah's relation to Abraham that is accentuated:

>   ... wise men   wordum secgað
>   þæt from Noe   nigoða wære
>   fæder Abrahames   on folctale.

> Þæt is se Abraham   se him engla god
> naman niwan asceop;   eac þon neah ond feor
> halige heapas   in gehyld bebead,
> werþeoda geweald[.]   (377-83a)

(... wise men relate that the father of Abraham was ninth from Noah in the
count of generations. That is the Abraham for whom the God of angels
created a new name; he also entrusted to his protection his holy hosts, near
and far, and power over the nation.)

In a baptismal context, Noah is an important *figura* of Christ, but in the
Exodus poem he is placed in a position subordinate to that of Abraham,
whose new name identified him as the father of all those who were to
form the universal church (cf. Genesis 17:5ff).

In the subsequent account of the sacrifice of Isaac, Abraham's role
is also central. Stanley R. Hauer has proposed that as a common type of
the crucifixion this event introduces into the poem an essential link
between baptism and the passion. Students of *Exodus* have remarked on
the striking omission of the passover feast, which in Scripture and typology is so closely connected with Israel's departure from Egypt. In Hauer's
view, the inclusion of the story of Abraham and Isaac is a bold and ingenious device eliminating the need to refer to the passover directly at the
point in the poem where it was to be expected chronologically but still
incorporating "the essential thematic significance of the event by means of
its typological associations with the material on Abraham and Isaac" (Hauer, 1981:89). The very plausible suggestion that the "patriarchal digression" reinforces the main story as the poet interprets it receives further
confirmation from the way he also makes use of the story of the sacrifice
of Isaac to draw attention to its alleged location, Mount Zion (l.386b). It is
identified as the place where God gave man the *"halige heahtrowe"* ('high
and holy pledge', l.388a) of his covenant. The poet instantly connects the
mountain in question with the site where Solomon later built the temple,
another type of the church. Solomon's role, too, is here subordinated to
that of Abraham.

As soon as the poet has again by implication shown his particular
interest in the *ecclesia*, he proceeds with the narrative of the sacrifice.
After Abraham's faith has been tested, the episode appropriately culmi-
nates in a speech in which the Angel of the Lord unfolds a glorious vision
of the universal church:

> Ne behwylfan mæg   heofon ond eorðe
> his wuldres word,   widdra ond siddra
> þonne befæðman mæge   foldan sceattas,
> eorðan ymbhwyrft   ond uprodor,

garsecges gin   ond þeos geomre lyft.
He að swereð,   engla þeoden,
wyrda waldend   ond wereda god,
soðfæst sigora,   þurh his sylfes lif,
þæt þines cynnes   ond cneowmaga,
randwiggendra,   rim ne cunnon
yldo ofer eorðan   ealle cræfte
to gesecgenne   soðum wordum,
nymðe hwylc þæs snottor   in sefan weorðe
þæt he ana mæge   ealle geriman
stanas on eorðan,   steorran on heofonum,
sæbeorga sand,   sealte yðe[.]   (427-42)

(Neither heaven nor earth can contain his [i.e. the Lord's] words of glory,
which are spread farther and wider than the regions of the world extend,
the circle of the earth and the firmament, the vastness of the sea, and this
sombre sky. An oath he—the Lord of angels, Ruler of all that happens,
and God of hosts, steadfast in victory—swears by his own life, that men
on earth for all their skill shall not be able to tell in true words the number
of your kin and your posterity, unless someone becomes so wise in his
heart that he alone can count all the stones on the earth, the stars in the
heavens, the sand of the dunes by the sea, and the salty waves.)

In this elaborate poetic rendering of Genesis 22:16-18 the many details
relating to number and distance keep the reader aware of Abraham's being
the founding father of the catholic community of believers gathered from
all the regions of the earth.

The centrality of Abraham in the entire so-called digression under-
lines the fact that the homeland promised to those rescued from the power
of God's enemy (cf. l.503b) is indeed also the church. Abraham himself is
in this context still described as an exile ("*he on wræce lifde*", l.383b),
but, in the words of the Scripture, he looked for "the city which has foundations, whose builder and founder is God" ("*fundamenta habentem civi-
tatem: cuius artifex et conditor Deus*"); he is identified as one of those
who, while "pilgrims and guests" ("*peregrini et hospites*") on earth, sought
the homeland which is the ultimate fulfilment of all *ecclesia* imagery
(Hebrews 11:10, 14). This overall typological perspective remains linked
to the exodus until the very end of the poem as we have it. Right after his
account of the fate of the Egyptians, the poet reports on the exhortation of
Moses to interpret historical events by unlocking them with spiritual keys
("*gastes cægon*", l.525b). His instructions clearly apply to the just completed *transitus*, for he delivers his speech standing "*on merehwearfe*" ('on
the shore of the sea', l.517a). He describes human life as the journey of
wandering exiles: "Eðellease / þysne gystsele   gihðum healdeð" ('Having
no homeland, they occupy this hall of passing guests', ll.534b-5). When

Moses continues, he is confident that the Israelites will reach their desired destination, the land of Canaan (l.555a), where they "gesittað *sigerice* ... *beorselas beorna*" ('shall in victory possess ... the beer-halls of warriors', ll.563a-4a). Their thoroughly Germanic celebration typologically represents the feasting of the church triumphant.[6]

The anticipated arrival of God's people in the land of Canaan is what the recurring Abraham motif has prepared us for; after they have crossed the Red Sea and are "*on lande*" (l.567b), they have in principle completed their pilgrimage. When on this very same shore, the gold-adorned "*Afrisc meowle*" (l.580b) participates in the general rejoicing, it makes perfect typological sense to regard her as a type of the universal church. In view of the rich abundance of *ecclesia* symbolism throughout the poem, such a conclusion is by no means fanciful and more than likely would, to use Cross and Tucker's expression, "occur naturally to any learned Christian's mind."

If at this point we take stock of the elements in the poem which, on the basis of substantial documentation, have been interpreted by students of *Exodus* as examples of the symbolism relating to the church, the list will include a battle in the sea, the binding and plundering of the Egyptians, the cluster of sail and veil imagery relating to the ark and the tabernacle, the several components of the so-called patriarchal digression, as well as the "*Afrisc meowle*" and the robe of Joseph.[7] As the role which the poet assigns to Abraham also confirms, the poem in its entirety focuses our attention on the congregation of all those who, having experienced the *transitus* in baptism, emerge victorious on the other side. Again and again, its richly varied imagery confirms that the Old English *Exodus* owes its essential thematic unity to the typology of the *ecclesia*.

---

[6] For evidence that in Old English literature beer-drinking often has very positive connotations, see Robinson (1985:74-80). He also makes the following important point: "Modern readers, to whom drinking seems more often a social problem than a social ritual, are apt to miss the significance of serving the cup to men" (1985:75). For a discussion suggesting that an Anglo-Saxon banquet hall can very well share the characteristics of the *ecclesia*, see Helder (1987).

[7] This list is by no means exhaustive. Possible additions include the typological function of Etham and the Ethiopians as well as of the allusions to creation and paradise. For more details, see Helder (1975).

REFERENCES

Biblia Vulgata. Ed. Alberto Colunga and Laurentio Turrado. Madrid: Biblioteca de Autores Cristianos. 1965.
Bright, James A. (1912). The Relation of the Caedmonian *Exodus* to the Liturgy. *Modern Language Notes* 27. 97-103.
Burlin, Robert B. (1968). *The Old English Advent: A Typological Commentary.* New Haven, CT: Yale University Press.
Cross, J.E. (1974). Review of *Anglo-Saxon England* 1 and 2. *Notes and Queries* N.S. 21. 186-8.
Cross, J.E., and S. I. Tucker (1960). Allegorical Tradition and the Old English *Exodus. Neophilologus* 44. 122-7.
Daniélou, Jean (1956). *The Bible and the Liturgy.* Notre Dame, IN: University of Notre Dame Press. (Transl. of *Bible et liturgie.* Paris: Cerf [1951].)
Earl, James W. (1970). Christian Traditions in the Old English *Exodus. Neuphilologische Mitteilungen* 71. 541-70.
Greenfield, Stanley B., and Daniel G. Calder (1986). *A New Critical History of Old English Literature.* With a Survey on the Anglo-Latin Background by Michael Lapidge. New York and London: New York University Press.
Hall, J.R. (1983). Old English *Exodus* and the Sea of Contradictions. *Mediaevalia* 9. 25-44.
Hauer, Stanley R. (1981). The Patriarchal Digression in the Old English *Exodus,* Lines 362-446. *Studies in Philology* 78. 77-90.
Helder, W. (1975). Etham and the Ethiopians in the Old English *Exodus. Annuale Mediaevale* 16. 5-23.
Helder, W. (1987). The Song of Creation in *Beowulf* and the Interpretation of Heorot. *English Studies in Canada* 13. 243-55.
Irving, Edward B., Jr. (ed.) (1953). *The Old English Exodus.* New Haven, CT: Yale University Press. (Repr. Hamden, CT: Archon Books. 1970).
Krapp, G.Ph. (ed.) (1931). *The Junius Manuscript.* The Anglo-Saxon Poetic Records, Vol. I. New York: Columbia University Press. (Repr., 1969).
Lee, Alvin A. (1972). *The Guest-Hall of Eden: Four Essays on the Design of Old English Poetry.* New Haven, CT: Yale University Press.
Lucas, Peter J. (1970). The Cloud in the Interpretation of the Old English *Exodus. English Studies* 51. 297-311.
Lucas, Peter J. (ed.) (1977). *Exodus.* Methuen's Old English Library. London: Methuen.
Robinson, Fred C. (1962). Notes on the Old English *Exodus. Anglia* 80. 363-78.
Robinson, Fred C. (1985). *Beowulf and the Appositive Style.* Knoxville, TN: University of Tennessee Press.
Vickrey, John F. (1972a). *Exodus* and the Battle in the Sea. *Traditio* 28. 119-40.
Vickrey, John F. (1972b). *Exodus* and the Treasure of Pharaoh. *Anglo-Saxon England* 1. 159-65.
Vickrey, John F. (1989). *Exodus* and the Robe of Joseph. *Studies in Philology* 86. 1-17.

CHANGING PERSPECTIVES ON A SAINT'S LIFE: *JULIANA*

ROLF H. BREMMER, JR.

I ain't no saint, so don't complain ...
I'm just a soul whose intentions are good,
Oh Lord, please, don't let me be misunderstood.
(from: "Don't let me be misunderstood", pop song).

A frequent meaning present-day dictionaries give for the word 'saint' is that of a person of blameless moral conduct, often implying a colourless person. Clearly, the word has suffered semantic erosion since medieval times. One of the most important aspects of religious life in Anglo-Saxon England, which has also found its reflection in the vernacular poetry, is the veneration, or cult, of saints. Saints in the medieval sense are men and women who through their exemplary lives and deaths were believed to have gained sufficient merits to be able to intercede with God in heaven for the benefit of individuals here on earth. There were two principal kinds of saints: confessors and martyrs. The category of confessors comprised exemplary believers who had conducted a life of asceticism and toil for the Christian faith. They had 'mortified their flesh' and in doing so had virtually become martyrs. The second group entailed Christians who had actually died a violent death for the sake of Christ.

Documentary evidence on saints, generally known as hagiography, comes down to us in the following forms: a written account of a confessor is known as a *Vita* or 'life', while that of a martyr is referred to as a *Passio* or 'passion'. There is also the genre of *Miracula*, usually a long list of miracles attributed to the intercessory power of a saint.[1]

Both the passion and the life find their origins in the early years of the Church, when Christians were being severely persecuted by the Roman Emperors and their govenors. Naturally, passions dominate the earliest accounts, and they were told and written down so that the day the women and men who had suffered death for their faith would be remembered. Such accounts simultaneously served the purpose of comforting and encouraging those for whom God might have such a death in store, and had the further useful effect of making the audience realize that their own situation was not as dramatic as that of the saint whose plight they had just

---

[1] For a useful introduction to the cult of saints in Anglo-Saxon England, see Lapidge (1991).

heard. As the numbers of saints increased, calendars were drawn up to keep track of them. Several of these calendars have been preserved from the England of the Anglo-Saxons. The earliest calendar extant is the one St Willibrord brought with him for private use when he sailed to the Continent in 690 to convert the Frisians.

A subsequent step in the written commemoration of saints was the martyrology, an elaborated calendar in which a short account was given of the main incidents in the life of the relevant saint and in which, usually, some miracles were related. A very early specimen of this genre is Bede's (Latin) *Martyrologium*. Several such martyrologies have survived, and at least one was eventually translated into Old English.[2] Only one poetical version of a calendar in the vernacular has come down to us, traditionally known as *The Menologium*, but perhaps better dubbed *The Old English Metrical Calendar*.[3] The poem of no more than 231 lines begins with Christ's birth, also to end with it as if to indicate that the entire year is embraced by Christ. Beside the most important common Christian liturgical feasts, it mentions a number of saints' days, mostly those of Christ's disciples. Of particular relevance for England alone are the sections on the missionary Augustine of Canterbury, and Pope Gregory the Great who had sent him. Though fairly enumerative in nature, the *OE Metrical Calendar* cannot be said to be dull as its diction is firmly grounded in the tradition of Old English poetry. Its placement in the manuscript—preceding a version of the *Anglo-Saxon Chronicle* (the C version; BL MS Cotton Tiberius B.i)—suggests a link with the royal court, a suggestion given weight by its concluding lines which state that the feasts enumerated are ordered by the king to be in force in all Britain. This connection with the royal ruler is further underpinned by the opening lines of the poem immediately following in the manuscript, *Maxims II*, which begins in small capitals: *CYNING SCEAL RICE HEALDAN* 'A king must rule his kingdom'.[4]

To give an impression of the contents of the *OE Metrical Calendar*, here follow the lines (quoted from Dobbie, 1942) that briefly account for St Helena's discovery of the Cross, an event retold at length in Cynewulf's *Elene*:

---

[2] The best edition of the *Old English Martyrology* is that of Kotzor (1981). More easily accessible, perhaps, but offering less, and certainly superseded by Kotzor's edition, is Herzfeld (1900). Kotzor (1986) demonstrates that Bede's martyrology is detailed but brief, while the author of the *OE Martyrology* tends to include episodes from his sources, with a preference for the miraculous and sensational.

[3] *Menologium* actually is the technical term for a martyrology of the Eastern Orthodox Church, cf. Lapidge (1991:262, n.12); Dobbie (1942:lxi-lxii).

[4] As pointed out by Bollard (1973).

And þæs embe twa niht   þætte tæhte God
Elenan eadigre   æþelust beama,
on þam þrowode   ðeoden engla
for manna lufan,   Meotud on galgan
be Fæder læfe.   (83-7a)

('And from then [i.e. the previous feast] about two days later, God revealed to the blessed Helena the noblest of trees, on which the Prince of angels suffered for the love of men, the Creator on the gallows, by his Father's consent.')

It would seem that to the poet Christ's passion on the cross is at least as important as Helena's finding the cross itself.[5] The poet immediately goes on to anchor the ecclesiastical feast of the Invention of the Cross into the natural calendar:

                    Swylce ymb fyrst wucan
butan anre niht   þætte yldum bringð
sigelbeorhte dagas   sumor to tune,
wærme gewyderu.   Þænne wangas hraðe
blostmum blowað,   swilce blis astihð
geond middangeard   manigra hada
cwicera cynna ...   (87b-94a)

('Likewise after a week's but one day, summer brings to the people sun-shiny days to their dwelling-places, warm weather conditions. Then the plains quickly bloom with blossoms; likewise, joy arises throughout the earth of many kinds of the species of creatures.')

The *OE Metrical Calendar* usually only receives the briefest of mentions in surveys of Old English literature, if anything, and it is never included in collections of translations of poetry. It is perhaps understandable that for modern literary tastes the *OE Metrical Calendar* has little to offer, but the critical neglect the poem has suffered does little to reflect the value it was given by the compiler of the manuscript.

The worship of saints as reflected in various literary sub-genres was an important element in the written culture of Anglo-Saxon England. Even the earliest English clerical writers like Aldhelm, Bede and Alcuin contributed substantially to the genre, in prose as well as in poetry, albeit in Latin. But no one has produced saints' lives so extensively as Ælfric, abbot of Eynsham, who even produced an extensive collection of homilies

---

[5] On the common Anglo-Saxon notion of Christ suffering on a tree or gallows instead of on the cross, cf. Bremmer (1991:410-11).

on the lives of saints in his rhythmical alliterative prose. Clearly, if men of such stature devoted their energy to the writing of hagiography, we are dealing with a major genre.

Several poetic saints' lives have survived, including lives of English saints. This in itself is surprising, for naturally most saints were 'imported' with the missionaries from the Mediterranean world. The Anglo-Saxons took great pride in their own saints as appears from their early hagiography activities. Bede composed (in Latin, of course) both a prose and a poetic life of St Cuthbert of Lindisfarne and Felix, a monk, produced a life of St Guthlac of Croyland, somewhere between the saint's death in 714 and 749 when King Ælfwald of East Anglia, for whom the life was written, died. Felix has firmly placed himself in the long tradition of hagiography. What few authentic details of Guthlac's life were known to him he fleshed out with a wide variety of events and circumstantial description taken from many sources, among which Bede's *Vita St Cuthberti* figures prominently (Roberts, 1979:9-10).[6] Much later, in the early eleventh century, Ælfric openly expresses his chauvinism in the epilogue to his *Passion of St Edmund* (No. XXXII in Skeat, 1900:332):

> Nis Angelcynn bedæled Drihtnes halgena,
> þonne on Englalande licgaþ swilce halgan
> swilce þæs halga cyning is, and Cuþberht se eadiga,
> and sancte Æþelþryþ on Elig, and eac hire sweostor,
> ansunde on lichaman, geleafan to trymminge.
> Synd eac fela oðre on Angelcynne halgan
> þe fela wundra wyrcaþ, swa swa hit is wide cuþ ...   (259-65)

> ('The English race is not deprived of the Lord's saints, for in England lie
> buried such saints as this holy king [i.e. Edmund] is: the blessed Cuthbert,
> St Æthelthryth in Ely, and also her sister, uncorrupted in body, for the
> confirmation of the faith. There are also many other saints in England, who
> bring about many miracles as is widely known ...')

The importance the Anglo-Saxons attached to the genre also appears from the fact that we have a number of vernacular lives cast in the shape of verse, thus constituting a religious counterpart to the secular heroic poetry. After all, every Christian, but especially a saint, was seen as a *miles Christi*, 'a soldier of Christ' (Hill, 1981). Indeed, it cannot be a matter of coincidence that we have more poetic saints' lives than heroic poems. In the broadest sense of the genre, the following survive: *Juliana, Elena* and the more encyclopaedic *Fates of the Apostles*, all three by

---

[6] On especially Bede as a hagiographer, see Lapidge (1986:19-20).

Cynewulf, and *Andreas*, whose author remains unknown—all of which have their origin in Continental hagiography. Native are the two poems dealing with St Guthlac of Croyland which nineteenth-century editors imaginatively designated *Guthlac A* and *Guthlac B*, respectively. *Guthlac A* deals with the saint's temptations and how he resisted them in his Fenland hermitage, while *Guthlac B* describes his death.

In a stricter sense, most of these poems can hardly be called saints' lives. *Elene* is more of a romance inasmuch as the story is structured on a quest, and does not end with the saint's death. The poem vividly describes how Constantine the Great was converted to Christianity, and how he encouraged his mother Helena to find the cross on which Christ suffered. Helena then organizes an expedition which brings her to Jerusalem. The local Jews there are reluctant to cooperate and it is only under torture that one of their representatives, Judas Cyriacus, reveals the place where the cross had been hidden by his forebears. When they dig for it, they find three crosses (including the two on which the criminals had been executed together with Jesus) and a miracle helps identify the 'true' cross. Judas Cyriacus is converted and becomes Patriarch of Jerusalem, while Helena, having successfully completed her mission, returns home with the four nails as trophies.

Andreas relates how the apostle St Andrew was summoned by an angel to go and liberate his fellow apostle St Matthew from prison in Mermedonia, a country inhabited by ferocious cannibals and situated, it would seem, in the margin of the inhabited world. The lengthy poem gives a lively account of Andrew's adventures and tortures there, but just like Helena, Andrew returns home safely after having converted the Mermedonians and thus having fulfilled his errand.

The Fates of the Apostles is not at all a saint's life, but briefly enumerates in some 100 lines how and where each of the twelve apostles met his death. In fact, it is a free translation of the *Breviarum Apostolorum*, a text popular throughout the Middle Ages.

According to Lapidge (1991:259), only *Juliana* would qualify as a saint's life in the narrow sense, and it is on this poem that I would like to concentrate. *Juliana* is one of the many items in the *Exeter Book*, and its text is unique. No vernacular prose version of her life has been preserved from Anglo-Saxon England. The poem was composed by Cynewulf, an author about whom we know next to nothing. He may have been a Mercian, and was certainly a learned man, which would seem to mean he was a monk (Sisam, 1953:6, 28). Knowledge of Cynewulf's origin could give us an indication of a date of composition, in all likelihood not long after 800, as Mercia was subsequently overrun by the Vikings. Cynewulf took as his source a Latin version, but exactly which one we do not know (cf. Whatley, 1990). It is generally assumed that Cynewulf had a version on his desk which was very much like that printed in the Bollandist *Acta Sanctorum* (repr. Strunk, 1904:33-49; trsl. Calder and Allen, 1976:121-32). Comparison with the Latin *Acta St Julianæ* allows us to see how Cynewulf responded to his source when he cast it into poetic form. Before going into this aspect of the poem, however, I will first take a closer look at the structure of a saint's life, which, in the case of *Juliana*, takes the shape of a *passio*.

Lapidge (1991:252-3) has given a useful outline of the plot of a passion:

> the saint, usually of noble birth, adopts Christianity in days when the state government is pagan; the saint is brought before a local magistrate or govenor and asked to recant his/ her Christianity by sacrificing to the gods; the saint refuses to do so, even on pain of numerable tortures (normally described in excruciating detail), and is eventually killed, usually by beheading.

Rather than making yet another plot summary of *Juliana*, let us see how Bede epitomized her story in his *Martyrologium*:

> And in Cumae was the birth of the holy virgin Juliana, who during the reign of Emperor Maximian was first beaten by her father Africanus, and severely tortured. Next, she was also beaten with rods, naked, by the Prefect Eleusius, whom she was to have as a spouse, and hung by her hair, and steeped with her head in molten lead, and again detained in a dungeon, where she clashed openly with the devil. And again summoned out, she survived torture on a wheel, flames of fires and a burning vessel, but gained martyrdom by beheading. All this happened indeed in Nicodemia, but after a short spell, she was translated to Campania through God's will.[7]

Practically all of Lapidge's ingredients are here. Only the reason for her suffering, that is, her being a Christian, is taken for granted: Juliana, during the reign of the pagan Emperor Maximian (305-311), is first cas-

---

[7] "Et in Cumis natale sanctæ Julianæ virginis, quæ tempore Maximiniani imperatoris primo a suo patre Africano cæsa, et graviter cruciata, deinde et a prefecto Eleusio, quem sponsum habuerat, nuda virgis cæsa, et a capilis suspensa est, et plumbo soluto capite perfusa, et rursum in carcerem recepta, ubi palam cum diabolo conflixit. Et rursus evocata rotarum tormenta, flammas ignium, ollam ferventem superavit, ac decollatione capitis martyrium consummavit. Quæ passa est quidem in Nicodemia, sed post paulum tempus Deo disponente in Campaniam translata" (*Patrologia Latina* 94, cols 843-4).

tigated by her father, then by her fiancé, the prefect—which makes clear that she belongs to the aristocracy. The tortures are enumerated at length, before she is decapitated.

Why is it that Lapidge's plot summary can so easily be filled in with the events of Juliana's life? The answer must be sought in the origin of saints' lives. As we have seen, the earliest passions often take the form of an account of a court procedure. However, fairly soon, particularly after Christianity had become the dominant religion in the Roman Empire during the reign of Constantine, accounts of martyrs were much in demand. Many such accounts had been preserved locally, and were handed down orally to next generations. In this process of oral transmission, the life adopted the features of a folktale. In a way, the lives took up a similar position among the early Christians as tales of heroes did among ethnic groups. What the hero was to them, the saint was to the young Church. As such the saint's life can be grouped together with the fairytale (or *Märchen*), which often hinges on the main character's mental ingenuity, and the hero tale, in which the protagonist usually is gifted with super-human powers with which he fights his supernatural opponents. All three groups concern stories of marvel.

Of course, the range of folktales is wider than that of saints' lives. Besides the many marvelous creatures and events that populate folktales, there are also tales of an aetiological nature, explaining the origin of names of towns or features in the landscape. The folktale often imparts historical character to something which has been handed down as oral tradition (Thompson, 1946:9). Just as hero tales relate the adventures of an outstanding warrior of a tribe in a crucial state of its existence, so too saints' lives celebrate the speeches and deeds, and especially the persever-ance of the "warriors of Christ", as members of the young "tribe" of the faithful. Thus, the new form of an old and well-tried narrative mode ful-filled the primaeval human urge for story telling and listening. Contrary to what might have been expected after the conversion to Christianity—the decline of the folktale—the legends of saints and martyrs gave new life to the "old and persistent narrative tradition among the common folk" (Thompson, 1946:282). Not only do we encounter fantastic feats in many saints' lives that often find a parallel in secular folktales (cf. Loomis, 1948), but also familiar oral narrative techniques, such as mnemonic devices, anticipation and repetition, are frequently met with.

One such feature is displayed by Cynewulf right at the beginning of his poem: "*Hwæt! We ðæt hyrdon   hæleð eahtian,/ deman dædhwæte ...*" 'Listen! We have heard heroes declare, bold men proclaim ...' (1-2a),[8]

---

[8] All quotations from *Juliana* are from Woolf (1977).

after which he continues to introduce the setting and the main characters. Cynewulf does not identify his source as a written document—which it demonstrably was—but hides himself behind the oral report of representatives of the warrior aristocracy. All reference to a literary origin, or indeed a literate society, are carefully obliterated by Cynewulf so as to give the poem the authority that would have been appreciated by an audience that was wont to listen to secular heroic tales. Tracing his source to heroes was intended to impress his audience. Using the vocabulary of Germanic heroic poetry only accommodated the easier new contents to an old and well-tried vessel.

Cynewulf has been seriously criticised for the way he has portrayed Juliana. "He seems barely fired emotionally or imaginatively by his heroine who is assigned little charisma", as Bradley (1982:302) remarks in the introduction to his translation of the poem. Rosemary Woolf, the latest editor of the poem, is even more severe in her judgment of Cynewulf's literary merits as displayed in *Juliana*. The almost total absence of imagery and the conventional heroic terms produce no "poetic progress": "beyond lie monotony or prose". *Juliana*, she thinks, "brings Old English poetry into a blind alley" (Woolf, 1977:19). Such critical opinions are the result of applying to the poem implicit aesthetic Wordsworthian standards that do no justice to either Cynewulf's intentions or to the literary reality that Cynewulf lived in and that is reflected by *Juliana*. Why did Cynewulf not give Juliana a personality of her own? Could he not have brought this about? In all likelihood he could have done so, but then he would have made at least two interventions: he would have drastically departed from the characterization he found in his written source, to which he sticks closely without admitting it. Moreover, he would have broken the "rules" of the structure of the folktale he was tacitly following. If we find Juliana lacking in emotional personality this is because she merely plays the role of an archetypal virgin saint, who runs the course that has already been dictated to the likes of her by many other tales before her. As we have seen, the narrative slots in a passion are already there (cf. Appendix). What remains to be done is filling them in with characters that act their roles of heroes and villains. In the present passion, these are Juliana (virgin, Christian), on the good side and Affricanus (wicked parent, pagan), Heliseus (suitor, persecutor, pagan) and the devil (supernatural foe), on the evil side. The evil characters all play a role of tempter (or: tester). Of necessity, such characters will remain 'flat'.

Keeping this in mind, the structure of the saint's life can be seen to be very much in line with that of a folktale. The elements of the fairytale, as established by one of the most influential scholars of the structure of fairytale narrative, Vladimir Propp (1968), can be briefly summarized as follows: the hero is forced to abandon his home; misfortune and unhappiness are the result; he enters into direct battle with the villain, is able to pull his trick and conquers him, thereby eliminating the original misfortune and unhappiness.

Substituting the elements presented by Propp with the details from *Juliana* would not seem a demanding task: through her unwillingness to marry Heliseus, her father Affricanus hands her over to the authorities to be punished (read: forced to leave home). In fact, her father is functioning as the "wicked parent" of folktales, who sets the chain-reaction of the plot in motion. Heliseus is his superior in evil, and the two are foreboding the worst enemy of all. In prison, Juliana fights with a demon, overcomes him (conquers villain), and eliminates her unhappiness by gaining the crown of martyrdom. A common feature of fairytales is that the hero must overcome obstacles in order that he may win his reward. These obstacles can be seen as tests, trying the hero's will-power and resolve. In Juliana's case, the first test is whether or not she will agree with the pre-arranged marriage which her father has organized for her with the prefect Heliseus. The lure of such a union is great: the spouse-to-be is an *æhtwelig æpeles cynnes / rice gerefa*, 'wealthy, powerful senator of noble lineage' (18-9a), who is in charge of the *hordgestreon*, 'treasure' (22). Besides being rich, Heliseus, as her prospective husband appears to be called, rules an *ealdordom / miclene and mærne*, 'princedom large and famous' (25-6a). Heliseus' status and wealth is stressed elsewhere: he is *goldspedig* 'rich in gold' (39); 'better than you [Juliana]', *æpelra for eorpan, æhtspedigra feohgestreona*, 'nobler in the eyes of the world, more wealthy in treasures' (101-2a). But despite this apparent advantage, Juliana from the start makes clear that all Heliseus' riches mean nothing to her compared to the respect she bears to God (35-7):

> heo þæs beornes lufan
> fæste wiðhogde,   þeah þe feohgestreon
> under hordlocan,   hyrsta unrim,
> æhte ofer eorþan.   (41b-4a)

('She firmly rejected the man's love, even though he possessed treasures in his coffer, a countless number of jewels on earth.')

Heleusius' immense treasures on earth are an allusion to the words of Christ who had said that we should not gather treasures on earth, where moth and rust devour them, but rather lay up treasures in heaven (Matthew 6:19-21). Thus Juliana successfully resists the first temptation, that of riches and worldly respect. With this refusal, the first conflict is there, and from it evolve all the following tests (or "adventures" in the folktale): she is flogged at her father's command (142ff), whipped at her fiancé's injunction, this time naked (187-8); hung by the hair from a high tree for six hours in the burning sunshine (227ff), and finally thrown into a dungeon. Here she meets with a devil, in angelic disguise, who tells her on God's behalf to give up her resistance and submit to her father's wishes (242ff). The demon's function here is that of the tempter, a crucial figure in folktales. The sudden and unexpected turn in her torments for a moment confuses Juliana, and we almost expect to see her succumb. Her confusion is brief, however, and after a short but intense prayer to God, a voice from heaven tells her to seize the (false) angel and squeeze the truth out of him.

Hand-to-hand combats with a devil in folktales are rare (Thompson, 1946:42), and give *Juliana* a welcome additional feature to the well-known pattern. With the strength of a bionic woman, Juliana manages to get the demon on his back and forces him to make a self-confession of all the havoc he has wrought in the course of history.[9] After the long intermezzo of her encounter with the demon (242-555), which is clearly the centre of the poem,[10] Juliana is brought to Heliseus once more and undergoes several more tortures (or "tests"): she is put on a wheel beset with swords and surrounded with flames. An angel rescues her, a feat which brings about the conversion of her torturers and, because of that, their subsequent beheading (now on a lost leaf). Next, she is put in a cauldron with boiling lead. However, when she is actually placed into it, the vessel explodes, causing the death of 75 bystanders.

When all these tortures prove to be of no avail and Juliana persists in her faith, she is at last decapitated. This time Heliseus' order is carried out successfully: Juliana has at long last got what she deserved for her obnoxiously clinging to her faith in Christ. But Heliseus' triumph is also Juliana's: she has finally gained her reward: her soul is carried to the *langan gefean* 'long joy' (670), that is, to life in heaven. In terms of the fairy-tale: the heroine has achieved her aims. Yet, Heliseus also gets what he deserves: he is drowned at sea, and conforms to a well-recognized pattern in the folktale. Stealing from a god or a saint or otherwise to attack a deity or sacred person is extremely dangerous. Death or punishment will follow certainly upon the violation of such a taboo, and often results in instant death or death by drowning or burning (cf. Thompson 1955:I,494, C51.2). Heliseus, by killing Juliana, has broken the taboo of

---

[9] "The Devil's Account" is a hagiographic motif, also found elsewhere in Old English literature, cf. Wright (1993:176). The contents of the devil's self-confession find a curious (incidental?) echo in a Rolling Stones' song, "Sympathy for the Devil".

[10] That is, almost three-sevenths of 731 surviving lines of the poem. Two leaves are missing in the MS, with perhaps a total of 140 lines (Woolf, 1977:1), so that with three-eighths the intermezzo still forms the central part in *Juliana*.

the immunity of God's possessions, and significantly ends up in the nether world.

*

When approached in terms of fairytale structure, *Juliana* can be seen to answer to the expected features, at least in its basic outline.[11] It may also help to explain why earlier critics have found little attraction in the psychological treatment Cynewulf has afforded the saint. On the other hand, such an approach leaves the modern reader with an unsatisfactory feeling, wondering what Cynewulf's role has been in handing down Juliana's story. Clear though it may be that he remained on the whole true to the basic plot as he found it in his Latin original, did he not literally sign the poem with his signature? And what is more, did he not write his name over its 755 lines? Dissatisfaction with critical opinions has brought about a reconsideration of the literary merits of the poem over the last twenty years, which allows us to read the poem in a more meaningful way than was thought possible.

One of the first successful new approaches was made by Wittig (1975), who pointed out that Cynewulf's concern was not so much to present a versified historic narrative of the Latin life as to rearrange the contents in such phrasings as to give the poem a 'figural narrative'. First, Cynewulf presents the general background: in the days of the Emperor Maximian, Christians were suffering from severe persecutions (2a-17). Next, he introduces the *dramatis personae*. Heliseus is the first to enter the scene, and his wealth and status are high-lighted, as we have already seen (18-26a). Then follows the introduction of Juliana, who is bent on preserving her virginity *fore Cristes lufan* 'for the love of Christ' (28-32).[12] The last main character, appearing almost casually, is Juliana's father Affricanus—we only learn his name at line 158—who appears to have betrothed Juliana to Heliseus for no other purpose than to gain from it socially. He is ignorant of his daughter's resolve not to marry (32-5). By stressing the qualities and activities of the main characters in the opening of the poem Cynewulf manages to create an extreme moral opposition between Juliana on the one hand, and, especially, Heliseus on the other.[13]

---

[11] Cf. Krappe's definition of the fairytale: "… a continued narrative (…) centering on one hero or heroine (…) who after a series of adventures in which the supernatural plays a conspicuous part, attains his goal and lives happy ever after" (Edmonson, 1971:144).

[12] The concept of virginity plays a major role in the poem. This should not be interpreted so much on a physical level but rather on a spiritual one, cf. Bugge (1975:52-4) and Olsen (1990:229).

[13] This diametrical contrast between vice and virtue is typically a structural feature of the

From a figural point of view Juliana stands for the 'City of God',
while Heliseus represents the 'City of the Devil', or, in other words, Juliana and Heliseus are figures of the Church and the World, respectively. In
fact, as Wittig demonstrates, a multi-figural reading of the poem is possible. From such a perspective, Juliana is not only a person from history,
but also a figure of Christ, the Church, as well as of the individual
believer. As a figure of Christ she is going through similar stages in her
Passion as Christ did. Her father having her flogged and then handed over
to Heliseus, who repeats the punishment, resembles Christ undergoing the
same at the hands of, first, the members of the Sanhedrin, and then from
Pontius Pilate. Just as Christ hung from a cross, Juliana hung from a high
tree. Juliana's being cast into prison reflects Christ's burial. The saint's
struggle with the devil and her victory, finally, reminds one of Christ's
Harrowing of Hell. It should be borne in mind that these similarities do
not make her equal to Christ, but point away from her to Christ, which
make her a type for Christ.

On another level, Juliana is also a figure of *Ecclesia*, the Church.
Her constantly confessing Christ, but also her instructing the pagans in the
principles of the faith (e.g. 638-69), exemplifies the duties of the Church.
The fact that she wants to keep her virginity for Christ parallels the idea
that the Church is Christ's bride. Her resistance against the devil and his
minions—real and fearful opponents then—, her suffering as well as her
subsequent victory reflect the actuality and future of the Church, respectively.

The effect Juliana's passion is meant to have on the individual is
testified to by Cynewulf himself in his epilogue, when he expresses the
need for her help (696) when he is being afflicted with despair, a state of
mind often associated with the devil. Will he or will he not go to heaven
after his death? At this crucial moment in life, the poet admits:

> Þonne arna biþearf,
> þæt me seo halge   wið þone hyhstan Cyning
> geþingige;   mec þæs þearf moniaþ,
> micel modes sorg.   (715b-9a)

('Then I have need of mercy, namely that the saint [i.e. Juliana] will
intercede for me with the highest King; need reminds me of this, a great
sorrow of heart.')

The effect of Juliana's passion on Cynewulf's religious experience should
be emulated by all individual believers who hear it.

---

passion, cf. Altman (1975).

Such a multi-figural reading, according to Wittig (1975:55), does not perhaps at once increase our aesthetic appreciation of the poem, but it should make us aware of the fact that Cynewulf selected and omitted certain elements from the *Vita*. In his editorial approach, Cynewulf manipulated his source to such an extent as to be able to apply his learning and imagination to bring out the multi-layered significance. To Wittig's mind (1975:47), the characters in *Juliana* remain 'flat', "because they are deliberately generalized". It would seem, therefore, that Wittig attributes the absence of psychological development of the poem's characters to Cynewulf's authorial strategy. I would suggest, however, that Cynewulf already found the characters 'flat' in his source, a characteristic which they naturally derive from their being actors in a folktale. It was exactly this flatness of character which enabled Cynewulf to superimpose on the protagonists a new and deeper significance.

Wittig's reading of *Juliana* opened the way to a revaluation of the traditional interpretations. If Cynewulf could manage to handle the raw material of his source so skilfully, his craft must also be visible in other respects. The previous generation of critics, as given voice by such an authority as C.L. Wrenn, considered *Juliana* prosaic and lacking in poetic quality in its clumsy presentation of a conflict between the saint and the devil. The only thrill Wrenn found in the poem, it would seem, was Cynewulf's runic signature, and the "still recognizable Germanic features" of the heroine (Wrenn, 1967: 125-26). Indeed, Cynewulf clearly updates (or anachronizes) the story by applying the familiar epithets of heroic verse to his characters. He turns Affricanus and Heliseus into Germanic warriors, for example, when they come together to discuss Juliana's refusal to marry Heliseus:

> Reord up astag,
> siþþan hy togædre garas hlændon,
> hildex1remman. (62b-64a)

('The discussion became loud, when they leaned their spears together, the warriors.')

In his source Cynewulf only found that the prefect called Juliana's father and told him word for word what she had said to him (Calder and Allen, 1976:123, I.2 beginning). Even more specifically, such Germanic colouring occurs in 683ff, when the men who had accompanied Heliseus on his fatal sea-voyage, ended up in hell, where they, the thegns (*þegnas*), the band of retainers (*geneotscolu*) had no need to expect to receive treasure (*feohgestealde*), rings (*beagas*) and ?dappled gold (*æpplede gold*) in the winehall (*winsele*) on the beerbenches (*beorsetle*). Though the terminology invites us to view Juliana as living in a Germanic world, we would be mistaken to interpret her as a Germanic heroine. The depiction of Juliana's world as Germanic was as inescapable to Cynewulf as it was to the Master of the Wakefield Cycle when he had Christ's nativity taking place on the Yorkshire Moors in *The Second Shepherd's Play* or when Pieter Bruegel painted the same event in a Flemish town with people skating on canals in the background; or, to remain closer to our subject, when the author of the thirteenth-century Middle English *Liflade of St Julienne* depicted Heliseus as a courtly lover in a feudal society (Price, 1987). Juliana's concern is not at all heroic in the same sense as *Beowulf*. True, *Juliana* shares similar folktale patterns with the hero tale (for *Beowulf*, cf. Shippey, 1969), yet the virtues attributed to the protagonists are manifestly Christian, and not heroic (Schneider, 1978), but contemporaneous Anglo-Saxon (Gillam, 1987). Indeed, modern studies of *Juliana* so much stress the position of Cynewulf's work as an intrinsic part of the discourse of early Medieval Christian learning and instruction that we would almost forget that the deep structure of its narrative plot ultimately finds its origin in the folktale.

REFERENCES

Altman, Charles J. (1975). Two Types of Opposition and the Structure of Latin Saints' Lives. *Medievalia & Humanistica* N.S. 6. 1-11.
Bollard, J.K. (1973). The Cotton *Maxims*. *Neophilologus* 57. 179-87.
Bradley, S.A.J. (tr. & ed.) (1982). *Anglo-Saxon Poetry*. Everyman's Library. London: Dent.
Bremmer, Jr., Rolf H. (1991). Hermes-Mercury and Woden-Odin as Inventors of Alphabets: A Neglected Parallel. In: *Old English Runes and their Continental Background*. Ed. Alfred Bammesberger. Heidelberg: Carl Winter. 409-19.
Bugge, John. (1975). *"Virginitas". An Essay in the History of a Medieval Idea*. The Hague: Martinus Nijhoff.
Calder, Daniel G. and Michael J.B. Allen (1976). *Sources and Analogues of Old English Poetry. The Major Latin Texts in Translation*. Cambridge: D.S. Brewer, and Totowa, NJ: Rowman and Littlefield.
Dobbie, Elliot Van Kirk (ed.) (1942). *Anglo-Saxon Minor Poems*. The Anglo-Saxon Poetic Records, vol. VI. New York: Columbia University Press.
Edmonson, Munro S. (1971). *Lore. An Introduction to the Science of Folklore and Literature*. New York: Holt, Rinehart and Winston.
Gillam, Doreen M.E. (1987). Love Triangle at Commedia: Some Sidelights on Cynewulf's Handling of Personal Relationships in *Juliana*. In: *Studies in Honour of René Derolez*. Ed. A.M. Simon-Vandenbergen. Gent: Seminarie voor Engelse en Oud-Germaanse Taalkunde, R.U.G. 190-215.
Hill, Joyce (1981). The Soldier of Christ in Old English Prose and Poetry. *Leeds Studies in English* N.S. 12. 57-80.
Kotzor, Günter (ed.) (1981). *Das altenglische Martyrologium*. Bayerische Akademie der Wissenschaften, Phil.-Hist. Klasse, Abh. N.F. 88 1/2, 2 vols. Munich.

Kotzor, Günter (1985). Anglo-Saxon Martyrologists at Work: Narrative Pattern and Prose Style in Bede and the *Old English Martyrology*. *Leeds Studies in English* N.S. 16. 152-73.

Lapidge, Michael (1986). The Anglo-Latin Background. In: Stanley B. Greenfield and Daniel G. Calder, *A New Critical History of Old English Literature*. New York and London: New York University Press. 5-37.

Lapidge, Michael. (1991). The Saintly Life in Anglo-Saxon England. In: *The Cambridge Companion to Old English Literature*. Ed. Malcolm Godden and Michael Lapidge. Cambridge: Cambridge University Press. 243-63.

Loomis, C. Grant (1948). *White Magic: An Introduction to the Folklore of Christian Legend*. Cambridge, MA: Medieval Academy of America.

Olsen, Alexandra Hennesey (1990). Cynewulf's Autonomous Women. A Reconsideration of *Elene* and *Juliana*. In: *New Readings on Women in Old English Literature*. Ed. Helen Damico and Alexandra Hennesey Olsen. Bloomington and Indianapolis: Indiana University Press. 222-32.

Price, J.G. (1987). *The Liflade of Seinte Juliene* and Hagiographic Convention. *Medievalia & Humanistica* N.S. 14. 37-58.

Propp, Vladimir I. (1968). *Morphology of the Folktale*. 2nd rev. ed. Austin and London: University of Texas Press.

Schneider, Claude (1978). Cynewulf's Devaluation of Heroic Tradition in *Juliana*. *Anglo-Saxon England* 7. 107-18.

Shippey, Thomas A. (1969). The Fairy-Tale Structure of *Beowulf*. *Notes and Queries* N.S. 16. 2-11.

Sisam, Kenneth (1953). *Studies in Old English Literature*. Oxford: Clarendon Press.

Skeat, Walter W. (ed.) (1900). *Ælfric's Lives of Saints*. Vol. 4. EETS, OS 114. London.

Strunk, Jr., William (1904). *The Juliana of Cynewulf*. Boston: D.C. Heath.

Thompson, Stith (1946). *The Folktale*. Berkeley, Los Angeles and London: University of California Press (repr. 1977).

Thompson, Stith (1955). *Motif-Index of Folk-Literature*. Rev. ed. Copenhagen: Rosenkilde and Bagger.

Whatley, E. Gordon (1990). Juliana. In: *Sources of Anglo-Saxon Literary Culture: A Trial Version*. Ed. Frederick M. Biggs, Thomas D. Hill and Paul E. Szarmach. Binghamton, NY: Center for Medieval and Early Renaissance Studies, SUNY. 13-5.

Wittig, Joseph (1975). Figural Narrative in Cynewulf's *Juliana*. *Anglo-Saxon England* 4. 37-55.

Woolf, Rosemary (ed.) (1977). *Juliana*. Rev. ed. Exeter: University of Exeter. [The 1977 revision is minimal compared with the 1st edition of 1955.]

Wrenn, Charles L. (1967). *A Study of Old English Literature*. London: Harrap.

Wright, Charles D. (1993). *The Irish Tradition in Old English Literature*. Cambridge: Cambridge University Press.

APPENDIX

Strunk (1904:xxx-xxxi) has given a useful illustration of how the personality of a saint was subservient to the larger structure of the early passion, which I quote here in full:

> [T]he circumstances and miracles of the *Acta St. Julianæ* appear again and again, with only slight modifications, in the lives of the other woman saints of the early Church. St. Juliana is only one of a throng of virgin martyrs with similar history. The typical virgin saint is a girl of noble rank

(St. Juliana, St. Agatha, St. Anastasia, St. Catherine, St. Basilia, St. Cyrilla), devout and learned (St. Julian, St. Susanna), sought in marriage by some heathen proconsul or prefect or prefect's son (St. Agatha, St. Juliana, St. Agnes), She rejects her suitor, and refuses to sacrifice to Apollo (St. Anastasia, St. Euphemia, St. Juliana). Brought before the prefect for trial, she adheres to her faith, whereupon she is subjected to atrocious torture and humiliation. She is stripped naked (St. Agnes, St. Barbara, St. Juliana), scourged and cudgelled (St. Agatha, St. Anastasia, St. Dorothea, St. Euphemia, St. Lucia); hung up by the hair (St. Juliana, St. Symphorosa); torn by a wheel in which are set swords or sharp hooks (St. Juliana, St. Catherine, St. Euphemia, St. Christina); placed in a hot cauldron (St. Juliana, St. Lucia, St. Fausta), and in the flames (St. Agnes, St. Juliana, St. Euphemia, St. Macra, St. Cecilia). Instead of harming her, the fire bursts out and consumes the bystanders (St. Agnes, St. Julian, St. Christina). Her executioners become converted by her constancy, and meet death for their faith (St. Julian, St. Anastasia, St. Fausta). After another imprisonment (St. Juliana, St. Lucia, St. Anastasia), she is beheaded (St. Agnes, St. Juliana, St. Dorothea, etc.; almost all perish in this way), and is thenceforward enrolled in the great army of the Church Triumphant, while her memory is tenderly and reverently cherished by the devout in this world.

NOTES ON CONTRIBUTORS

Henk Aertsen is a Lecturer in English at the Vrije Universiteit, Amsterdam.

Rolf H. Bremmer, Jr., is a Lecturer in English at the University of Leiden.

Mildred Budny is Director of The Richard Rawlinson Center for Anglo-Saxon Studies at Western Michigan University, Kalamazoo, MI, where she is also Associate Professor of History.

Graham D. Caie is Professor of English at the University of Glasgow.

Allen J. Frantzen is Professor of English at Loyola University, Chicago.

Joseph Harris is Professor of English and Folklore at Harvard University, Cambridge, MA.

William Helder is a teacher of English at Guido de Brès High School, Hamilton, Ontario.

Thomas D. Hill is Professor of English and Medieval Studies at Cornell University, Ithaca, NY.

David F. Johnson is Assistant Professor of English at Florida State University, Tallahassee, FL.

T.A. Shippey is Professor of English at the University of Leeds.

Wim Tigges is a Lecturer in English at the University of Leiden.